W9-ANW-217

Rick Steves.

SNAPSHOT

Madrid & Toledo

CONTENTS

INTRODUCTION

This Snapshot guide, excerpted from my guidebook *Rick Steves Spain*, introduces you to majestic Madrid. Spain's capital is home to some of Europe's top art treasures (the Prado Museum's collection, plus Picasso's *Guernica* in the Reina Sofía) and a lively selection of characteristic tapas bars, where you can assemble a memorable feast of Spanish specialties. Explore the city's cozy-feeling historic core, tour its lavish Royal Palace, and beat the heat on a rowboat at the lush and inviting Retiro Park.

This book also covers several side-trips from Madrid. Toledo, the hill-capping onetime capital of Spain, features one of the country's most magnificent cathedrals, a medieval vibe, and top paintings by favorite son El Greco. Northwest of Madrid, you'll find Spain's grandest palace at the Inquisition-era El Escorial, a jarring jolt of the 20th century at Franco's Valley of the Fallen, and a pair of charming towns: Segovia, with its towering Roman aqueduct, and Ávila, encircled by a medieval wall.

To help you have the best trip possible, I've included the following topics in this book:

• **Planning Your Time,** with advice on how to make the most of your limited time

• **Orientation,** including tourist information offices (abbreviated as TI), tips on public transportation, local tour options, and helpful hints

• **Sights** with ratings:

▲▲▲—Don't miss

▲▲—Try hard to see

▲—Worthwhile if you can make it

No rating—Worth knowing about

• **Sleeping** and **Eating,** with good-value recommendations in every price range

• **Connections,** with tips on trains, buses, and driving

Practicalities, near the end of this book, has information on money, staying connected, lodging, restaurants, transportation, and other helpful hints, plus Spanish survival phrases.

To travel smartly, read this little book in its entirety before you go. It's my hope that this guide will make your trip more meaningful and rewarding. Traveling like a temporary local, you'll get the absolute most out of every mile, minute, and dollar.

Buen viaje!

MADRID

Today's Madrid is upbeat and vibrant. You'll feel it. Look around, just about everyone has a twinkle in their eyes.

Madrid is the hub of Spain. This modern capital—Europe's second-highest, at more than 2,000 feet above sea level—is home to more than 3 million people, with about 6 million living in greater Madrid.

Like its population, the city is relatively young. In medieval times, it was just another village, wedged between the powerful kingdoms of Castile and Aragon. When newlyweds Ferdinand and Isabel united those kingdoms (in 1469), Madrid—sitting at the center of Spain—became the focal point of a budding nation. By 1561, Spain ruled the world's most powerful empire, and King Philip II moved his capital from tiny Toledo to spacious Madrid. Successive kings transformed the city into a European capital. By 1900, Madrid had 575,000 people, concentrated within a small area. In the mid-20th century, the city exploded with migrants from the countryside, creating today's modern sprawl. Fortunately for tourists, the historic core survives intact and is easy to navigate.

Madrid is working hard to make itself more livable. Massive urban-improvement projects such as pedestrianized streets, parks, commuter lines, and Metro stations are transforming the city. The investment is making once-dodgy neighborhoods safe and turning ramshackle zones into trendy ones. The broken concrete and traffic chaos of Madrid's not-so-distant past are gone. Even with Spain's financial woes, funding for the upkeep of this great city center has been maintained. Madrid feels orderly and welcoming.

Dive headlong into the grandeur and intimate charm of Madrid. Feel the vibe in Puerta del Sol, the pulsing heart of modern Madrid and of Spain itself. The lavish Royal Palace, with its gilded rooms and frescoed ceilings, rivals Versailles. The Prado has Europe's top collection of paintings, and nearby hangs Picasso's chilling masterpiece, *Guernica*. Retiro Park invites you to take a shady siesta and hopscotch through a mosaic of lovers, families, skateboarders, pets walking their masters, and expert bench-sitters. Save time for Madrid's elegant shops and people-friendly pedestrian zones. On Sundays, cheer for the bull at a bullfight or bargain like mad at a megasize flea market. Swelter through the hot, hot summers or bundle up for the cold winters. Save some energy for after dark, when Madrileños pack the streets for an evening paseo that can continue past midnight. Lively Madrid has enough street-singing, bar-hopping, and people-watching vitality to give any visitor a boost of youth.

PLANNING YOUR TIME

Madrid is worth two days and three nights on even the fastest trip. Divide your time among the city's top three attractions: the Royal Palace (worth a half-day), the Prado Museum (also worth a half-day), and the contemporary bar-hopping scene.

For good day-trip possibilities from Madrid, see the next two chapters (Northwest of Madrid and Toledo).

Day 1

Morning: Take a brisk, 20-minute good-morning-Madrid walk along the pedestrianized Calle de las Huertas from Puerta del Sol to the Prado. Spend the rest of the morning at the Prado (reserve in advance).

Afternoon: Enjoy an afternoon siesta in Retiro Park. Then tackle modern art at the Reina Sofía, which displays Picasso's *Guernica* (closed Tue). Ride bus #27 from this area out through Madrid's modern section to Puerta de Europa for a dose of the nontouristy, no-nonsense big city.

Evening: End your day with a progressive tapas dinner at a series of characteristic bars.

Day 2

Morning: Follow my self-guided walk, which loops to and from Puerta del Sol, with a tour through the Royal Palace in the middle.

Afternoon: Your afternoon is free for other sights or shopping. Be out at the magic hour—just before sunset—for the evening paseo when beautifully lit people fill Madrid.

Evening: Take in a flamenco or zarzuela performance.

Orientation to Madrid

Puerta del Sol marks the center of Madrid. No major sight is more than a 20-minute walk or a €7 taxi ride from this central square. Get out your map and frame off Madrid's historic core: To the west of Puerta del Sol is the Royal Palace. To the east, you'll find the Prado Museum, along with the Reina Sofía museum. North of Puerta del Sol is Gran Vía, a broad east-west boulevard bubbling with shops and cinemas. Between Gran Vía and Puerta del Sol is a lively pedestrian shopping zone. And southwest of Puerta del Sol is Plaza Mayor, the center of a 17th-century, slow-down-and-smell-the-cobbles district.

This entire historic core around Puerta del Sol—Gran Vía, Plaza Mayor, the Prado, and the Royal Palace—is easily covered on foot. A wonderful chain of pedestrian streets crosses the city east to west, from the Prado to Plaza Mayor (along Calle de las Huertas) and from Puerta del Sol to the Royal Palace (on Calle del Arenal). Stretching north from Gran Vía, Calle de Fuencarral is a trendy shopping and strolling pedestrian street.

TOURIST INFORMATION

Madrid offers city TIs run by the Madrid City Council, and regional TIs run by the privately owned Turismo Madrid. Both are helpful, but you'll get more biased information from Turismo Madrid.

City-run TIs share a website (www.esmadrid.com), a central phone number (tel. 914-544-410), and hours (daily 9:30-20:30 or later); exceptions are noted in the listings below. The best and most central city TI is on **Plaza Mayor.** They can help direct travelers to the nearby foreign tourist assistance office (SATE; see "Helpful Hints" for details).

Madrid's other city-run TIs are at **Plaza de Colón** (in the underground passage accessed from Paseo de la Castellana and Calle de Goya), **Palacio de Cibeles** (inside, up the stairs, and to the right), **Plaza de Cibeles** (at Paseo del Prado), and **Paseo del Arte** (on Plaza Sánchez Bustillo, near the Reina Sofía museum). Small TIs inside funky little glass buildings are scattered throughout the city in busy tourist spots, such as at the Reina Sofía's modern entrance, near the Neptune Fountain and Prado Museum, and on Plaza Callao. Travelers will find city TIs at the **airport** (Terminals 2 and 4, daily 9:00-20:00).

Regional Turismo Madrid TIs share a website (www.turismomadrid.es) and are located near the **Prado Museum** (Duque de Medinaceli, across from Palace Hotel, Mon-Sat 8:00-15:00, Sun 9:00-14:00), **Chamartín train station** (near track 20, Mon-Sat 8:00-20:00, Sun 9:00-14:00), and **Atocha train station**

MADRID

(AVE arrivals side, Mon-Sat 8:00-20:00, Sun 9:00-20:00). There are also regional TIs at the **airport** (Terminals 1 and 4, Mon-Sat 9:00-20:00, Sun 9:00-14:00).

At most TIs, you can get the *Es Madrid* English-language monthly, which lists events around town. Pick up and use the free Metro map and the separate *Public Transport* map (which includes detailed bus transportation routes throughout the city center).

Entertainment Guides: For arts and culture listings, the TI's printed material is pretty good, but you can also pick up the more practical Spanish-language weekly entertainment guide *Guía del Ocio* (€1, sold at newsstands) or visit www.guiadelocio.com. It lists daily live music *("Conciertos"),* museums (under *"Arte"*—with the latest times, prices, and special exhibits), restaurants (an exhaustive listing), TV schedules, and movies ("V.O." means original version, *"V.O. en inglés sub"* means a movie is played in English with Spanish subtitles rather than dubbed).

ARRIVAL IN MADRID

For more information on arriving at or departing from Madrid, see "Madrid Connections," at the end of this chapter.

By Train: Madrid's two train stations, Chamartín and Atocha, are both on Metro and *cercanías* (suburban train) lines with easy access to downtown Madrid. Chamartín handles most international trains and the AVE (AH-vay) train to and from Segovia. Atocha generally covers southern Spain, as well as the AVE trains to and from Barcelona, Córdoba, Sevilla, and Toledo. Many train tickets include a *cercanías* connection to or from the train station.

Traveling Between Chamartín and Atocha Stations: You can take the Metro (line 1, 30-40 minutes, €1.50, but the *cercanías* trains are faster (6/hour, 13 minutes, Atocha-Chamartín lines C1, C3, C4, C7, C8, and C10 each connect the two stations, lines C3 and C4 also stop at Sol—Madrid's central square, €1.70). If you have a rail pass or any regular train ticket to Madrid, you can get a free transfer. Go to the *Cercanías* touch-screen ticket machine and choose *combinado cercanías,* then either scan the bar code of your train ticket or punch in a code (labeled *combinado cercanías),* and choose your destination. These trains depart from Atocha's track 6 and generally Chamartín's track 1, 3, 8, or 9—but check the *Salidas Inmediatas* board to be sure.

By Bus: Madrid has several bus stations, each one handy to a Metro station: Estación Sur de Autobuses (for Ávila, Salamanca, and Granada; Metro: Méndez Álvaro); Plaza Elíptica (for Toledo, Metro: Plaza Elíptica); Moncloa (for El Escorial, Metro: Moncloa); and Avenida de América (for Pamplona and Burgos, Metro:

MADRID

Greater Madrid

CHAMARTÍN TRAIN STATION
PUERTA DE EUROPA "TWIN TOWERS"
Chamartín
M-30
To Barajas Airport Terminal 4

Plaza de Castilla

CASTELLANA
ALBERTO ALCOCER

BERNABÉU STADIUM
C. ESPINA
#27
Santiago Bernabéu

PRÍNCIPE DE VERGARA

To Barajas Airport, Barcelona & ❹
A-2

To El Escorial & Segovia via A-6

MUSEUM OF THE AMERICAS
❸ Moncloa
CLOTHING MUSEUM
HERMITAGE OF S. ANTONIO DE LA FLORIDA (GOYA'S TOMB)
TEMPLE OF DEBOD

BERMUDEZ
J. ABASCAL
Iglesia M
SOROLLA MUSEUM

Avenida de América M
LAS VENTAS BULLRING
Ventas M

ALCALÁ

HISTORY MUSEUM
MALASAÑA
Plaza Colón

O'DONNELL

M-30

PRÍNCIPE PÍO TRAIN & BUS STATIONS ❷
Príncipe Pío
Casa de Campo

Plaza de España
GRAN VÍA
#27
RECOLETOS

Retiro Park

Sol ★ Puerta del Sol
PRADO

ROYAL PALACE
Plaza Mayor
EL RASTRO
ATOCHA
ACACIAS
Atocha RENFE M

ROYAL TAPESTRY FACTORY

MEDITERRANEO
A-3

See detail maps

Menéndez Pelayo M

ATOCHA TRAIN STATION

STA. MARIA DE LA CABEZA

MÉNDEZ ÁLVARO
BARCELONA

Méndez Álvaro M ❶

To Barajas Airport Terminal 4

Manzanares River
M-30

G. RICARDOS
To ❺ & Toledo via N-401
A-42

Bus Stations
❶ Estación Sur de Autobuses
❷ Príncipe Pío Station
❸ Moncloa Station
❹ To Avenida de América Station
❺ To Plaza Elíptica Station

--- Bus #27 Self-Guided Tour

Not all Metro stations are shown

2 Kilometers
2 Miles

A-4

To Toledo, Sevilla & Barcelona via AVE trains

Avenida de América). If you take a taxi from the station to your hotel, you'll pay a €3 supplement.

By Plane: Both international and domestic flights arrive at Madrid's Barajas Airport. Options for getting into town include public bus, *cercanías* train, Metro, taxi, and minibus shuttle.

HELPFUL HINTS

Sightseeing Tips: While the Prado and palace are open daily, the Reina Sofía (with Picasso's *Guernica*) is closed on Tuesday, and other sights are closed on Monday, including the Monasterio de San Lorenzo de El Escorial, outside of Madrid (see next chapter). If you're here on a Sunday, consider going to the flea market (year-round) and/or a bullfight (some Sun in March-mid-Oct; generally daily during San Isidro festival in May-early June).

Theft Alert: Be wary of pickpockets—anywhere, anytime. Areas of particular risk are Puerta del Sol (the central square), El Rastro (the flea market), Gran Vía (the paseo zone: Plaza del Callao to Plaza de España), the Ópera Metro station (or anywhere on the Metro), bus #27, the airport, and any crowded street. Be alert to the people around you: Someone wearing a heavy jacket in the summer is likely a pickpocket. Teenagers may dress like Americans and work the areas around the three big art museums; being under 18, they can't be charged in any meaningful way by the police. Assume any fight or commotion is a scam to distract people about to become victims of a pickpocket. Wear your money belt. For help if you get ripped off, see the next listing.

Tourist Emergency Aid: SATE is an assistance service for tourists who might need, for any reason, to visit a police station or lodge a complaint. Help ranges from canceling stolen credit cards to assistance in reporting a crime (central police station, daily 9:00-24:00, near Plaza de Santo Domingo at Calle Leganitos 19). They can help you get to the police station and will even act as an interpreter if you have trouble communicating with the police. Or you can call in your report to the SATE line (24-hour tel. 902-102-112, English spoken once you get connected to a person), then go to the police station (where they'll likely speak only Spanish) to sign your statement.

You may see a police station in the Sol Metro station.

Prostitution: Diverse by European standards, Madrid is spilling over with immigrants from South America, North Africa, and Eastern Europe. Many young women come here, fall on hard times, and end up on the streets. While it's illegal to make money from someone else selling sex (i.e., pimping), prostitutes over 18 can solicit legally. Calle de la Montera (leading from Puerta del Sol to Plaza Red de San Luis) is lined with what looks like a bunch of high-school girls skipping out of school for a cigarette break. Don't stray north of Gran Vía around Calle de la Luna and Plaza Santa María Soledad—while the streets may look inviting, this area is a meat-eating flower.

One-Stop Shopping at El Corte Inglés: Madrid's dominant department store is El Corte Inglés, filling three huge buildings in the commercial pedestrian zone just off Puerta del Sol. Building 3—full of sports equipment, books, and home furnishings—is closest to the Puerta del Sol. Building 2, a block up from Puerta del Sol on Calle Preciados, has a handy info desk at the door (with Madrid maps), a travel agency/box office for local events, souvenirs, toiletries, a post office, men and women's fashion, a boring cafeteria, and a vast supermarket in the basement with a fancy "Club del Gourmet" section for edible souvenirs. Farther north on Calle del Carmen toward Plaza del Callao is Building 1, which has electronics, another travel agency/box office, and the "Gourmet Experience"—a floor filled with fun eateries and a rooftop terrace for diners.

All El Corte Inglés department stores are open daily (Mon-Sat 10:00-22:00, Sun 11:00-21:00, tel. 913-798-000, www.elcorteingles.es). Locals figure you'll find anything you need at El Corte Inglés. Salespeople wear flag pins indicating which languages they speak. If doing serious shopping here, ask about their discounts (10 percent for tourists) and VAT refund policy (21 percent but with a minimum purchase requirement that you can accumulate over multiple shopping trips).

Wi-Fi: Plaza Mayor has free Wi-Fi, as does the Palacio de Cibeles and the Thyssen-Bornemisza Museum. You can get online on all Madrid buses and trains—look for *Wi-Fi gratis* signs.

Bookstores: For books in English, try **FNAC Callao** (Calle Preciados 28, tel. 902-100-632), **Casa del Libro** (English on basement floor, Gran Vía 29, tel. 902-026-402), and **El Corte Inglés** (guidebooks and some fiction, in its Building 3 Books/Librería branch kitty-corner from main store, fronting Puerta del Sol—see listing above).

Laundry: For a self-service laundry, try **Colada Express** at Calle Campomanes 9 (free Wi-Fi, daily 9:00-22:00, tel. 657-876-464) or **Lavandería** at Calle León 6 (self-service, Mon-Sat 9:00-22:00, Sun 12:00-15:00; full-service, Mon-Sat 9:00-14:00 & 15:00-20:00, tel. 914-299-545).

Travel Agencies: The grand department store **El Corte Inglés** has

MADRID

Central Madrid

To Plaza de España

GRAN VIA

CALLE TORIJA

PALACIO DEL SENADO

Jardines de Sabatini

Plaza de Santo Domingo

JACOMETREZO

Callao M

LA ENCARNACIÓN

CALLE DE LA BOLA

CALLE ARRIETA

STO. DOMINGO

Santo Domingo M

PRECIADOS

PST. S. MARTIN

S. QUINTÍN

C. CAMPOMANES

C. D. PERAL

ROYAL PALACE

Plaza de Oriente

FELIPE V

TEATRO REAL

Plaza Isabel II

FLORA

Plaza San Martín

CARLOS II

CALLE DE BAILÉN

REQUENA

VERGARA

Plaza Ramales

C. SER. LUZON

INDEPENDENCIA

ESCALINATA

Ópera M

CALLE HILERAS

CALLE DEL

Plaza de la Armería

Plaza Herradores

SAN GINES

C. BORD.

COLOR.

ALMUDENA CATHEDRAL

FACTOR

SAN NICOLAS

CALLE MAYOR

N

200 Meters

200 Yards

CALLE

Plaza de la Villa

CITY HALL

MERCADO DE SAN MIGUEL

Plaza Mayor

ZARAGOZA

CONVENT

PUÑONROSTRO

MESONES BARS

CUCHILLEROS

CALLE DE TOLEDO

CALLE DE SEGOVIA

SACRAMENTO

Plaza Conde Barajas

CONCEPCIÓN

Plaza Puerta Cerrada

CALLE

COLEGIATA

C. MORERIA

COST. DE S. ANDRÉS

C. NUNCIO

SAN ISIDRO

C. REDONDILLA

C. ALMENDRO

CALLE DON PEDRO

CALLE CAVA BAJA

C. CAVA ALTA

La Latina M

CALLE DUQUE

Plaza de San Francisco

CRA. S. FRANCISCO

C. JUANELO

C. CEBADA

DE

TOLEDO

Plaza de Cascorro

C. ÁNGEL

C. DE EMBAJADORES

CALLE STA. ANA

EL RASTRO FLEA MARKET

CALLE

CALLE RIBERA

CALLE AGUILA

C. D. CALATRAVA

C. FREY

two travel agencies (air and rail tickets, but not reservations for rail-pass holders, €2 fee; Building 2—first floor, Building 1—third floor; see "One-Stop Shopping at El Corte Inglés," earlier). They also have a travel agency in the Atocha train station. These are fast and easy places to buy AVE and other train tickets.

GETTING AROUND MADRID

Madrid has excellent public transit. Pick up the Metro map (free, available at TIs or at Metro info booths in stations with staff); for buses get the fine *Public Transport* map (free at TIs). The metropolitan Madrid transit website (www.crtm.es) covers all public transportation options (Metro, bus, and suburban rail).

By Metro: The city's broad streets can be hot and exhausting. A subway trip of even a stop or two saves time and energy. Madrid's Metro is simple, speedy, and cheap. It costs €1.50 for a ride within zone A, which covers most of the city, but not trains out to the airport. The 10-ride, €12.20 Metrobus ticket can be shared by several travelers with the same destination and works on both the Metro and buses. Buy single-ride tickets in the Metro (from easy-to-use machines or ticket booths—just pick your destination from the alphabetized list and follow the simple prompts), at newspaper stands, or at Estanco tobacco shops. Insert your ticket in the turnstile, then retrieve it and pass through. The Metro runs from 6:00 to 1:30 in the morning. At all times, be alert to thieves, who thrive in crowded stations.

Study your Metro map—the simplified map on the previous page can get you started. Lines are color-coded and numbered; use end-of-the-line station names to choose your direction of travel. Once in the Metro station, signs direct you to the train line and direction (e.g., Linea 1, *Valdecarros*). To transfer, follow signs in the station leading to connecting lines. Once you reach your final stop, look for the green *salida* signs pointing to the exits. Use the helpful neighborhood maps to choose the right *salida* and save yourself lots of walking. Metro info: www.metromadrid.es.

By Bus: City buses, though not as easy as the Metro, can be useful (€1.50 tickets sold on bus, €12.20 for a 10-ride Metrobus ticket, bus maps at TI or info booth on Puerta del Sol, poster-size maps usually posted at bus stops, buses run 6:00-24:00, much less frequent *Buho* buses run all night). The EMT Madrid app finds the

MADRID

Madrid Metro

To Salamanca, San Sebastián,
Santiago de Compostela,
Barcelona, Lisbon &
other destinations

(Light Blue)
1
Chamartín RENFE
Pinar de
Chamartín

To Airport
Terminal 4

Valdeacederas

Plaza de
Castilla

Tetuán

Not to Scale

Alvarado

(Red)
2
Cuatro
Caminas

(Yellow)
3

To
Alameda de
Osuna

Moncloa
Argüelles

Canal   Iglesia

Noviciado

BULL RING

(Green)
5
Ventas

Bilbao
Tribunal   A. Mar-
tinez

Chueca   Goya

(Red)
2

To
Las
Rosas

Plaza de
España

Gran Vía

Santo Domingo

Ópera

Callao

Sol

ROYAL
PALACE

PLAZA
MAYOR

La Latina   Lavapiés

Sevilla   Banco de
España

Retiro

To
Airport

#27   PRADO

RETIRO
PARK

Tirso de
Molina

To
Casa de
Campo

Antón Martín

To Airport
Terminal 4

Embajadores

REINA
SOFÍA

Atocha

5
(Green)

Puerta de
Toledo

#27

Atocha RENFE

Menéndez
Pelayo

GRAY CIRCLE
INDICATES
CENTRAL MADRID

Legazpi
Villaverde
Alto

3
(Yellow)

To Toledo, Sevilla,
Barcelona (AVE)
& other destinations

Pacífico

Valdecarros

1
(Light Blue)

Bus #27

To
Airport

Metro Line 1 (Light Blue)
Metro Line 2 (Red)
Metro Line 3 (Yellow)
Metro Line 5 (Green)
Bus
#M1 Electric Bus
Rail (Long distance)
Rail (Cercanías Commuter Line)

Not all lines and
stations are shown

closest stops and lines and gives accurate wait times, plus there's a version in English. Bus info: www.emtmadrid.es.

By Taxi or Uber: Madrid's 15,000 taxis are reasonably priced and easy to hail. A green light on the roof indicates that a taxi is available. Foursomes travel as cheaply by taxi as by Metro. For example, a ride from the Royal Palace to the Prado costs about €7. After the drop charge (about €3), the per-kilometer rate depends on the time: *Tarifa 1* (€1.05/kilometer) is charged Mon-Fri 7:00-21:00; *Tarifa 2* (€1.20/kilometer) is valid after 21:00 and on Saturdays, Sundays, and holidays. If your cabbie uses anything other than *Tarifa 1* on weekdays (shown as an isolated "1" on the meter), you're being cheated.

Rates can be higher if you go outside Madrid. There's a flat rate of €30 between the city center and any one of the airport terminals. Other legitimate charges include the €3 supplement for leaving any train or bus station, €20 per hour for waiting, and a maximum of €5 if you call to have the taxi come to you. Make sure the meter is turned on as soon as you get into the cab so the driver can't tack anything onto the official rate. If the driver starts adding up "extras," look for the sticker detailing all legitimate surcharges (which should be on the passenger window).

Madrid is the only city in Spain where **Uber** operates, and prices are generally similar to taxis.

Tours in Madrid

∩ To sightsee on your own, download my free Madrid audio tour.

ON FOOT
Food and Walking Tours
Letango Tours offers private tours, packages, and stays all over Spain with a focus on families and groups. Carlos Galvin, a Spaniard who led tours for my groups for more than a decade, his wife Jennifer from Seattle, and their team of guides in Madrid offer a kid-friendly "Madrid Discoveries" tour that mixes a market walk and history with a culinary-and-tapas introduction (€275/group, up to 5 people, kids free, 3-plus hours). They also lead tours to Barcelona, whitewashed villages, wine country, and more (www.letango.com, tours@letango.com).

At **Madridivine,** David Gillison enthusiastically shares his love for his adopted city through food and walking tours of historic Madrid. He connects you with locals, food, and wine from an insider's viewpoint (€200/group, up to 7 people, 3-hour tour, food and drinks extra—usually around €35-40, www.madridivine.com/ricksteves, madridivineinfo@gmail.com).

Julià Travel offers various walking and food tours, including one on Hapsburg Madrid and another that allows you to skip the line at the Prado (from €28, www.juliatravel.com). See Julià Travel's listing under "On Wheels," below, for info about their bus tours.

Local Guides

Frederico and Cristina, along with their team, are licensed guides who lead city walks. Frederico specializes in family tours of Madrid and engaging kids and teens in museums, and Cristina excels at intertwining history and art (prices per group: €160/2 hours, €200/4 hours, €240/6 hours). They also lead tours to nearby towns (with public or private transit, mobile 649-936-222, www.spainfred.com, info@spainfred.com).

Across Madrid is run by Almudena Cros, a well-travelled academic Madrileña. She offers several specialized tours including one on the Spanish Civil War that draws on her family's history. She also gives a good Prado tour for kids (generally €70/person, maximum 8 people, €50 extra for private tour, book well in advance, mobile 652-576-423, www.acrossmadrid.com, info@acrossmadrid.com).

Stephen Drake-Jones, an eccentric British expat, has led walks of historic old Madrid almost daily for decades. A historian with a passion for the Duke of Wellington (the general who stopped Napoleon), Stephen loves to teach history. For €75 you get a 3.5-hour tour with three stops for drinks and tapas (call it lunch; daily at 11:00, maximum 8 people). You can also book a private version of this tour (€190/2 people) or one of his many themed tours (Spanish Civil War, Hemingway's Madrid, and more; www.wellsoc.org, mobile 609-143-203, chairman@wellsoc.org).

Other good licensed local guides include: **Inés Muñiz Martin** (guiding since 1997 and a third-generation Madrileña, €120-185/2-5 hours, 25 percent more on weekends and holidays, mobile 629-147-370, www.immguidedtours.com, info@immguidedtours.com), and **Susana Jarabo** (with a master's in art history, €200/4 hours; extra charge to tour by bike, scooter, or Segway; available March-Aug, mobile 667-027-722, susanjarabo@yahoo.es).

ON WHEELS
Hop-On, Hop-Off Bus

Madrid City Tour makes two different hop-on, hop-off circuits through the city: historic and modern. Buy a ticket from the driver (€21/1 day, €25/2 consecutive days), and you can hop from sight to sight and route to route as you like, listening to a recorded English commentary along the way (15-21 stops, about 90 minutes, with buses departing every 15 minutes). The two routes intersect at the south side of Puerta del Sol and in front of Starbucks across from

Madrid at a Glance

▲▲▲**Royal Palace** Spain's sumptuous, lavishly furnished national palace. **Hours:** Daily 10:00-20:00, Oct-March 10:00-18:00. See page 35.

▲▲▲**Prado Museum** One of the world's great museums, loaded with masterpieces by Diego Velázquez, Francisco de Goya, El Greco, Hieronymus Bosch, Albrecht Dürer, and more. **Hours:** Mon-Sat 10:00-20:00, Sun until 19:00. See page 46.

▲▲▲**Centro de Arte Reina Sofía** Modern-art museum featuring Picasso's epic masterpiece *Guernica.* **Hours:** Mon and Wed-Sat 10:00-21:00, Sun 10:00-19:00, closed Tue. See page 61.

▲▲▲**Paseo** Evening stroll among the Madrileños. **Hours:** Sundown until the wee hours. See page 78.

▲▲**Puerta del Sol** Madrid's lively central square. See page 18.

▲▲**Thyssen-Bornemisza Museum** A great complement to the Prado, with lesser-known yet still impressive works and an especially good Impressionist collection. **Hours:** Mon 12:00-16:00, Tue-Sun 10:00-19:00, Sat until 21:00 in summer (exhibits only). See page 60.

▲▲**National Archaeological Museum** Traces the history of Iberia through artifacts. **Hours:** Tue-Sat 9:30-20:00, Sun 9:30-15:00, closed Mon. See page 69.

▲▲**Sorolla Museum** Delightful, intimate collection of portraits and landscapes by Spanish artist Joaquín Sorolla. **Hours:** Tue-Sat 9:30-20:00, Sun 10:00-15:00, closed Mon. See page 71.

▲**Bullfight** Spain's controversial pastime. **Hours:** Scattered Sundays and holidays March-mid-Oct, plus almost daily in May-early June. See page 74.

the Prado (daily March-Oct 9:30-22:00, Nov-Feb 10:00-18:00, tel. 917-791-888, www.madridcitytour.es).

Big-Bus City Sightseeing Tours

Julià Travel leads bus tours departing from Calle San Nicolás near Plaza de Ramales, just south of Plaza de Oriente (office open Mon-Fri 8:00-19:00, Sat-Sun 8:00-15:00, tel. 915-599-605). Their city offerings include a 2.5-hour Madrid tour with a live guide in two or three languages (€27, one stop for a drink at Hard Rock Café, one

▲▲**Flamenco** Captivating music and dance performances, at various venues throughout the city. **Hours:** Shows every night, some places closed on Sun. See page 79.

▲▲**Plaza Mayor** Historic cobbled square. See page 22.

▲▲**Retiro Park** Festive green escape from the city, with rental rowboats and great people-watching. **Hours:** Closes at dusk. See page 67.

▲**Royal Botanical Garden** A relaxing museum of plants, with specimens from around the world. **Hours:** Daily 10:00-21:00, shorter hours off-season. See page 68.

▲**Naval Museum** Seafaring history of a country famous for its Armada. **Hours:** Tue-Sun 10:00-19:00, until 15:00 in Aug, closed Mon. See page 68.

▲**Museum of the Americas** Pre-Columbian and colonial artifacts from the New World. **Hours:** Tue-Sat 9:30-15:00, Thu until 19:00, Sun 10:00-15:00, closed Mon. See page 69.

▲**Hermitage of San Antonio de la Florida** Church with Goya's tomb, plus frescoes by the artist. **Hours:** Tue-Sun 9:30-20:00, closed Mon. See page 70.

▲**Madrid History Museum** The city's story told through old paintings, maps, fascinating photos, and historic artifacts. **Hours:** Tue-Sun 10:00-20:00, closed Mon. See page 71.

▲**El Rastro** Europe's biggest flea market, filled with bargains and pickpockets. **Hours:** Sun 9:00-15:00, best before 11:00. See page 76.

▲**Zarzuela** Madrid's delightful light opera. **Hours:** Evenings. See page 78.

shopping stop, no museum visits, daily at 9:00 and 15:00, no reservation required—just show up 15 minutes before departure). See their website for other tours and services (www.juliatravel.com).

Self-Guided Tours by Bus or Minibus
A ride on public **bus #27** from the museum neighborhood up Paseo del Prado and Paseo de la Castellana to the Puerta de Europa and back gives visitors a glimpse of the modern side of Madrid, while a

MADRID

ride on electric **minibus #M1** takes you through the characteristic, gritty old center.

Walks in Madrid

Two self-guided walks provide a look at two different sides of Madrid. For a taste of old Madrid, start with my "Puerta del Sol to Royal Palace Loop," which winds through the historic center. My "Gran Vía Walk" lets you glimpse a more modern side of Spain's capital.

🎧 Download my free Madrid audio tour, which complements this section.

PUERTA DEL SOL TO ROYAL PALACE LOOP

Madrid's historic center is pedestrian-friendly and filled with spacious squares, a trendy market, bulls' heads in a bar, and a cookie-dispensing convent. Allow about two hours for this self-guided, mile-long triangular walk. You'll start and finish on Madrid's central square, Puerta del Sol (Metro: Sol).

• *Start in the middle of the square, by the equestrian statue of King Charles III, and survey the scene.*

❶ Puerta del Sol

The bustling Puerta del Sol, rated ▲▲, is Madrid's—and Spain's—center. It's a hub for the Metro, *cercanías* (local) trains, revelers,

pickpockets, and characters dressed as cartoon characters (who hit up little kids so their parents end up paying for a photo op). You'll also notice that it's a meeting point for many "free tours" with their color-coded umbrellas. In recent years, the square has undergone a facelift to become a mostly pedestrianized, wide-open space...without a bench or spot of shade in sight. Nearly traffic-free, it's a popular site for political demonstrations. Don't be surprised if you come across a large, peaceful protest here.

The equestrian statue in the middle of the square honors **King Charles III** (1716-1788) whose enlightened urban policies earned him the affectionate nickname "the best mayor of Madrid." He decorated the squares with beautiful fountains, got those meddlesome Jesuits out of city government, established the public-school system, mandated underground sewers, opened his private Retiro Park to the general public, built the Prado, made the Royal Palace the wonder of Europe, and generally cleaned up Madrid.

Head to the slightly uphill end of the square and find the **statue of a bear** pawing a tree—a symbol of Madrid since medieval times. Bears used to live in the royal hunting grounds outside the city. And the *madroño* trees produce a berry that makes the traditional *madroño* liqueur.

Charles III faces a red-and-white building with a bell tower. This was Madrid's first post office, which he founded in the 1760s. Today it's the **county governor's office,** home to the president who governs greater Madrid. The building is notorious for having once been dictator Francisco Franco's police headquarters. A tragic number of those detained and interrogated by the Franco police tried to "escape" by jumping out its windows to their deaths.

Appreciate the **harmonious architecture** of the buildings that circle the square—yellow-cream, four stories, balconies of iron, shuttered windows, and balustrades along the rooflines.

Crowds fill the square on New Year's Eve as the rest of Spain watches the Times Square-style action on TV. The bell atop the governor's office chimes 12 times, while Madrileños eat one grape for each ring to bring good luck through each of the next 12 months.

• *Cross the square and street to the governor's office.*

Look at the curb directly in front of the entrance to the governor's office. The marker is **"kilometer zero,"** the symbolic center of Spain (with the country's six main highways indicated). Standing on the zero marker with your back to the governor's office, get oriented visually: At twelve o'clock (straight ahead), notice the thriving pedestrian commercial zone (with the huge El Corte Inglés department store). Look up to see the famous Tío Pepe sign—advertising the famous sherry from Andalucía since the 1930s. At two o'clock starts the seedier Calle de la Montera, a street with shady characters and prostitutes that leads to the trendy, pedestrianized Calle de Fuencarral. At three o'clock is the biggest Apple store in Europe; the Prado is about a mile farther to your right. At ten o'clock, the pedestrianized Calle del Arenal Street (which leads to the Royal Palace) dumps into this square...just where you will end this walk.

Now turn around. On either side of the entrance to the governor's office are **two white marble plaques** tied to important dates, expressing thanks from the regional government to its citizens for assisting in times of dire need. To the left of the entry, a plaque on the wall honors those who helped during the terrorist bombings of March 11, 2004 (we have our 9/11—Spain commemorates its 3/11). A similar plaque on the right marks the spot where the war against Napoleon started in 1808. When Napoleon invaded Spain and tried to appoint his brother (rather than the Spanish heir) as king of Spain, an angry crowd gathered outside this building. The French soldiers attacked and simply massacred the mob. Painter

MADRID

To Plaza de España & Madrid Tower

S. QUINTÍN

LA ENCARNACIÓN

CALLE ARRIETA

STO. DOMINGO

C. D. PERAL

Campo Del Moro

ROYAL PALACE

CALLE DE BAILÉN

PHILIP IV STATUE

FELIPE V

CARLOS II

ROYAL THEATER

Plaza Isabel II

OLD CINEMA

10

11

Plaza de Oriente

CAFÉ DE ORIENTE

VERGARA

12

Ópera

Plaza de la Armería

REQUENA

Plaza Ramales

C. SEN. LUZON

INDEPENDENCIA

ESCALINATA

Plaza Herradores

ROYAL PALACE ENTRANCE

FACTOR

SAN NICOLÁS

MAIN ENTRANCE

ALMUDENA CATHEDRAL

9

Plaza de la Villa

CALLE

SAN MIGUEL MARKET

PUÑONROSTRO

5

SIDE ENTRANCE

CUESTA DE LA VEGA

100 Meters
100 Yards

8

TOWN HALL

7

ASSASSINATION ATTEMPT MEMORIAL

CALLE SACRAMENTO

6

CONVENT

Plaza Conde Barajas

1 Puerta del Sol
2 Calle de Postas
3 Plaza Mayor

4 La Torre del Oro Bar Andalú
5 Mesones & Mercado de San Miguel
6 Church & Convent of Corpus Christi

Francisco de Goya, who worked just up the street, observed the event and captured the tragedy in his paintings *Second of May, 1808* and *Third of May, 1808,* now in the Prado.

Finally, notice the hats of the civil guardsmen at the entry. The hats have square backs, and it's said that they were cleverly designed so that the guards can lean against the wall while enjoying a cigarette.

On the corner of Puerta del Sol and Calle Mayor (downhill end of Puerta del Sol) is the busy, recommended *confitería* **La Mallorquina,** "*fundada en 1.894.*" Go inside for a tempting peek at racks with goodies hot out of the oven. Enjoy observing the churning energy at the bar lined with Madrileños popping in for a fast coffee and a sweet treat. The shop is famous for its cream-filled *Napolitana* pastry. Or sample Madrid's answer to doughnuts, *rosquillas* (*tontas* means "silly"—plain, and *listas* means "all dressed up and ready to go"—with icing). The café upstairs is more genteel, with nice views of the square.

From inside the shop, look back toward the entrance and notice the tile above the door with the 18th-century view of Puerta

Puerta del Sol to Royal Palace Loop

MADRID

⑦ Town Hall
⑧ Assassination Attempt Memorial
⑨ Almudena Cathedral
⑩ Royal Palace

⑪ Plaza de Oriente
⑫ Plaza de Isabel II
⑬ Calle del Arenal

del Sol. Compare this with today's view out the door. This was before the square was widened, when a church stood at its top end.

Puerta del Sol ("Gate of the Sun") is named for a long-gone gate with the rising sun carved onto it, which once stood at the eastern edge of the old city. From here, we begin our walk through the historic town that dates back to medieval times.

• *Head west on busy Calle Mayor, just past McDonald's, and veer left up the pedestrian-only street called...*

❷ Calle de Postas

The street sign shows the post coach heading for that famous first post office. Medieval street signs posted on the lower corners of buildings included pictures so the illiterate (and monolingual tourists) could "read" them. Fifty yards up the street on the left, at Calle San Cristóbal, is Pans & Company, a popular Catalan sandwich chain offering lots of healthy choices. While Spaniards tend to consider American fast food unhealthy—both culturally and physically—they love it. McDonald's and Burger King are thriving in Spain.

MADRID

• *Continue up Calle de Postas, and take a slight right on Calle de la Sal through the arcade, where you emerge into...*

❸ Plaza Mayor

This square, worth ▲▲, is a vast, cobbled, traffic-free chunk of 17th-century Spain. In early modern times, this was Madrid's

main square. The **equestrian statue** (wearing a ruffled collar) honors Philip III, who (in 1619) transformed the old marketplace into a Baroque plaza. The square is 140 yards long and 100 yards wide, enclosed by three-story buildings with symmetrical windows, balconies, slate roofs, and steepled towers. Each side of the square is uniform, as if a grand palace were turned inside-out. This distinct "look," pioneered by architect Juan de Herrera (who finished El Escorial), is found all over Madrid.

This site served as the city's 17th-century open-air theater. Upon this stage, much Spanish history has been played out: bullfights, fires, royal pageantry, and events of the gruesome **Inquisition.** Worn-down reliefs on the seatbacks under the lampposts illustrate the story. During the Inquisition, many were tried here—suspected heretics, Protestants, Jews, tour guides without a local license, and Muslims whose "conversion" to Christianity was dubious. The guilty were paraded around the square before their executions, wearing billboards listing their many sins (bleachers were built for bigger audiences, while the wealthy rented balconies). The heretics were burned, and later, criminals were slowly strangled as they held a crucifix, hearing the reassuring words of a priest as the life was squeezed out of them with a garrote. Up to 50,000 people could crowd into this square for such spectacles.

The square's buildings are mainly private apartments. Want one? Costs run from €400,000 for a tiny attic studio to €2 million and up for a 2,500-square-foot flat. The square is painted a democratic shade of burgundy—the result of a citywide vote. Since the end of decades of dictatorship in 1975, there's been a passion for voting here. Three different colors were painted as samples on the walls of this square, and the city voted for its favorite.

The building to Philip's left, on the north side beneath the twin towers, was once home to the baker's guild and now houses the **TI,** which is wonderfully air-conditioned.

A **stamp-and-coin market** bustles at Plaza Mayor on Sundays (10:00-14:00). Day or night, Plaza Mayor is a colorful place to enjoy an affordable cup of coffee or overpriced food. Throughout Spain, lesser *plazas mayores* provide peaceful pools in the whitewater river of Spanish life. We'll cross the square, leaving through the far corner on the right-hand side, with a quick stop along that arcade on the way.

❹ La Torre del Oro Bar Andalú

For some interesting, if gruesome, bullfighting lore, step into La Torre del Oro Bar Andalú. This bar is a good place to finish off your Plaza Mayor visit (at #26, a few doors to the left of the TI). The bar has *Andalú* (Andalusian) ambience and an entertaining—if gruff—staff. Warning: They may push expensive tapas on tourists. The price list posted outside the door makes your costs perfectly clear: "*barra*" indicates the price at the bar; "*terraza*" is the price at an outdoor table. Step inside, stand at the bar, and order a drink—a *caña* (small draft beer) shouldn't cost more than €2.50.

The interior is a temple to bullfighting, festooned with gory decor. Notice the breathtaking action captured in the many photographs. Look under the stuffed head of Barbero the bull (center, facing the bar). At eye level you'll see a *puntilla*, the knife used to put poor Barbero out of his misery at the arena. The plaque explains: weight, birth date, owner, date of death, which matador killed him, and the location.

Just to the left of Barbero is a photo of longtime dictator Franco with the famous bullfighter Manuel Benítez Pérez—bet-

ter known as El Cordobés, the Elvis of bullfighters and a working-class hero.

At the top of the stairs going down to the WC, find the photo of El Cordobés and Robert Kennedy—looking like brothers. Three feet to the left of them (and elsewhere in the bar) is a shot of Che Guevara enjoying a bullfight.

Below and left of the Kennedy photo is a picture of El Cordobés' illegitimate son being gored. Disowned by El Cordobés senior, yet still using his dad's famous name after a court battle, the junior El Cordobés is one of this generation's top fighters.

At the end of the bar, in a glass case, is the "suit of lights" the great El Cordobés wore in an ill-fated 1967 fight, in which the bull gored him. El Cordobés survived; the bull didn't. Find the photo of Franco with El Cordobés at the far end, to the left of Segador the bull.

In the case with the "suit of lights," notice the photo of a matador (not El Cordobés) horrifyingly hooked by a bull's horn. For a series of photos showing this episode (and the same matador healed afterward), look to the right of Barbero back by the front door.

Below that series is a strip of photos showing José Tomás—a hero of this generation (with the cute if bloody face)—getting his groin gored. Tomás is renowned for his daring intimacy with the bull's horns—as illustrated here.

Leaving the bull bar, turn right and notice the **La Favorita hat shop** (at #25). See the plaque in the pavement honoring the shop, which has served the public since 1894.

Consider taking a break at one of the tables on Madrid's grandest square. Cafetería Margerit (nearby) occupies Plaza Mayor's sunniest corner and is a good place to enjoy a coffee with the view. The scene is easily worth the extra euro you'll pay for the drink.

• *Leave Plaza Mayor on Calle de Ciudad Rodrigo (at the northwest corner of the square), passing a series of solid turn-of-the-20th-century storefronts and sandwich joints, such as* **Casa Rúa,** *famous for their* cheap *bocadillos de calamares—fried squid rings on a small baguette.*

Mistura Ice Cream *(across the lane at Ciudad Rodrigo 6) serves fine coffee and quality ice cream, rolling your choice of topping into the ice cream with a cold-stone ritual that locals enjoy. Its cellar is called the "chill zone" for good reason—an oasis of cool and peace, ideal for enjoying your treat.*

Emerging from the arcade, turn left and head downhill toward the iron covered market hall. Before entering the market, look downhill to the left down a street called Cava de San Miguel.

❺ Mesones and Mercado de San Miguel

Lining the street called Cava de San Miguel is a series of traditional dive bars called **mesones.** If you like singing, sangria, and sloppy people, come back after 22:00 to visit one. These cave-like bars, stretching far back from the street, get packed with Madrileños out on dates who—emboldened by sangria and the setting—are prone to suddenly breaking out in song. It's a lowbrow, electric-keyboard, karaoke-type ambience, best on Friday and Saturday nights. The odd shape of these bars isn't a contrivance for the sake of atmosphere—Plaza Mayor was built on a slope, and these underground vaults are part of a structural system that braces the leveled plaza.

For a much more refined setting, pop into the Mercado de San Miguel (daily 10:00-24:00). This historic iron-and-glass structure from 1916 stands on the site of an even earlier marketplace. Renovated in the 21st century, the city's oldest surviving market hall now hosts some 30 high-end vendors of fresh produce, gourmet foods, wines by the glass, tapas, and full meals. Locals and tourists alike pause here for its food, natural-light ambience, and social scene.

Go on an edible scavenger hunt by simply grazing down the center aisle. You'll find: fish tapas, gazpacho and *pimientos de Padrón*, artisan cheeses, and lots of olives. Skewer them on a toothpick and they're called *banderillas*—for the decorated spear a bullfighter thrusts into the bull's neck. The smallest olives are Campo Real—the Madrid favorite. You'll find a draft *vermut* (Vermouth) bar with kegs of the sweet local dessert wine, along with sangria and sherry (V.O.R.S. means, literally, very old rare sherry—dry and full-bodied). Finally, the San Onofre bar is for your sweet tooth. *¡Que aproveche!*

• *After you walk through the market and leave through the exit farthest from Plaza Mayor, turn left, heading downhill on Calle del Conde de Miranda. At the first corner, turn right and cross the small plaza to the brick church in the far corner.*

❻ Church and Convent of Corpus Christi

The proud coats of arms over the main entry announce the rich family that built this Hieronymite church and convent in 1607. In 17th-century Spain, the most prestigious thing a noble family could do was build and maintain a convent. To harvest all the goodwill created in your community, you'd want your family's insignia right there for all to see. (You can see the donating couple, like a 17th-century Bill and Melinda Gates, kneeling before the communion wafer in the central panel over the entrance.) Inside is a cool and quiet oasis with a Last Supper altarpiece.

Now for a unique shopping experience. A half-block to the right from the church entrance is its associated convent—it's the big brown door on the left, at Calle del Codo 3 (Mon-Sat 9:30-13:00 & 16:30-18:30, closed Sun). The sign reads: *Venta de Dulces* (Sweets for Sale). To buy goodies from the cloistered nuns, buzz the *monjas* button, then wait patiently for the sister to respond over the intercom. Say *"dulces"* (DOOL-thays), and she'll let you in. When the lock buzzes, push open the door. It will be dark—look for a glowing light switch to turn on the lights. Walk straight in and to the left, then follow the sign to the *torno*—the lazy Susan that lets the sisters sell their baked goods without being seen. Scan the menu, announce your choice to the sequestered sister (she may tell you she has only one or two of the options available), place your money on the *torno,* and your goodies (and change) will appear. *Galletas* (shortbread cookies) are the least expensive item (a *medio*-kilo costs about €10). Or try the *pastas de almendra* (almond cookies).

• *Continue uphill on Calle del Codo (where, in centuries past, those in need of bits of armor shopped—see the tiled street sign on the building) and turn left, heading toward the Plaza de la Villa. Before entering the square, no-tice an **old door** to the left of the **Real Sociedad Económica** sign, made of wood lined with metal. This is consid-ered the oldest door in town on Madrid's oldest building—inhabited since 1480.*

It's set in a Moorish keyhole arch. Look up at what was a prison tower. Now continue into the square called Plaza de la Villa, dominated by Madrid's...

❼ Town Hall

The impressive structure features Madrid's distinctive architectural style—symmetrical square towers, topped with steeples and a slate roof...Castilian Baroque. The building was Madrid's Town Hall. Over the doorway, the three coats of arms sport many symbols of Madrid's rulers: Habsburg crowns on each, castles of Castile (in center shield), and the city symbol—the berry-eating bear (shield on left). This square was the ruling center of medieval Madrid in the centuries before it became an important capital.

Imagine how Philip II took this city by surprise in 1561 when he decided to move the capital of Europe's largest empire (even bigger than ancient Rome at the time) from Toledo to humble Ma-drid. To better administer their empire, the Habsburgs went on a building spree. But because their empire was drained of its riches by prolonged religious wars, they built Madrid with cheap brick instead of elegant granite. Baroque buildings in Spain didn't need to be over-the-top propagandistic structures like elsewhere, as the people here didn't need much encouragement to stay loyal to the Church.

The statue in the garden is of Philip II's admiral, Don Alvaro de Bazán—mastermind of the Christian victory over the Turk-ish Ottomans at the naval battle of Lepanto in 1571. This pivotal battle, fought off the coast of Greece, slowed the Ottoman threat to Christian Europe. However, mere months after Bazán's death in 1588, his "invincible" Spanish Armada was destroyed by Eng-land...and Spain's empire began its slow fade.

• *By the way, a cute little shop selling traditional monk- and nun-made pastries is just down the lane (**El Jardín del Convento**, at Calle del Cordón 1, on the back side of the cloistered convent you dropped by ear-lier). From here, walk along busy Calle Mayor, which leads downhill toward the Royal Palace. Along the way, at #80, you'll pass a fine lit-*

tle shop specializing in books about Madrid. A few blocks down Calle Mayor, on a tiny square, you'll find the...

❽ Assassination Attempt Memorial

This statue memorializes a 1906 assassination attempt. The target was Spain's King Alfonso XIII and his bride, Victoria Eugenie, as they paraded by on their wedding day. While the crowd was throwing flowers, an anarchist (as terrorists used to be called) threw a bouquet lashed to a bomb from a balcony at #84 (across the street). He missed the royal newlyweds, but killed 28 people. Gory photos of the event hang inside the Casa Ciriaco restaurant, which now occupies #84 (photos to the right of the entrance, or in an outside window). The king and queen went on to live to a ripe old age, producing many great-grandchildren, including the current king, Felipe VI.

• *Continue down Calle Mayor one more block to a busy street, Calle de Bailén. Take in the big, domed...*

❾ Almudena Cathedral (Catedral de Nuestra Señora de la Almudena)

Madrid's massive, gray-and-white cathedral (110 yards long and 80 yards high) opened in 1993, 100 years after workers started building it. This is the side entrance for tourists. Climbing the steps to the church courtyard, you'll come to a monument to Pope John Paul II's 1993 visit, when he consecrated Almudena—ending Madrid's 300-year stretch of requests for a cathedral of its own.

If you go inside (€1 donation requested), stop in the center, immediately under the dome, and face the altar. Beyond it, colorful paintings—rushed to completion for the pope's '93 visit—brighten the apse. In the right transept the faithful venerate a 15th-century Gothic altarpiece with a favorite statue of the Virgin Mary—a striking treasure considering the otherwise 20th-century Neo-Gothic interior. Gape up at the glittering 5,000-pipe organ in the rear of the nave.

The church's historic highlight is the 13th-century coffin (empty, painted leather on wood, in a chapel behind the altar) of Madrid's patron saint, Isidro. A humble farmer, the exceptionally devout Isidro was said to have been helped by angels who did the plowing for him while he prayed. Forty years after he died, this coffin was opened, and his body was found to have been miraculously preserved. This convinced the pope to canonize Isidro as the patron saint of Madrid and of farmers, with May 15 as his feast day.

• *Leave the church from the transept where you entered and turn left. Hike around the church to its rarely used front door. Climb the cathedral's front steps and face the imposing...*

❿ Royal Palace

Since the ninth century, this spot has been Madrid's center of power: from Moorish castle to Christian fortress to Renaissance palace to the current structure, built in the 18th century. With its expansive courtyard surrounded by imposing Baroque architecture, it represents the wealth of Spain before its decline. Its 2,800 rooms, totaling nearly 1.5 million square feet, make it Europe's largest palace. Stretching toward the mountains on the left is the vast Casa del Campo (a former royal hunting ground and now city park).

• *You could visit the palace now, using my self-guided tour.*

*Or, to follow the rest of this walk back to Puerta del Sol, continue one long block north up Calle de Bailén (walking alongside the palace) toward the **Madrid Tower** skyscraper. This was a big deal in the 1950s when it was one of the tallest buildings in Europe (460 feet tall) and the pride of Franco and his fascist regime. The tower marks Plaza de España, and the end of my "Gran Vía Walk." To Spaniards, this symbolizes the boom time the country enjoyed when it sided with the West during the Cold War (allowing the US and not the USSR to build military bases in Spain). Walk to where the street opens up and turn right, facing the statue, park, and royal theater.*

⓫ Plaza de Oriente

As its name suggests, this square faces east. The grand yet people-friendly plaza is typical of today's Europe, where energetic governments are converting car-congested wastelands into inviting public spaces like this. Where's the traffic? Under your feet. A past mayor of Madrid earned the nickname "The Mole" for all the digging he did.

Notice the quiet. You're surrounded by more than three million people, yet you can hear the birds, bells, and fountain. The park is decorated with statues of Visigothic kings who ruled from the fifth to eighth century. Romans allowed them to administer their province of Hispania on the condition that they'd provide food and weapons to the empire. The Visigoths inherited real power after Rome fell, but lost it to invading Moors in 711. The fine bronze equestrian statue of Philip IV was a striking technical feat in its day, as the horse stood up on its hind legs (possible only with the help of Galileo's clever calculations and by using the tail for more support). The king faces Madrid's opera house, the 1,700-seat **Royal Theater** (Teatro Real), rebuilt in 1997.

• *Walk along the Royal Theater, on the right side, to the...*

⓬ Plaza de Isabel II

This square is marked by a statue of Isabel II, who ruled Spain in the 19th century and was a great patron of the arts. Although she's immortalized here, Isabel had a rocky reign, marked by uprisings and political intrigue. A revolution in 1868 forced her to abdicate, and she lived out her life in exile.

Facing the opera house is a grand **old cinema** (now closed). During the dictatorial days of Franco, movies were always dubbed in Spanish, making them easier to censor. (In one famously awkward example, Franco's censors were scandalized by a film that implied a man and a woman were having an affair, so they edited the voice track to make the characters into brother and sister. But the onscreen chemistry was still sexually charged—and the censors inadvertently turned an illicit relationship into an incestuous one.) Movies in Spain are still mostly dubbed (to see a movie here without dubbing, look for "V.O.", which means "original version").

• *From here, follow Calle del Arenal, walking gradually uphill. You're heading straight to Puerta del Sol.*

⓭ Calle del Arenal

As depicted on the tiled street signs, this was the "street of sand"— where sand was stockpiled during construction. Each cross street is named for a medieval craft that, historically, was plied along that lane (for example, "Calle de Bordadores" means "Street of the Embroiderers"). Wander slowly uphill. As you stroll, imagine this street as a traffic inferno—which it was until the city pedestrianized it a decade ago (and now monitor it with police cameras atop posts at intersections). Notice also how orderly the side streets are. Where a mess of cars once lodged chaotically on the sidewalks, orderly bollards *(bolardos)* now keep vehicles off the walkways. The fancier facades (such as the former International Hotel at #19) are in the "eclectic" style (Spanish for Historicism—meaning a new interest in old styles) of the late 19th century.

Continue 200 yards up Calle del Arenal to a brick church on the right. As you walk, consider how many people are simply out strolling. The paseo is a strong tradition in this culture—people of all generations enjoy being out, together, strolling. And local governments continue to provide more and more pedestrianized boulevards to make the paseo better than ever.

The brick **St. Ginés Church** (on the right) means temptation to most locals. It marks the turn to the best *chocolatería* in town. From the uphill corner of the church, look to the end of the lane where—like a high-calorie red-light zone—a neon sign spells out *Chocolatería San Ginés*...every local's favorite place for hot chocolate and *churros* (always open). Also notice the charming bookshop clinging like a barnacle to the wall of the church. It's been selling books on this spot since 1650.

Next door is the **Joy Eslava disco,** a former theater famous

MADRID

Spain's Royal Families: From Habsburg to Bourbon

Spain as we know it was born when four long-established medieval kingdoms were joined by the 1469 marriage of Isabel, ruler of Castile and León, and Ferdinand, ruler of Aragon and Navarre. The so-called "Catholic Monarchs" (Reyes Católicos) wasted no time in driving the Islamic Moors out of Spain (the Reconquista). By 1492, Isabel and Ferdinand had conquered a fifth kingdom, Granada, establishing more or less the same borders that Spain has today.

This was an age when "foreign policy" was conducted, in part, by marrying royal children into other royal families. Among the dynastic marriages of their children, Isabel and Ferdinand arranged for their third child, Juana "the Mad," to marry the crown prince of Austria, Philip "the Fair." This was a huge coup for the Spanish royal family. A member of the Habsburg dynasty, Philip was heir to the Holy Roman Empire, which then encompassed much of today's Austria, Czech Republic, Hungary, Transylvania, the Low Countries, southern Italy, and more. And when Juana's brothers died, making her ruler of the kingdoms of Spain, it paved the way for her son, Charles, to inherit the kingdoms of his four grandparents—creating a vast realm and famously making him the most powerful man in Europe. He ruled as Charles I (king of Spain, from 1516) and Charles V (Holy Roman Emperor, from 1519).

He was followed by Philip II, Philip III, Philip IV, and finally Charles II. Over this period, Spain rested on its Golden Age laurels, eventually squandering much of its wealth and losing some of its holdings. Arguably the most inbred of an already very inbred dynasty (his parents were uncle and niece), Charles II was weak, sickly, and unable to have children, ending the 200-year Habsburg dynasty in Spain with his death in 1700.

Charles II willed the Spanish crown to the Bourbons of France, and his grandnephew Philip of Anjou, whose granddaddy was the "Sun King" Louis XIV of France, took the throne. But the rest of

for operettas in the Gilbert and Sullivan days and now a popular club. In Spain, you can do it all when you're 18 (buy tobacco, drink, drive, serve in the military). This place is an alcohol-free disco for the younger kids until midnight, when it becomes a thriving adult space, with the theater floor and balconies all teeming with clubbers. Their slogan: "Go big or go home."

The Starbucks on the opposite corner (at #14) is popular with young locals for its inviting ambience and American-style muffins (and free Wi-Fi), even though the coffee is too tame for many Spaniards.

Kitty corner (at #7) is **Ferpal,** an old-school deli with an in-

Europe feared allowing the already powerful Louis XIV to add Spain (and its vast New World holdings) to his empire. Austria, the Germanic States, Holland, England, and Catalunya backed a different choice (Archduke Charles of Austria). So began the War of Spanish Succession (1700-1714), involving all of Europe. The French eventually prevailed, but with the signing of the Treaty of Utrecht (1713), Philip had to give up any claim to the throne of France. This let him keep the Spanish crown but ensured that his heirs—the future Spanish Bourbon dynasty—couldn't become too powerful by merging with the French Bourbons.

In 1714, the French-speaking Philip became the first king of the Bourbon dynasty in Spain (with the name Philip V). He breathed much-needed new life into the monarchy, which had grown ineffectual and corrupt under the inbred Habsburgs. When the old wooden Habsburg royal palace burned on Christmas Eve of 1734, Philip (who was born at Versailles) built a new and spectacular late-Baroque-style palace as a bold symbol of his new dynasty. This is the palace that wows visitors to Madrid today. Construction was finished in 1764, and Philip V's son Charles III was the palace's first occupant. Charles III's decorations are what you'll see if you visit the palace's interior.

The Bourbon palace remained the home of Spain's kings from 1764 until 1931, when democratic elections led to the Second Spanish Republic and forced King Alfonso XIII into exile. After Francisco Franco took power in 1939, he sidelined the royals by making himself ruler-for-life. But later he handpicked as his successor Alfonso XIII's grandson, the Bourbon Prince Juan Carlos, whom Franco believed would continue his hardline policies. When Franco died in 1975, Juan Carlos surprised everyone by voluntarily turning the real power back over to Spain's parliament. Today Spain is a constitutional monarchy with a figurehead Bourbon king, Felipe VI, son of Juan Carlos I, who abdicated the throne in 2014.

viting bar and easy takeout options. Wallpapered with ham hocks, it's famous for selling the finest Spanish cheeses, hams, and other tasty treats. Spanish saffron is half what you'd pay for it back in the US. While they sell quality sandwiches, cheap and ready-made, it's fun to buy some bread and—after a little tasting—choose a ham or cheese for a memorable picnic or snack. If you're lucky, you may get to taste a tiny bit of Spain's best ham (Ibérico de Bellota). Close your eyes and let the taste fly you to a land of very happy acorn-fed pigs.

Across the street, in a little mall (at #8), a lovable mouse cherished by Spanish children is celebrated with a six-inch-tall bronze statue in the lobby. Upstairs is the fanciful **Casita Museo de Ratón Pérez** (€3, daily, Spanish only) with a fun window display. A steady stream of adoring children and their parents pour through here to learn about the wondrous mouse that is Spain's tooth fairy.

Just uphill (at #6) is an official retailer of **Real Madrid** football (soccer) paraphernalia. Many Europeans come to Madrid primarily to see its 80,000-seat Bernabéu Stadium. Madrid has crosstown rival teams (similar to Chicago's Cubs and White Sox, or New York's Yankees and Mets). Atlético de Madrid is the working-class underdog (like the Mets), while Real Madrid (the Yankees of Spanish football) has piles of money and wins piles of championships. Step inside to see posters of the happy team posing with the latest trophy.

Across the street at #3 is **Pronovias,** a famous Spanish wedding-dress shop that attracts brides-to-be from across Europe. These days, the current generation of Spaniards often just shack up without getting married. Those who do get married are more practical—preferring a down payment on a condo to a fancy wedding with a costly dress.

• *You're just a few steps from where you started this walk, at Puerta del Sol. Back in the square, you're met by a statue popularly known as* La Mariblanca. *This mythological Spanish Venus—with Madrid's coat of arms at her feet—stands tall amid all the modernity, as if protecting the people of this great city.*

GRAN VÍA WALK

For a walk down Spain's version of Fifth Avenue, stroll the Gran Vía. Built primarily between 1910 and the 1930s, this boulevard, worth ▲, affords a fun view of early 20th-century architecture and a chance to be on the street with workaday Madrileños. I've broken this self-guided walk into five sections, each of which was the ultimate in its day.

• *Start at the skyscraper at Calle de Alcalá #42 (Metro: Banco de España).*

❶ Circulo de Bellas Artes

This 1920s skyscraper has a venerable café on its ground floor (free entry to enjoy its belle époque-style interior) and the best rooftop view around. Ride the **elevator** to the seventh-floor roof terrace/lounge and bar (€4, Mon-Fri 9:30-21:00, Sat-Sun from 11:00). Stand under a black Art Deco statue of Minerva, perhaps put here to associate Madrid with this mythological protectress of culture and high thinking, and survey the city. Start in the far left and work your way around the perimeter for a clockwise tour.

Looking down to the left, you'll see the gold-fringed dome of the landmark Metropolis building (inspired by Hotel Negresco in

Nice), once the headquarters of an insurance company. It stands at the start of the Gran Vía and its cancan of proud facades celebrating the good times in pre-civil war Spain. On the horizon, the Guadarrama Mountains hide Segovia. Farther to the right, in the distance, skyscrapers mark the city's north gate, Puerta de Europa (with its striking slanted twin towers peeking from behind other towers). Round the terrace corner. The big traffic circle and fountain below are part of Plaza de Cibeles, with its ornate and bombastic cultural center and observation deck (Palacio de Cibeles—built in 1910 as the post-office headquarters, and since 2006 the Madrid City Hall). Behind that is the vast Retiro Park. Farther to the right (at the next corner of the terrace), the big low-slung building surrounded by green is the Prado Museum.

• *Descend the elevator and cross the busy boulevard immediately in front of Círculo de Bellas Artes to reach the start of Gran Vía.*

❷ 1910s Gran Vía

This first stretch, from the Banco de España Metro stop to the Gran Vía Metro stop, was built in the 1910s as a strip of luxury stores. The Bar Chicote (at #12) is a classic cocktail bar that welcomed Hemingway and the stars of the day. While the people-watching and window-shopping can be enthralling, be sure to look up and enjoy the beautiful facades, too.

❸ 1920s Gran Vía

The second stretch, from the Gran Vía Metro stop to the Callao Metro stop, starts where two recently pedestrianized streets meet up. To the right, Calle de Fuencarral is the trendiest pedestrian zone in town, with famous brand-name shops and a young vibe. To the left, Calle de la Montera is notorious for its prostitutes. The action pulses from the McDonald's down a block or so. Some find it an eye-opening little detour.

The 14-story **Telefónica skyscraper** is nearly 300 feet tall. Perched here at the highest point around, it seems even taller. It was one of the city's first skyscrapers (the tallest in Spain until the 1950s) with a big New York City feel—and with a tiny Baroque balcony, as if to remind us we're still in Spain. Telefónica was Spain's only telephone company through the Franco age (and was notorious for overbilling people, with nothing itemized and no accountability). Today it's one of Spain's few giant blue-chip corporations.

With plenty of money and a need for corporate goodwill, the building houses the free **Espacio Fundación Telefónica** (Tue-Sun 10:00-20:00, closed Mon), with an art gallery, kid-friendly special exhibits, and a fun permanent exhibit telling the story of telecommunications, from telegraphs to iPhones. This exhibit fills the second floor amid exposed steel beams—a space where a thousand "09 girls," as operators were called back then, once worked.

Farther along is a strip of department stores, including **Primark,** the first modern department store in town. Just before the Callao Metro station, at #37, step into the **H&M** department store for a dose of a grand old theater lobby.

❹ 1930s Gran Vía

The final stretch, from the Callao Metro stop to Plaza de España, is considered the "American Gran Vía," built in the 1930s to emulate the buildings of Chicago and New York City. The **Schweppes** building (Art Deco in the Chicago style, with its round facade and curved windows) was radical and innovative in 1933. This section of Gran Vía is the Spanish version of Broadway, with all the big theaters and plays. These theaters survive thanks to Spanish translations of Broadway shows, productions which get a huge second life here and in Latin America.

Across from the Teatro Lope de Vega (at #60) is a quasi fascist-style building (#57). It's a bank from 1930 capped with a stern statue that looks like an ad for using a good, solid piggy bank. Looking up the street toward the Madrid Tower, the buildings become even more severe.

The **Dear Hotel** (at #80) has a restaurant on its 14th floor

Gran Vía Walk

1 Círculo de Bellas Artes
2 1910s Gran Vía (Banco de España to Gran Vía Metro)
3 1920s Gran Vía (Gran Vía to Callao Metro)
4 1930s Gran Vía (Callao to Plaza de España Metro)
5 Plaza de España

and a rooftop lounge and small bar above that. (Walk confidently through the hotel lobby, ride the elevator to the top, pass through the restaurant, and climb the stairs from the terrace outside to the rooftop.) The views from here are among the best in town.

5 Plaza de España

The end of Gran Vía is marked by Plaza de España (with a Metro station of the same name). While statues of the epic Spanish characters Don Quixote and Sancho Panza (part of a Cervantes monument) are ignored in the park, two Franco-era buildings do their best to scrape the sky above. Franco wanted to show he could keep up with America, so he had the Spain Tower (shorter) and Madrid Tower (taller) built in the 1950s. But they reminded people more of Moscow than the USA. The future of the Plaza de España looks brighter than its past. Major renovation plans are in the works to limit traffic, invite more pedestrians, and link it up with some of the city's bike paths.

Sights in Madrid

▲▲▲ROYAL PALACE

Spain's Royal Palace (Palacio Real) is Europe's third-greatest palace, after Versailles and Vienna's Schönbrunn. It has arguably the most sumptuous original interior, packed with tourists and royal antiques.

The palace is the product of many kings over several centuries. Philip II (1527-1598) made a wooden fortress on this site his governing center when he established Madrid as Spain's capital. When that palace burned down, the current structure was built by King Philip V (1683-1746). Philip V wanted to make it his own private Versailles, to match his French upbringing: He was born in Versailles—the grandson of Louis XIV—and ordered his tapas

in French. His son, Charles III (whose statue graces Puerta del Sol), added interior decor in the Italian style, since he'd spent his formative years in Italy. These civilized Bourbon kings were trying to raise Spain to the cultural level of the rest of Europe. They hired foreign artists to oversee construction and established local Spanish porcelain and tapestry factories to copy works done in Paris or Brussels. Over the years, the palace was expanded and enriched, as each Spanish king tried to outdo his predecessor.

Today's palace is ridiculously supersized—with 2,800 rooms, tons of luxurious tapestries, a king's ransom of chandeliers, frescoes by Tiepolo, priceless porcelain, and bronze decor covered in gold leaf. While these days the royal family lives in a mansion a few miles away, this place still functions as the ceremonial palace, used for formal state receptions, royal weddings, and tourists' daydreams.

Cost and Hours: €10, €11 if there are special exhibits; open daily 10:00-20:00, Oct-March 10:00-18:00, last entry one hour before closing; from Puerta del Sol, walk 15 minutes down pedestrianized Calle del Arenal (Metro: Ópera); palace can close for royal functions—confirm in advance.

Information: Tel. 914-548-800, www.patrimonionacional.es.

Crowd-Beating Tips: The palace is free for locals—and most crowded—Monday-Thursday 18:00-20:00 in summer and 16:00-18:00 in winter. On any day, arrive early or go late to avoid lines and crowds.

Visitor Information: Short English descriptions posted in each room complement what I describe in my tour. The museum guidebook demonstrates a passion for meaningless data.

Tours: The excellent €4 **audioguide** is much more interesting than the museum guidebook. Or download in advance the helpful **app,** "Royal Palace of Madrid," that takes you through the palace in three segments ($2 fee). You can also join a €4 **guided tour.** Check the time of the next English-language tour and decide as

Royal Palace

Plaza de Caballerizas

Not to Scale

MADRID

Campo del Moro–Plaza Incógnita

Courtyard

CALLE BAILÉN

N

Plaza de la Armería

To ㉑

❶ Exterior
❷ Grand Stairs
❸ Royal Guard/
  Halberdiers Room
❹ Hall of Columns
❺ Drawing Room
❻ Antechamber
❼ Gasparini Room
❽ Charles III Salon
❾ Porcelain Room
❿ Yellow Lounge
⓫ Gala Dining Room
⓬ Cinema Room
⓭ Silver Room
⓮ Crockery &
  Crystal Rooms
⓯ Courtyard
⓰ Royal Chapel
⓱ Queen's Boudoir
⓲ Stradivarius Room
⓳ Crown Room
⓴ Throne Room
㉑ To Armory

you buy your ticket; the tours are dry, depart sporadically, and aren't worth a long wait.

Services: Free lockers and a WC are just past the ticket booth. Upstairs you'll find a more serious bookstore with good books on Spanish history.

Eating: Though the palace has a refreshing air-conditioned cafeteria upstairs (with salad bar), I prefer to walk a few minutes and find a place near the Royal Theater or on Calle del Arenal. Another great option is **$$ Café de Oriente,** boasting good lunch specials and fin-de-siècle elegance immediately across the park from the Royal Palace.

◑ Self-Guided Tour

You'll follow a simple one-way circuit on a single floor covering more than 20 rooms.

• *Buy your ticket, pass through the bookstore, stand in the middle of the vast open-air courtyard, and face the palace entrance.*

❶ Palace Exterior: The palace sports the French-Italian Baroque architecture so popular in the 18th century—heavy columns, classical-looking statues, a balustrade roofline, and false-front entrance. The entire building is made of gray-and-white local stone (very little wood) to prevent the kind of fire that leveled the previous castle. Imagine the place in its heyday, with a courtyard full of soldiers on parade, or a lantern-lit scene of horse carriages arriving for a ball.

• *Enter the palace and show your ticket.*

Palace Lobby: In the old days, horse-drawn carriages would drop you off here. Today, stretch limos do the same thing for gala events. (If you're taking a guided palace tour, this is where you wait to begin.) The modern black bust in the corner is of Juan Carlos I, a "people's king," who is credited with bringing democracy to Spain after 36 years under dictator Franco. (Juan Carlos passed the throne to his son in 2014.)

❷ Grand Stairs: Gazing up the imposing staircase, you can see that Spain's kings wanted to make a big first impression.

Whenever high-end dignitaries arrive, fancy carpets are rolled down the stairs (notice the little metal bar-holding hooks). Begin your ascent, up steps that are intentionally shallow, making your climb slow and regal. Overhead, the white-and-blue ceiling fresco gradually opens up to your view. It shows the Spanish king, sitting on clouds, surrounded by female Virtues.

At the first landing, the burgundy coat of arms represents Felipe VI, the son of Spain's previous king, Juan Carlos. J. C. knew Spain was ripe for democracy after Francisco Franco's dictatorial regime. Rather than become "Juan the Brief" (as some were nicknaming him), he returned real power to the parliament. You'll see his (figure) head on the back of some Spanish €1 and €2 coins.

Continue up to the top of the stairs. Before entering the first room, look to the right of the door to find a white marble bust of J. C.'s great-great-g-g-g-great-grandfather Philip V, who began the Bourbon dynasty in Spain in 1700 and had this palace built.

❸ **Royal Guard/Halberdiers Room:** The palace guards used to hang out in this relatively simple room. Notice the two fake doors, added to give the room symmetry. The old clocks—still in working order—are part of a collection of hundreds amassed as a hobby by Spain's royal family. Throughout the palace, the themes chosen for the ceiling frescoes relate to the function of the room they decorate. In this room, the ceiling fresco is the first we'll see in a series by the great Venetian painter Giambattista Tiepolo. It depicts the legendary hero Aeneas (in red, with the narrow face of Charles III) standing in the clouds of heaven, gazing up at his mother Venus (with the face of Charles' own mother).

Notice the carpets in this room. Although much of what you see in the palace dates from the 18th century, the carpet on the left (folded over to show the stitching) is new, from 1991. It was produced by Madrid's royal tapestry factory, the same works that made the older original carpet (displayed next to the modern one). Though recently produced, the new carpet was woven the traditional way—by hand.

❹ **Hall of Columns:** Originally a ballroom and dining room, today this space is used for formal ceremonies and intimate concerts. This is where Spain formally joined the European Union in 1985 (the fancy table used for the event is in the Crown Room) and honored its national soccer team after their 2010 World Cup victory. The tapestries (like most you'll see in the palace) are 17th-century Belgian, from designs by Raphael.

The central theme in the ceiling fresco (by Jaquinto, following Tiepolo's style) is Apollo driving the chariot of the sun, while Bacchus enjoys wine, women, and song with a convivial gang. This is a reminder that the mark of a good king is to drive the chariot of state as smartly as Apollo, while providing an environment where the people can enjoy life to the fullest.

• *The next several rooms were the living quarters of King Charles III (r. 1759-1788). First comes his ❺ drawing room (with red-and-gold walls), where the king would enjoy the company of a similarly great ruler—the Roman emperor Trajan—depicted "triumphing" on the ceiling. The heroics of Trajan, one of two Roman emperors born in Spain, naturally made the king feel good. Next, you enter the blue-walled...*

❻ **Antechamber:** This was Charles III's dining room. The four paintings—all original by Francisco de Goya—are of Charles III's son and successor, King Charles IV (looking a bit like a dim-witted George Washington), and his wife, María Luisa (who wore

Charles III (1716-1788)

Of the many monarchs who've enlarged or redecorated the Royal Palace, it was Charles III who set the tone for its Baroque-Rococo interior. Charles' mother was Italian, and he spent his formative years in Italy. When he became Spain's king, he brought along sophisticated Italian artists to decorate his new home—the painter Tiepolo, the architect Sabatini, and the decorator Gasparini. They created some of the most elaborate, jaw-dropping rooms tourists see in the palace today.

Charles was an enlightened ruler who tried to reform Spain along democratic principles. He failed. After his death, Spain dwindled into repressive irrelevance. But over the centuries, each of his successors labored to top Charles in ostentatious decoration, making Madrid's Royal Palace his greatest legacy.

the pants in the palace). María Luisa was famously hands-on, tough, and businesslike, while Charles IV was pretty wimpy as far as kings go. To meet the demand for his work, Goya made other copies of these portraits, which you'll see in the Prado.

The 12-foot-tall clock—showing Cronus, God of time, in porcelain, bronze, and mahogany—sits on a music box. Reminding us of how time flies, Cronus is shown both as a child and as an old man. The palace's clocks are wound—and reset—once a week (they grow progressively less accurate as the week goes on).

The gilded decor you see throughout the palace is bronze with gold leaf. Velázquez's famous painting, *Las Meninas* (which you'll marvel at in the Prado), originally hung in this room.

❼ Gasparini Room: (Gasp!) The entire room is designed, top to bottom, as a single gold-green-rose ensemble: from the frescoed ceiling to the painted stucco figures, silk-embroidered walls, chandelier, furniture, and multicolored marble floor. Each marble was quarried in, and therefore represents, a different region of Spain. Birds overhead spread their wings, vines sprout, and fruit bulges from the surface. With curlicues everywhere (including their reflection in the mirrors), the room dazzles the eye and mind. It's a triumph of the Rococo style, with exotic motifs such as the Chinese people sculpted into the corners of the ceiling. (These figures, like many in the palace, were formed from stucco, or wet plaster.) The fabric gracing the walls was recently restored. Sixty people spent three years replacing the rotten silk fabric and then embroidering back on the silver, silk, and gold threads.

Note the micro-mosaic table—a typical royal or aristocratic souvenir from any visit to Rome in the mid-1800s. The chandelier, the biggest in the palace, is mesmerizing, especially with its glittering canopy of crystal reflecting in the wall mirrors.

This was the king's dressing room. For a divine monarch, dressing was a public affair. The court bigwigs would assemble here as the king, standing on a platform—notice the height of the mirrors—would pull on his leotards and toy with his wig.

• *In the next room, the silk wallpaper is from modern times—the intertwined "J. C. S." indicates the former monarchs Juan Carlos I and Sofía. Pass through the silk room to reach...*

❽ **Charles III Salon:** Charles III died here in his bed in 1788. His grandson, Ferdinand VII, redid the room to honor the great man. The room's blue color scheme recalls the blue-clad monks of Charles' religious order. A portrait of Charles (in blue) hangs on the wall. The ceiling fresco shows Charles establishing his order, with its various (female) Virtues. At the base of the ceiling (near the harp player) find the baby in his mother's arms—that would be Ferdy himself, the long-sought male heir, preparing to continue Charles' dynasty.

The chandelier is in the shape of the fleur-de-lis (the symbol of the Bourbon family) capped with a Spanish crown. As you exit the room, notice the thick walls between rooms. These hid service corridors for servants, who scurried about mostly unseen.

❾ **Porcelain Room:** This tiny but lavish room is paneled with green-white-gold porcelain garlands, vines, babies, and mythological figures. The entire ensemble was disassembled for safety during the civil war. (Find the little screws in the greenery that hides the seams between panels.) Notice the clock in the center with Atlas supporting the world on his shoulders.

❿ **Yellow Lounge:** This was a study for Charles III. The properly cut crystal of the chandelier shows all the colors of the rainbow. Stand under it, look up, and sway slowly to see the colors glitter. This is not a particularly precious room. But its decor pops because the lights are generally left on. Imagine the entire palace as brilliant as this when fully lit. As you leave the room, look back at the chandelier to notice its design of a temple with a fountain inside.

• *Next comes the...*

⓫ **Gala Dining Room:** Up to 12 times a year, the king entertains as many as 144 guests at this bowling lane-size table,

Tiepolo's Frescoes

In 1762, King Charles III invited Europe's most celebrated palace painter, Giambattista Tiepolo (1696-1770), to decorate three rooms in the newly built palace.

Sixty-six-year-old Tiepolo made the trip from Italy with his two well-known sons as assistants. They spent four years atop scaffolding decorating in the fresco technique, troweling plaster on the ceiling and quickly painting it before it dried.

Tiepolo's translucent ceilings seem to open up to a cloud-filled heaven, where Spanish royals cavort with Greek gods and pudgy cherubs. Tiepolo used every trick to "fool the eye" (trompe l'oeil), creating dizzying skyscapes of figures tumbling at every angle. He mixes 2-D painting with 3-D stucco figures that spill over the picture frame. His colorful, curvaceous ceilings blend seamlessly with the flamboyant furniture of the room below. Tiepolo's Royal Palace frescoes are often cited as the final flowering of Baroque and Rococo art.

which can be extended to the length of the room. The parquet floor was the preferred dancing surface when balls were held in this fabulous room. Note the vases from China, the tapestries, and the ceiling fresco depicting Christopher Columbus kneeling before Ferdinand and Isabel, presenting exotic souvenirs and his new, red-skinned friends. Imagine this hall in action when a foreign dignitary dines here. The king and queen preside from the center of the room. Find their chairs (slightly higher than the rest). The tables are set with fine crystal and cutlery (which we'll see a couple of rooms later). And the whole place glitters as the 15 chandeliers (and their 900 bulbs) are fired up. (The royal kitchens, where the gala dinners were prepared, may be open for viewing; ask the staff where to enter.)

• *Pass through the next room, known as the* ⓬ ***Cinema Room*** *because the royal family once enjoyed Sunday afternoons at the movies here. The royal string ensemble played here to entertain during formal dinners. From here, if the next two rooms are open, move into the...*

⓭ **Silver Room:** Some of this 19th-century silver tableware—knives and forks, bowls, salt and pepper shakers, and the big punch bowl—is used in the Gala Dining Room on special occasions. If you look carefully, you can see quirky royal necessities, including a baby's silver rattle and fancy candle snuffers.

• Head straight ahead to the...

❹ **Crockery and Crystal Rooms:** Philip V's collection of china is the oldest and rarest of the various pieces on display; it came from China before that country was opened to the West. Since Chinese crockery was in such demand, any self-respecting European royal family had to have its own porcelain works (such as France's Sèvres or Germany's Meissen) to produce high-quality knockoffs (and cutesy Hummel-like figurines). The porcelain technique itself was kept a royal secret. As you leave, check out Isabel II's excellent 19th-century crystal ware.

• Exit to the hallway and notice the interior courtyard you've been circling one room at a time.

❺ **Courtyard:** You can see how the royal family lived in the spacious middle floor while staff was upstairs. The kitchens, garage, and storerooms were on the ground level. The new king, Felipe VI, married a commoner (for love) and celebrated their wedding party in this courtyard, which was decorated as if another palace room. Spain's royals take their roles and responsibilities seriously—making a point to be approachable and empathizing with their subjects—and are very popular.

• Between statues of two of the giants of Spanish royal history (Isabel and Ferdinand), you'll enter the...

❻ **Royal Chapel:** This chapel is used for private concerts and funerals. The royal coffin sits here before making the sad trip to El Escorial to join the rest of Spain's past royalty (see next chapter). The glass case contains the entire body of St. Felix, given to the Spanish king by the pope in the 19th century. Note the "crying room" in the back for royal babies. While the royals rarely worship here (they prefer the cathedral adjacent to the palace), the thrones are here just in case.

• Pass through the ❼ *Queen's Boudoir—where royal ladies hung out—and into the...*

❽ **Stradivarius Room:** Of all the instruments made by Antonius Stradivarius (1644-1737), only 300 survive. This is the world's best collection and the only matching quartet set: two violins, a viola, and a cello. Charles III, a cultured man, fiddled around with these. Today, a single Stradivarius instrument might sell for $15 million.

• Continue into the room at the far left.

❾ **Crown Room:** The stunning crown of Bourbon Charles III, and the scepter of the last Hapsburg king, Charles II, are displayed in a glass case in the middle. Look for the 2014 proclamations of Juan Carlos' abdication of the crown and Felipe VI's acceptance as king of Spain. Notice which writing implement each man chose to sign with: Juan Carlos' traditional classic pen and Felipe VI's modern one. The fine inlaid marble table in this room is important

MADRID

to Spaniards because it was used when King Juan Carlos signed the treaty finalizing Spain's entry into the European Union in 1985.

• *Walk back through the Stradivarius Room and into the courtyard hallway. Continue your visit through the Antechamber, where ambassadors would wait to present themselves, and the Small Official Chambers, where officials are received by royalty and have their photos taken. Walk through two rooms—the blue official antechamber with royal portraits and busts of Juan Carlos, Sofía, and Felipe VI, and the red official waiting room with tapestries, paintings, and a Tiepolo ceiling fresco—to reach the grand finale, the...*

⓴ **Throne Room:** This room, where the Spanish monarchs preside, is one of the palace's most glorious. And it holds many of the oldest and most precious things in the palace: silver-and-crystal chandeliers (from Venice's Murano Island), elaborate lions, and black bronze statues from the fortress that stood here before the 1734 fire. The 12 mirrors, impressively large in their day, each represent a different month.

The throne stands under a gilded canopy, on a raised platform, guarded by four lions (symbols of power found throughout the palace). The coat of arms above the throne shows the complexity of the Spanish empire across Europe—which, in the early 18th century, included Naples, Sicily, parts of the Netherlands, and more. Though the room was decorated under Charles III (late 18th century), the throne itself dates only from 1977. In Spain, a new throne is built for each king or queen, complete with a gilded portrait on the back. The room's chairs also indicate the previous monarchs—"JC I" and "Sofía." With Juan Carlos' abdication, the chairs may not have changed names yet.

Today, this room is where the king's guests salute him before they move on to dinner. He receives them relatively informally... standing at floor level, rather than seated up on the throne.

The ceiling fresco (1764) is the last great work by Tiepolo, who died in Madrid in 1770. His vast painting (88 × 32 feet) celebrates the vast Spanish empire—upon which the sun also never set. The Greek gods look down from the clouds, overseeing Spain's empire, whose territories are represented by the people ringing the edges of the ceiling. Find the Native American (hint: follow the rainbow to the macho red-caped conquistador who motions to someone he has conquered). From the near end of the room (where tourists stand), look up to admire Tiepolo's skill at making a pillar seem to shoot straight up into the sky. The pillar's pedestal has an inscription celebrating Tiepolo's boss, Charles III ("Carole Magna"). Notice how the painting spills over the gilded wood frame, where 3-D statues recline alongside 2-D painted figures. All of the throne room's decorations—the fresco, gold garlands, mythological statues, wall medallions—unite in a multimedia extravaganza.

• *Exit the palace down the same grand stairway you climbed at the start. Cross the big courtyard, heading to the far-right corner to the...*

㉑ Armory: Here you'll find weapons and armor belonging to many great Spanish historical figures. While some of it was actually for fighting, remember that the great royal pastimes included hunting and tournaments, and armor was largely for sport or ceremony. Much of this armor dates from Habsburg times, before this palace was built (it came here from the earlier fortress or from El Escorial). Circle the big room clockwise.

In the three glass cases on the left, you'll see the oldest pieces in the collection, from the 15th century. In the central case (case III), the shield, sword, belt, and dagger belonged to Boabdil, the last Moorish king, who surrendered Granada in 1492. In case IV, the armor and swords belonged to Ferdinand, the husband of Isabel, and Boabdil's contemporary.

The center of the room is filled with knights in armor on horseback—mostly suited up for tournament play. Many of the pieces belonged to the two great kings who ruled Spain at its 16th-century peak, Charles I and his son Philip II.

The long wall on the left displays the personal armor wardrobe of Charles I (a.k.a. the Holy Roman Emperor Charles V). At the far end, you'll meet Charles on horseback. The mannequin of the king wears the same armor and assumes the same pose as in Titian's famous painting of him (in the Prado).

The opposite wall showcases the armor and weapons of Philip II, the king who watched Spain start its long slide downward. Philip, who impoverished Spain with his wars against the Protestants, anticipated that debt collectors would ransack his estate after his death and specifically protected his impressive collection of armor by founding this armory.

The tapestry above the armor once warmed the walls of the otherwise stark palace that predated this one. Tapestries traveled ahead of royals to decorate their living space. They made many palaces "fit for a king" back when the only way to effectively govern was to be on the road a lot.

Downstairs is more armor, a mixed collection mostly from the 17th century. You'll find early guns and Asian armor. The pint-size armor you may see wasn't for children to fight in. It's training armor for noble youngsters, who as adults would be expected to ride, fight, and play gracefully in these clunky getups. Before you leave, notice the life-saving breastplates dimpled with bullet dents (to right of exit door).

• *Climb the steps from the armory exit to the viewpoint.*

View of the Gardens: Looking down from this high bluff, it's clear why rulers have built on this strategically located spot (great for protecting the historic capital, Toledo) since the ninth century.

The vast palace backyard, once the king's hunting ground, is now a city park, dotted with fountains.

• *Walk to the center of the huge square and face the palace. Notice how the palace of the king faces the palace of the bishop (the cathedral). Whew. After all those rooms, frescoes, chandeliers, knickknacks, kings, and history, consider a final stop in the palace's upstairs café for a well-deserved rest.*

BETWEEN THE ROYAL PALACE AND PUERTA DEL SOL
Descalzas Royal Monastery (Monasterio de las Descalzas Reales)

Madrid's most visit-worthy monastery was founded in the 16th century by Philip II's sister, Joan of Habsburg (known to Spaniards as Juana and to Austrians as Joanna). She's buried here. The monastery's chapels are decorated with fine art, Rubens-designed tapestries, and the heirlooms of the wealthy women who joined the order (the nuns were required to give a dowry). Because this is still a working Franciscan monastery, tourists can enter only when the nuns vacate the cloister, and the number of daily visitors is limited. The scheduled tours often sell out—so try to buy your ticket right at 10:00 for morning tours or 16:00 for afternoon tours (advance tickets available online, but usually for Spanish-language tours only; check www.patrimonionacional.es).

Cost and Hours: €6, visits guided in Spanish or English depending on demand, Tue-Sat 10:00-14:00 & 16:00-18:30, Sun 10:00-15:00, closed Mon, last entry one hour before closing, Plaza de las Descalzas Reales 1, near the Ópera Metro stop and just a short walk from Puerta del Sol, tel. 914-548-800.

MADRID'S MUSEUM NEIGHBORHOOD

Three great museums, all within a 10-minute walk of one another, cluster in east Madrid. The Prado is Europe's top collection of paintings. The Thyssen-Bornemisza sweeps through European art from old masters to moderns. And the Centro de Arte Reina Sofía has a choice selection of modern art, starring Picasso's famous *Guernica*.

Combo-Ticket: If visiting all three museums, you can save a few euros by buying the **Paseo del Arte** combo-ticket (€28, sold at all three museums, good for a year). Note that the Prado is free to enter every evening, the Reina Sofía has free hours every night but Tuesday (when it's closed), and the Thyssen-Bornemisza is free on Monday afternoons (see specifics in following listings).

▲▲▲Prado Museum (Museo Nacional del Prado)

With more than 3,000 canvases, including entire rooms of masterpieces by superstar painters, the Prado (PRAH-doh) is my vote for the greatest collection anywhere of paintings by the European masters. The Prado is *the* place to enjoy the great Spanish painter Francisco de Goya, and it's also the home of Diego Velázquez's *Las Meninas,* considered by many to be the world's finest painting, period. In addition to Spanish works, you'll find paintings by Italian and Flemish masters, including Hieronymus Bosch's fantastical *Garden of Earthly Delights* altarpiece.

Cost: €15, additional (obligatory) fee for occasional temporary exhibits, free Mon-Sat 18:00-20:00 and Sun 17:00-19:00, temporary exhibits discounted during free hours, under age 18 always free.

Hours: Mon-Sat 10:00-20:00, Sun until 19:00.

Information: Tel. 913-302-800, www.museodelprado.es.

Crowd-Beating Tips: It's generally less crowded at lunchtime (13:00-16:00), when there are fewer groups, and on weekdays. It can be busy on free evenings and weekends. Ticket-buying lines can be long. You can save time by booking an entry time in advance online or by phone (www.museodelprado.es, print out ticket; or tel. 902-107-077, get a reference number). Same-day advance purchase is possible if space is available. Alternately, you can buy a Paseo del Arte combo-ticket (described earlier) online or at the less-crowded Thyssen-Bornemisza or Reina Sofía museums. Temporary exhibits are included at the Prado, but you must show the Paseo del Arte combo-ticket at the Prado ticket office to get an entry ticket.

Getting There: It's at the Paseo del Prado. The nearest Metro stops are Banco de España (line 2) and Atocha (line 1), each a five-minute walk from the museum. It's a 15-minute walk from Puerta del Sol.

Getting In: While there are several entrances, you must buy tickets at the Goya (north) entrance. (Even at free-entry times, you need to pick up a gratis ticket at the Goya ticket window.) Once you have your ticket, you can enter at the Goya, Jerónimos, or Velázquez entrance. Those who book in advance can pick up their tickets at the adjacent Jerónimos entrance, skipping the main line. The Murillo entrance is generally reserved for student groups. Your bags will be scanned as you enter.

Tours: Given the ever-changing locations of paintings, the €3.50 **audioguide** is a helpful supplement to my self-guided tour, and a good investment, allowing you to wander and dial up com-

MADRID

Madrid's Museum Neighborhood

1. Mercure Madrid Centro Hotel Lope de Vega
2. Urban Sea Hotel Atocha 113
3. Hostales Gonzalo & Cervantes
4. Restaurante Palacio de Cibeles, Terrace Cibeles & Colección Cibeles
5. Calle de Jesús Tapas Bars
6. El Brillante
7. VIPS Café (under Palace Hotel)

mentary on 250 masterpieces as you come across them. Skip the Prado's Second Canvas smartphone **app.**

Services: The Jerónimos entrance has an information desk, bag check, audioguides, bookshop, WCs, and café. Larger bags must be checked.

No-no's: No drinks, food, backpacks, or large umbrellas are allowed inside.

Cuisine Art: The self-service **$$** cafeteria and restaurant are open daily (Mon-Sat 10:00-19:30, Sun 10:00-18:30, main dishes, salads, and sandwiches, hot dishes served only 12:30-16:00). A block west of the Prado, you'll find **$$ VIPS,** a bright, popular chain restaurant, handy for a cheap and filling salad. Engulfed in a shop selling books and candy, this is a high-energy, no-charm eatery (daily 9:00-24:00, across the boulevard from northern end of Prado at Plaza de Canova del Castillo, under Palace Hotel). Next door is Spain's first Starbucks, opened in 2001. A strip of wonderful **$$** tapas bars is just a few blocks east of the museum, lining Calle de Jésús. If you want to take a break outside the museum for lunch, you can reenter the museum on the same ticket as long as you get it stamped at a desk marked *"Educación,"* near the Jerónimos entrance.

❍ Self-Guided Tour

Thanks to Gene Openshaw for writing the following tour.

Centuries of powerful kings (and lots of New World gold) funded the Prado, the greatest painting museum in the world. You'll see first-class Italian Renaissance art (especially Titian), Northern art (Bosch, Rubens, Dürer), and Spanish art (El Greco, Velázquez, Goya). This huge museum is not laid out chronologically, so this tour will not be either. Instead, we'll hit the highlights with a minimum of walking. Paintings are moved around frequently—if you can't find a particular one, ask a guard.

• *Pick up a museum map as you enter. Once inside, make your way to the main gallery on the ground floor. Plans are in the works to renumber the rooms, but even if the room numbers are different than those on the map in this book, the paintings should be in the same physical locations. Follow your map and signs to Sala 49. Look for the following paintings in Room 49 and the adjoining galleries.*

Italian Renaissance

During its Golden Age (the 1500s), Spain may have been Europe's richest country, but Italy was still the most cultured. Spain's kings loved how Italian Renaissance artists captured a three-dimensional world on a two-dimensional canvas, bringing Bible scenes to life and celebrating real people and their emotions.

Raphael (1483-1520) was the undisputed master of realism. When he painted *Portrait of a Cardinal* (*El Cardenal,* c. 1510), he

MADRID

Prado Museum Overview

Note: Numbers indicate room numbers

Second Floor

GOYA TAPESTRIES 85, 90-94 ⊠

▥▥ **Stairs**
⊠ **Elevator**

MURILLO 16-17

VELÁZQUEZ 10-12, 14-15 ⊠ WC

EL GRECO 8b-10b

RUBENS 28-29

ROTUNDA

GALERÍA CENTRAL

⊠

(VELÁZQUEZ, RUBENS, TITIAN, ETC.)

TITIAN 40-42

⊠ GOYA 32, 36

GOYA ENTRANCE UPPER

First Floor

WC

JERÓNIMOS (MAIN) ENTRANCE ➤

INFO BOOTH ■

GIFT SHOP ■   CAFÉ ■

MURILLO ENTRANCE (GROUPS)

LOBBY

GOYA ENTRANCE LOWER

NORTHERN ART 55-58

⊠ ■ WC
INFO BOOTH

ROTUNDA
⊠

ITALIAN RENAISSANCE GALERÍA NORTE

ROOM 49

SPANISH GALERÍA SUR 90-99

GOYA 65-67

VELÁZQUEZ ENTRANCE

Not to Scale

Ground Floor

showed the sly Vatican functionary with a day's growth of beard and an air of superiority, locking eyes with the viewer. The cardinal's slightly turned torso is as big as a statue. Nearby are several versions of *Holy Family* and other paintings by Raphael.

Fra Angelico's *The Annunciation* (*La Anunciación,* c. 1426) is in nearby Room 56b. It's half medieval piety, half Renaissance realism. In the crude Garden of Eden scene (on the left), a scrawny, sinful First Couple hovers unrealistically above the foliage, awaiting eviction. The angel's Annunciation to Mary (right side) is more Renaissance, both with its upbeat message (that Jesus will be born to redeem sinners like Adam and Eve) and in the budding photorealism, set beneath 3-D arches. (Still, aren't the receding bars of the porch's ceiling a bit off? Painting three dimensions wasn't that easy.)

Also in Room 56b, the tiny *Dormition of the Virgin (El Transito de la Virgen)*, by **Andrea Mantegna** (c. 1431-1506), shows his mastery of Renaissance perspective. The apostles crowd into the room to mourn the last moments of the Virgin Mary's life. The receding floor tiles and open window in the back create the subconscious effect of Mary's soul finding its way out into the serene distance.

• *Find examples of Northern European art, including Dürer, in Room 55b.*

Northern Art

Albrecht Dürer's *Self-Portrait (Autorretrato)*, from 1498, is possibly the first time an artist depicted himself. The artist, age 26, is

German, but he's all dolled up in a fancy Italian hat and permed hair. He'd recently returned from Italy and wanted to impress his countrymen with his sophistication. Dürer (1471-1528) wasn't simply vain. He'd grown accustomed, as an artist in Renaissance Italy, to being treated like a prince. Note Dürer's signature, the pyramid-shaped "A. D." (D inside the A), on the windowsill.

Dürer's 1507 panel paintings of Adam and Eve are the first full-size nudes in Northern European art. Like Greek statues, they pose in their separate niches, with three-dimensional, anatomically correct bodies. This was a bold humanist proclamation that the body is good, man is good, and the things of the world are good.

• *Backtrack through Room 56b, and go through Rooms 57b and 57 to Room 58.*

Descent from the Cross (El Descendimiento) by **Rogier van der Weyden** (c. 1399-1464) is a masterpiece. The Flemish painter reveals the psychological drama of this biblical event by placing the characters of real people in a contemporary (1435) scene. The Flemish were masters of detail, as you can see in the cloth, jewels, faces, and even tears. These effects are all enhanced by the artist's choice of oil paint, a relatively new and vibrant medium especially suited to conveying textural realism and intense color. The creative composition suggests that, in losing her son, Mary suffered along with Jesus, which is conveyed by showing their bodies in the same position. Note the realism, especially in the mournful faces, and the gorgeous arc of Mary Magdalene's pose (far right). As the Netherlands was then a part of the Spanish empire, this painting ended up in Madrid.

• *Continue to Room 56a, dedicated to...*

Hieronymus Bosch (c. 1450-1516), in his cryptic triptych *The Garden of Earthly Delights* (*El Jardín de las Delicias,* c. 1505), relates the message that the pleasures of life are fleeting, and we'd better avoid them or we'll wind up in hell.

This is a triptych—a three-paneled altarpiece, with a central image and two hinged outer panels. When the panels are closed, another image is revealed on their back side. All four images work together to teach a religious message. First notice the back side of this otherwise colorful work. It's a black-and-white scene depicting Creation on Day Three—before God added animals and humans to the mix. So, imagine the altarpiece closed. All is mellow. Then open it up, bring on the people, and splash into the colorful *Garden of Earthly Delights.*

On the left is Paradise, showing naked Adam and Eve before original sin. Everything is in its place, with animals behaving

virtuously. Innocent Adam and Eve get married, with God himself performing the ceremony.

The central panel is a riot of hedonistic men and women on a perpetual spring break. Men on horseback ride round and round, searching for but never reaching the elusive Fountain of Youth. Others frolic in earth's "Garden," oblivious to where they came from (left) and where they may end up (exit...right).

Now, go to Hell (right panel). It's a burning Dante's Inferno-inspired wasteland where geneticmutant demons torture sinners. Everyone gets their just desserts, like the glutton who is eaten and re-eaten eternally, the musician strung up on his own harp, and the gamblers with their table forever overturned. In the center, hell is literally frozen over. A creature with a broken eggshell body hosting a tavern, tree-trunk legs, and a hat featuring a bagpipe (symbolic of hedonism) stares out—it's the face of Bosch himself.

If you like this Bosch, you'll enjoy the others in this gallery. The table in the center features his *Seven Deadly Sins* (*Los Pecados*

Capitales, late 15th century). Each of the four corners has a theme: death, judgment, paradise, and hell. The fascinating wheel, with Christ in the center, names the sins in Latin (lust, envy, gluttony, and so on), and illustrates each with a vivid scene that works as a slice of 15th-century Dutch life.

Another triptych, *The Hay Wain* (*El Carro de Heno,* c. 1516), stands nearby. Like *The Garden of Earthly Delights,* and with the same vivid imagery, it teaches morality in what must have been a very effective and frightening way back when Bosch painted it.

• *But you can escape this room. Continue through the next few galleries and into the red lobby. Find the elevators on the right, and go up to level 1. Exiting the elevator, turn left into Room 11. This is one of several rooms with work by Velázquez, but* Las Meninas *is around the corner to the right in the large, lozenge-shaped Room 12.*

Spanish Masters

Diego Velázquez (vel-LAHTH-keth, 1599-1660) was the photo-journalist of court painters, capturing the Spanish king and his court in formal portraits that take on aspects of a candid snapshot. Room 12 is filled with the portraits Velázquez was called on to produce. Kings and princes prance like Roman emperors. Get up close and notice that his remarkably detailed costumes are nothing but a few messy splotches of paint—the proto-Impressionism Velázquez helped pioneer.

The room's centerpiece, and perhaps the most important painting in the museum, is Velázquez's *Maids of Honor* (*Las Meninas,* c.

1656). It's a peek at nannies caring for Princess Margarita and, at the same time, a behind-the-scenes look at Velázquez at work. One hot summer day in 1656, Velázquez (at left, with paintbrush and Dalí moustache) stands at his easel and stares out at the people he's painting—the king and queen. They would have been standing about where we are, and we see only their reflection in the mirror at the back of the room. Their daughter (blonde hair, in center) watches her parents being painted, joined by her servants *(meninas),* dwarves, and the family dog. At that very moment, a man happens to pass by the doorway at back and pauses to look in. Why's he there? Probably just to give the painting more depth.

This frozen moment is lit by the window on the right, splitting the room into bright and shaded planes that recede into the distance. The main characters look right at us, making us part of the scene, seemingly able to walk around, behind, and among the characters. Notice the exquisitely painted mastiff.

If you stand in the center of the room, the 3-D effect is most striking. This is art come to life.

• *Facing this painting, leave to the left and go into Room 10.*

Look around this gallery and see how Velázquez enjoyed capturing light—and capturing the moment. *The Feast of Bacchus* (*Los Borrachos,* c. 1628-29) is a cell-phone snapshot in a blue-collar bar, with a couple of peasants mugging for a photo-op with a Greek god—Bacchus, the god of wine. This was an early work, before Velázquez got his court-painter gig. A personal homage to the hardworking farmers enjoying the fruit of their labor, it shows how Velázquez had a heart for real people and believed they deserved portraits, too. Notice the almost-sacramental presence of the ultrarealistic bowl of wine in the center, as Bacchus, with the honest gut, crowns a fellow hedonist.

• *Backtrack through the big gallery with* Las Meninas *to Room 14.*

Velázquez's boss, King Philip IV, had an affair, got caught, and repented by commissioning *The Crucified Christ* (*Cristo Crucificado,* c. 1632). Christ hangs his head, humbly accepting his punishment. Philip would have been left to stare at the slowly dripping blood, contemplating how long Christ had to suffer to atone for Philip's sins. This is an interesting death scene. There's no anguish, no tension, no torture. Light seems to emanate from Jesus as if nothing else matters. The crown of thorns and the cloth wrapped around his waist are particularly vivid. Above it all, a sign reads in three languages: *"Jesus of Nazareth, King of the Jews."*

• *The nearby rooms (16 and 17) are filled with Murillo paintings. Look for a couple of his immaculately conceived virgins.*

Bartolomé Murillo (1618-1682) put a human face on the abstract Catholic doctrine that Mary was conceived and born free of original sin. Murillo painted several versions of the *Immaculate Conception,* of which the Prado has five that sometimes rotate. *The Immaculate Conception of Los Venerables* (*La Inmaculada Concepción de los Venerables,* c. 1678) hangs in Room 16, and another version is installed in Room 17. Murillo's "immaculate" virgin floats in a cloud of Ivory Soap cleanliness, radiating youth and wholesome goodness. She wears the usual colors of the Virgin Mary—white for purity and blue for divinity. Sweet and escapist, Murillo's work was a hit, and it must have been very comforting to the wretched people of post-plague Sevilla (his hometown was hit hard in 1647-1652).

• *Go back to Room 14, cross the large stairwell (where there are WCs) into the main gallery (Rooms 28 and 29) for lots of fleshy excitement, courtesy of Peter Paul Rubens.*

Northern Baroque

A native of Flanders, **Peter Paul Rubens** (1577-1640) painted Baroque-style art meant to play on the emotions, titillate the senses, and carry you away. His paintings surge with Baroque energy and ripple with waves of figures. Surveying his big, boisterous canvases, you'll notice his trademarks: sex, violence, action, emotion, bright colors, and ample bodies, with the wind machine set on full. Gods are melodramatic, and nymphs flee half-human predators. Rubens painted the most beautiful women of his day—well-fed, no tan lines, squirt-gun breasts, and very sexy.

Rubens' *The Three Graces* (*Las Tres Gracias*, c. 1630-1635) celebrates cellulite. The ample, glowing bodies intertwine as the women exchange meaningful glances. The Grace at the left is Rubens' young second wife, Hélène Fourment, who shows up regularly in his paintings.

• *From the main gallery with the Rubens, look to the near end of the hall, where Goya's royal portraits hang. We'll end up there. But first, head the other way to Titian and El Greco. Titians line the main gallery, and the El Grecos are in Rooms 8b, 9b, and 10b.*

Spanish Mystic

El Greco (1541-1614) was born in Greece (his name is Spanish for "The Greek"), trained in Venice, then settled in Toledo—60 miles from Madrid. His paintings are like Byzantine icons drenched in Venetian color and fused in the fires of Spanish mysticism. The El Greco paintings displayed here rotate, but they all glow with his unique style.

In *Christ Carrying the Cross* (*Cristo Abrazado a la Cruz*, c. 1602), Jesus accepts his fate, trudging toward death with blood running

down his neck. He hugs the cross and directs his gaze along the crossbar. His upturned eyes (sparkling with a streak of white paint) lock onto his next stop—heaven.

The Adoration of the Shepherds (*La Adoración de los Pastores*, c. 1614), originally painted for El Greco's own burial chapel in Toledo, has the artist's typical two-tiered composition—heaven above, earth below. The long, skinny shepherds are stretched unnaturally in between, flickering like flames toward heaven.

The Nobleman with His Hand on His Chest (*El Caballero de la Mano al Pecho*, c. 1580) shows an elegant and somewhat arrogant man whose hand has the middle fingers touching—El Greco's trademark way of expressing elegance (or was it the 16th-century symbol for "Live long and prosper"?). The signature is on the right in faint Greek letters—"Doménikos Theotokópoulos," El Greco's real name.

• *Return to the main gallery. Spot several Titian paintings in Rooms 25-26, and meander through the Italian wing, including Venetian portraits in Rooms 40-44. Continue down the main gallery to the center, under the dome (and opposite* Las Meninas)*, where Charles I sits royally on horseback.*

Venetian Painter to the Court

Spain's Golden Age kings Charles I (a.k.a. Charles V) and Philip II were both staunch Catholics, but that didn't stop them from amassing this sometimes surprisingly racy collection. Both kings sat for portraits by the Venetian master **Titian** (c. 1485-1576).

In *The Emperor Charles V at Mühlberg* (*Carlos V en la Batalla de Mühlberg*, 1548), the king rears on his horse, raises his lance, and rides out to crush an army of Lutherans. Charles, having inherited many kingdoms and baronies through his family connections, was the world's most powerful man in the 1500s. (You can see the suit of armor depicted in the painting in the Royal Palace.)

In contrast (just to the left), Charles I's son, *Philip II* (*Felipe II,* c. 1550-1551), looks pale, suspicious, and lonely—a scholarly and complex figure. He built the austere, monastic palace at El Escorial, but also indulged himself with Titian's bevy of Renaissance Playmates—a sampling of which is here in the Prado.

These are the faces of the Counter-Reformation. While father and son ruled very differently, both had underbites, a product of royal inbreeding (which Titian painted...but very delicately).

• *Now walk to the far end of the main gallery and enter the round Room 32, where you'll see royal portraits by Goya. The museum's exciting Goya collection is on three levels at this end of the building: classic Goya (royal portraits and* La Maja*), on this floor; early cartoons, upstairs; and his dark and political work, downstairs.*

Painter of Kings and Demons

Follow the complex **Francisco de Goya** (1746-1828) through the stages of his life—from dutiful court painter, to political rebel and scandal maker, to the disillusioned genius of his "black paintings."

In the group portrait *The Family of Charles IV* (*La Familia de Carlos IV,* 1800), the royals are all decked out in their Sunday best.

Goya himself stands at his easel to the far left, painting the court (a tribute to Velázquez in *Las Meninas*) and revealing the shallowness beneath the fancy trappings. Charles, with his ridiculous hairpiece and goofy smile, was a vacuous, henpecked husband. His toothless yet domineering queen upstages him, arrogantly stretching her swanlike neck. The other adults, with their bland faces, are bug-eyed with stupidity.

Surrounding you in this same room are other portraits of the king and queen. Also notice the sketch paintings, quick studies done with the subjects posing for Goya. He used these for reference to complete his larger, more finished canvases.

• *Exit to the right across a small hallway and enter Room 36, where you'll find Goya's most scandalous work.*

Rumors flew that Goya was fooling around with the vivacious Duchess of Alba, who may have been the model for two similar paintings, *Nude Maja* (*La Maja Desnuda,* c. 1800) and *Clothed Maja* (*La Maja Vestida,* c. 1808). A *maja* was a trendy, working-class girl. Whether she's a duchess or a *maja*, Goya painted a naked lady—an actual person rather than some mythic Venus. And that was enough to risk incurring the wrath of the Inquisition. The nude stretches in a Titian-esque pose to display her charms, the pale body with realistic pubic hair highlighted by cool green sheets. (Notice the artist's skillful rendering of the transparent fabric on the pillow.) According to a believable legend, the two paintings were displayed in a double frame, with the *Clothed Maja* sliding over the front to hide the *Nude Maja* from Inquisitive minds.

• *Find the nearby staircase and elevator, and head up to level 2 to Rooms 85-87 and 90-94 for more Goya.*

These rooms display Goya's designs for tapestries (known as "cartoons") for nobles' palaces. As you stroll around, the scenes make it clear that, while revolution was brewing in America and France, Spain's lords and ladies were playing, blissfully ignorant of the changing times. Dressed in their "Goya-style" attire, they're picnicking, dancing, flying kites, playing paddleball and Blind Man's Bluff, or just relaxing in the sun—as in the well-known *The Parasol* (*El Quitasol*, Room 85 or 94).

• *For more Goya, take the stairs or elevator down to level 0. Room 66 leads into Goya's final paintings, with a darker edge. But first go to Room 65, which takes you to powerful military scenes.*

Goya became a political liberal, a champion of democracy. He was crushed when France's hero of the French Revolution,

Napoleon, morphed into a tyrant and invaded Spain. In the *Second of May, 1808* (*El 2 de Mayo de 1808*, 1814), Madrid's citizens rise up to protest the occupation in Puerta del Sol, and the French send in their dreaded Egyptian mercenaries. They plow through the dense tangle of Madrileños, who have nowhere to run. The next day, the *Third of May, 1808* (*El 3 de Mayo de 1808*, 1814), the French rounded up ringleaders and executed them. The colorless firing squad—a faceless machine of death—mows them down, and they fall in bloody, tangled heaps. Goya throws a harsh prison-yard floodlight on the main victim, who spreads his arms Christ-like to ask, "Why?"

Politically, Goya was split—he was a Spaniard, but he knew France was leading Europe into the modern age. His art, while political, has no Spanish or French flags. It's a universal comment on the horror of war. Many consider Goya the last classical and first modern painter...the first painter with a social conscience.

• *About-face to the "black paintings" in Room 67.*

Depressed and deaf from syphilis, Goya retired to his small home and smeared its walls with his "black paintings"—dark in color and in mood. During this period in his life, Goya would paint his nightmares...literally. The style is considered Romantic—emphasizing emotion over beauty—but it foreshadows 20th-century Surrealism with its bizarre imagery, expressionistic and thick brushstrokes, and cynical outlook.

Stepping into Room 67, you are surrounded by art from Goya's dark period. These paintings are the actual murals from the walls of his house, transferred onto canvas. Imagine this in your living room. Goya painted what he felt with a radical technique unburdened by reality—a century before his time. And he painted without being paid for it—perhaps the first great paintings done not for hire or for sale. We know frustratingly little about these works because Goya wrote nothing about them.

Dark forces convened continually in Goya's dining room, where *The Great He-Goat* (*El Aquelarre/El Gran Cabrón,* c. 1820-1823) hung. The witches, who look like skeletons, swirl in a frenzy around a dark, Satanic goat in monk's clothing who presides over the obscene rituals. The black goat represents the devil and stokes the frenzy of his wild-eyed subjects. Amid this adoration and lust, a noble lady (far right) folds her hands primly in her lap ("I thought this was a Tupperware party!"). Or, perhaps it's a pep rally for her execution, maybe inspired by the chaos that accompanied Plaza Mayor executions. Nobody knows for sure.

In *Fight to the Death with Clubs* (*Duelo a Garrotazos,* c. 1820-1823), two giants stand face-to-face, buried up to their knees, and flail at each other with clubs. It's a standoff between superpowers in the never-ending cycle of war—a vision of a tough time when people on the streets would kill for a piece of bread.

In *Saturn* (*Saturno,* c. 1820-1823), the king of the Roman gods—fearful that his progeny would overthrow him—eats one of his offspring. Saturn, also known as Cronus (Time), may symbolize how time devours us all. Either way, the painting brings new meaning to the term "child's portion."

The Drowning Dog (*Perro Semihundido,* c.

1820-1823) is, according to some, the hinge between classical art and modern art. The dog, so full of feeling and sadness, is being swallowed by quicksand...much as, to Goya, the modern age was overtaking a more classical era. And look closely at the dog. It also can be seen as a turning point for Goya. Perhaps he's bottomed out—he's been overwhelmed by depression, but his spirit has survived. With the portrait of this dog, color is returning.

• *Head back to Room 66, and look on the right.*

The last painting we have by Goya is *The Milkmaid of Bordeaux* (*La Lechera de Burdeos,* c. 1827). Somehow, Goya pulled out of his depression and moved to France, where he lived until his death at 82. While painting as an old man, color returned to his palette. His social commentary, his passion for painting what he felt (more than what he was hired to do), and, as you see here, the freedom of his brushstrokes explain why many consider Francesco de Goya to be the first modern artist.

• *There's a lot more to the Prado, but there's also a lot more to Madrid. The choice is yours.*

▲▲Thyssen-Bornemisza Museum (Museo del Arte Thyssen-Bornemisza)

Locals call this stunning museum simply the Thyssen (TEE-sun). It displays the impressive collection that Baron Thyssen (a wealthy German married to a former Miss Spain) sold to Spain for $350 million. The museum offers a unique chance to enjoy the sweep of all of art history—including a good sampling of the "isms" of the 20th century—in one collection. It's basically minor works by major artists and major works by minor artists. (Major works by major artists are in the Prado.) But art lovers appreciate how the good baron's art complements the Prado's collection by filling in where the Prado is weak—such as Impressionism, which is the Thyssen's forte.

Cost and Hours: €12, includes temporary exhibits, timed ticket required for temporary exhibits, free for kids under age 12, free on Mon; permanent collection open Mon 12:00-16:00, Tue-Sun 10:00-19:00, Sat until 21:00 (exhibits only); audioguide-€5 for permanent collection, €4 for temporary exhibits, €7 for both; Second Canvas Thyssen is a decent, free smartphone app that explains major works with text and audio—use museum's free Wi-Fi to access; kitty-corner from the Prado at Paseo del Prado 8 in Palacio de Villahermosa (Metro: Banco de España); tel. 902-760-511, www.museothyssen.org.

Services: The museum has free baggage storage (bags must fit through a small x-ray machine), a cafeteria and restaurant, free Wi-Fi, and a shop/bookstore.

Visiting the Museum: After purchasing your ticket, continue

MADRID

down the wide main hall past larger-than-life paintings of former monarchs Juan Carlos I and Sofía, and at the end of the hall, paintings of the baron (who died in 2002) and his art-collecting baroness, Carmen. At the info desk, pick up a museum map. Each of the three floors is divided into two separate areas: the permanent collection (numbered rooms) and additions from the baroness since the 1980s (lettered rooms). Ascend to the top floor and work your way down, taking a delightful walk through art history. Visit the rooms on each floor in numerical order, from Primitive Italian (Room 1) to Surrealism and Pop Art (Room 45-47).

Connecting the Thyssen and Reina Sofía: If you're heading to the Reina Sofía and you're tired, hail a cab at the gate to zip straight there, or take bus #27, which stops in the square with the Neptune fountain, in front of the Starbucks (ride to the end of Paseo del Prado, get off at the McDonald's, and cross the street, going away from the Royal Botanical Garden, to Plaza Sánchez Bustillo and the museum).

▲▲▲Centro de Arte Reina Sofía

Home to Picasso's *Guernica,* the Reina Sofía is one of Europe's most enjoyable modern-art museums. Its exceptional collection
of 20th-century art is housed in what was Madrid's first public hospital. The focus is on 20th-century Spanish artists—Picasso, Dalí, Miró, Gris, and Tàpies—but you'll also find plenty of works by Kandinsky, Braque, and many other giants of modern art.

The curator, who has a passion for cinema, has paired paintings with films from the same decade, which play continuously in nearby rooms. This provides a fascinating insight into the social context that inspired the art of Spain's tumultuous 20th century. Those
with an appetite for modern and contemporary art can spend several delightful hours in this museum.

Cost: €8 (includes most temporary exhibits), €3 if you're under 18 or over 65, €4 for temporary exhibit only, free Mon and Wed-Sat 19:00-21:00, Sun 15:00-19:00 (free times are often crowded, and you must pick up a ticket).

Hours: Mon and Wed-Sat 10:00-21:00, Sun 10:00-19:00 (fourth floor not accessible Sun after 15:00), closed Tue.

Information: Tel. 917-741-000, www.museoreinasofia.es.

Getting There: It's a block from the Atocha Metro stop, on Plaza Sánchez Bustillo (at Calle de Santa Isabel 52). In the Metro station, follow signs for the Reina Sofía exit. Emerging from the Metro, walk straight ahead a half-block and look for an opening between the group of buildings. You'll see the tall, exterior glass elevators that flank the museum's main entrance.

A second entrance in the newer section of the building sometimes has shorter lines, especially during the museum's free hours. Facing the glass elevators, walk left around the old building to the large gates of the red-and-black Nouvel Building.

Tours: The hardworking audioguide is €4.50.

Services: Bag storage is free. The *librería* just outside the Nouvel wing has a larger selection of Picasso and Surrealist reproductions than the main gift shop at the entrance.

Cuisine Art: The museum's **$$** café (a long block around the left from the main entrance) is a standout for its tasty cuisine. The square immediately in front of the museum is ringed by fine places for a simple meal or drink. My favorite is **$$ El Brillante,** a classic dive offering pricey tapas and baguette sandwiches. But everyone comes for the fried squid sandwiches (evidenced by the older *señoras* with mouthfuls of *calamares*). Sit at the simple bar or at an outdoor table (long hours daily, two entrances—one on Plaza Sánchez Bustillo, the other at Plaza del Emperador Carlos V 8, tel. 915-286-966). Also nearby is my favorite strip of tapas bars, on Calle de Jesús.

❷ Self-Guided Tour

Pick up a free map and use the good information sheets to supplement this tour.

The permanent collection is divided into three groups: art from 1900 to 1945 (second floor), art from 1945 to 1968 (fourth floor), and art from 1962 to 1982 (adjoining Nouvel wing, which also has space for bigger installations). Temporary exhibits are on the first and third floors.

While the collection is roughly chronological, it's displayed thematically. The second-floor grand hallway leads around a courtyard connecting a series of rooms, each clearly labeled with a theme. For a good first visit, ride the fancy glass elevator to level 2 and tour that floor clockwise (Goya, Surrealism, Cubism, Picasso's *Guernica*), and then finish with post-WWII art on level 4.
• *Begin in Room 201, with examples of...*

Proto-Modern Goya

The installations at many museums can leave you scratching your head in frustration. But the wonderful curator of the Reina Sofía insightfully begins your look at modern art with Goya engravings. That's because Goya is a proto-modernist—the first painter with a social conscience, the first to show inner feelings, and the first to deal with social reality. He painted because he had something to say, not just to get a paycheck.

• *Browse through the next rooms, whose underlying theme is the conflict between tradition (the powerful Church) and progress (social modernization). Find your way to Room 205 and...*

Surrealism and Salvador Dalí

In 1914 a generation marched enthusiastically into combat, believing the Great War would be the "war to end all wars." Many artists embraced this fight, volunteered to serve, and died for the cause. But when it was over, it was clear: World War I brought no lasting change. Frustrated, many survivors turned their backs on society.

In the postwar years, a class of artists abandoned the outer world and looked inside (with inspiration from Freud). They painted mindscapes rather than landscapes. They had learned that reality is deeper than what you first "see." These were the Surrealists. To "see" their art, you need to vary your position: your physical perspective and your mental perspective. See it happy, sad, before coffee, after coffee.

In the Dalí room, you'll see the artist's distinct, Surrealist, melting-object style. Dalí places familiar items in a stark landscape, creating an eerie effect. Figures morph into misplaced faces and body parts. Background and foreground play mind games—is it an animal (seen one way) or a man's face? A waterfall or a pair of legs? It's a wide shot...no, it's a close-up. Look long at paintings like Dalí's *Endless Enigma* (1938) and *The Invisible Man* (c. 1933); they take different viewers to different places.

The Great Masturbator (1929-1932) is psychologically exhausting, depicting in its Surrealism a lonely, highly sexual genius in love with his muse, Gala (while she was still married to a French poet). This is the first famous Surrealist painting.

During this productive period, Dalí was working on the classic Surrealist film *Un Chien Andalou* (*The Andalusian Dog*, 1928) with his collaborator Luis Buñuel (the film plays in Room 203). Both men were members of the Generation of '27, a group of nonconformist Spanish bohemians whose creative interests had a huge influence on art and literature in their era.

• *Skirt back around the courtyard to find Room 210 and...*

Cubism

Cubism was born in the first decade of the 20th century. You could make a good case that the changes in society in the year 1900 were more profound than those we lived through in 2000. Trains and cars brought speed to life. Electricity brought light. Einstein introduced us to abstract ideas. Photography captured reality. And art broke away. At the turn of the century there were two ways to express art: line (Picasso) and color (Matisse)—but it was still in two dimensions. With Cubism, three dimensions are shown in two. Imagine walking around a statue to take in all the angles, and then attempting to put it on a 2-D plane. With Cubism, everyone sees things differently. To appreciate it, take your time and free your imagination.

Room 210 shows the birth of Cubism—a movement in which Spaniards were very much at the forefront (with works by Picasso, Braque, Léger, and Gris). To literally see a 2-D picture plane leap to life, watch the Lumière brothers' early film *Partie d'Écarté* (c. 1898).

• *In Room 206, you come to what is likely the reason for your visit...*

Picasso's *Guernica*

Perhaps the single most impressive piece of art in Spain is Pablo Picasso's *Guernica* (1937). The monumental canvas—one of Europe's must-see sights—is not only a piece of art but a piece of history, capturing the horror of modern war in a modern style.

While it's become a timeless classic representing all war, it was born in response to a specific conflict—the civil war (1936-1939), which pitted the democratically elected Second Republican government against the fascist general Francisco Franco. Franco won and ended up ruling Spain with an iron fist for the next 36 years. At the time Franco cemented his power, *Guernica* was touring internationally as part of a fundraiser for the Republican cause. With Spain's political situation deteriorating and World War II looming, Picasso in 1939 named New York's Museum of Modern Art as the depository for the work. It was only after Franco's death, in 1975, that *Guernica* ended its decades of exile. In 1981 the painting finally arrived in Spain (where it had never before been), and it now stands as Spain's national piece of art.

Guernica—The Bombing: On April 26, 1937, Guernica—a Basque market town in northern Spain and an important Republican center—was the target of the world's first saturation-bombing raid on civilians. Franco gave permission to his fascist confederate Adolf Hitler to use the town as a guinea pig to try out Germany's new air force. The raid leveled the town, causing destruction that was unheard of at the time (though by 1944 it would be commonplace).

News of the bombing reached Picasso in Paris, where coincidentally he was just beginning work on a painting commission awarded by the Republican government. Picasso scrapped his earlier plans and immediately set to work sketching scenes of the destruction as he imagined it. In a matter of weeks he put these bomb-shattered shards together into a large mural (286 square feet). For the first time, the world could see the destructive force of the rising fascist movement—a prelude to World War II.

Guernica—The Painting: The bombs are falling, shattering the quiet village. ❶ A woman looks up at the sky (far right), ❷ horses scream (center), and ❸ a man falls from a horse and dies, while ❹ a wounded woman drags herself through the streets. She tries to escape, but her leg is too thick, dragging her down, like trying to run from something in a nightmare. ❺ On the left, a bull—a symbol of Spain—ponders it all, watching over ❻ a mother and her dead baby...a modern pietà. ❼ A woman in the center sticks her head out to see what's going on. The whole scene is lit from above by the ❽ stark light of a bare bulb. Picasso's painting threw a light on the brutality of Hitler and Franco, and suddenly the whole world was watching.

Picasso's abstract, Cubist style reinforces the message. It's as if he'd picked up the shattered shards and pasted them onto a canvas. The black-and-white tones are as gritty as the black-and-white newspaper photos that reported the bombing. The drab colors create a depressing, almost nauseating mood.

Picasso chose images with universal symbolism, making the work a commentary on all wars. Picasso himself said that the central horse, with the spear in its back, symbolizes humanity succumbing to brute force. The fallen rider's arm is severed and his sword is broken, more symbols of defeat. The bull, normally a proud symbol of strength and independence, is impotent and frightened. Between the bull and the horse, the faint dove of peace can do nothing but cry.

The bombing of Guernica—like the entire civil war—was an exercise in brutality. As one side captured a town, it might systematically round up every man, old and young—including priests—line them up, and shoot them in revenge for atrocities by the other side.

Thousands of people attended the Paris exhibition, and *Guernica* caused an immediate sensation. They could see the horror of modern war technology, the vain struggle of the Spanish Republicans, and the cold indifference of the fascist war machine. Picasso vowed never to return to Spain while Franco ruled (the dictator outlived him).

With each passing year, the canvas seemed more and more prophetic—honoring not just the hundreds or thousands who died in Guernica, but also the estimated 500,000 victims of Spain's bitter civil war and the 55 million worldwide who perished in World War II. Picasso put a human face on what we now call "collateral damage."

• *After seeing Guernica, view the additional exhibits that put the painting in its social context.*

Other Picasso Exhibits

On the back wall on the *Guernica* room is a line of **photos** showing the evolution of the painting, from Picasso's first concept to the final mural. The photos were taken in his Paris studio by Dora Maar, Picasso's mistress-du-jour (and whose portrait by Picasso hangs nearby). Notice how his work evolved from the defiant fist in early versions to a broken sword with a flower.

The room behind *Guernica* contains **studies** Picasso did for the painting. These studies are filled with motifs that turn up in the final canvas—iron-nail tears, weeping women, and screaming horses. Picasso returned to these images in his work for the rest of his life. He believed that everyone struggles internally with aspects of the horse and bull: rationality and brutality, humanity and animalism. The Minotaur—half-man and half-bull—powerfully captures Picasso's poet/rapist vision of man. Having lived through the brutality of the age—World War I, the Spanish Civil War, and World War II—his outlook is understandable.

In the far end of this hall, you'll also find a **model of the Spanish Pavilion** at the 1937 Paris exposition where *Guernica* was first displayed (look inside to see Picasso's work). Picasso originally toyed with painting an allegory on the theme of the artist's studio for the expo. But the bombing of Guernica jolted him into the realization that Spain was a country torn by war. Thanks to *Guernica*, the pavilion became a vessel for propaganda and a fundraising tool against Franco.

Nearby the Spanish Pavilion, you'll see posters and political cartoons that are pro-communist and anti-Franco. Made the same year as *Guernica* and the year after, these touch on timeless themes related to rich elites, industrialists, agricultural reform, and the military industrial complex versus the common man, as well as promoting autonomy for Catalunya and the Basque Country.

The remaining rooms display pieces from contemporary artists reacting to the conflict of the time, whether through explicit commentary or through new, innovative styles inspired by the changing political and social culture.

• *Head up to level 4, where the permanent collection continues.*

Post-WWII Art

After World War II, the center of the art world moved from Paris to New York City. Spain was ruled by a dictatorship, and the avant-garde could not be so *avant*. The organizing theme in this part of the museum is "Art in a Divided World." On this floor, especially, you'll want to take full advantage of the English information sheets in each room and the narration provided by your audioguide.

You'll see Kandinsky as a bridge into abstract art and the Abstract Expressionism of Jackson Pollock and company. You'll find late works by Picasso and Miró (from the 1960s and 1970s) scattered throughout this floor. You can also see photographs and watch films documenting Spain's slow recovery from its devastating civil war. The physical and psychological damage of the war weighed on Spain for decades afterward.

• *End your visit in the...*

Nouvel Wing

The newest wing of the museum features art from the 1960s through the 1980s, with a thematic focus on the complexity and plurality of modern times. While these galleries have fewer household names, the pieces displayed demonstrate the many aesthetic directions of more recent modern art.

NEAR THE PRADO (AND BEYOND)

Several other worthy sights are located in and around the museum neighborhood. This is also where my self-guided bus tour along Paseo de la Castellana to the modern skyscraper part of Madrid starts.

▲▲Retiro Park (Parque del Buen Retiro)

Once the private domain of royalty, this majestic park has been a favorite of Madrid's commoners since Charles III decided to share it with his subjects in the late 18th century. Siesta in this 300-acre green-and-breezy escape from the city. At midday on Saturday and Sunday, the area around the lake becomes a street carnival, with jugglers, puppeteers, and lots of local color. These peaceful gardens offer great picnicking and people-watching (closes at dusk). From the Retiro Metro stop, walk to the big lake (El Estanque), where you can rent a rowboat. Enjoy the 19th-century glass-and-iron Crystal Palace, which often hosts free exhibits and installations. Past the lake, a grand boulevard of statues leads to the Prado.

▲Royal Botanical Garden (Real Jardín Botánico)

After your Prado visit, you can take a lush and fragrant break in this sculpted park. Wander among trees from around the world, originally gathered by—who else?—the enlightened King Charles III. This garden was established when the Prado's building housed the natural science museum. A flier in English explains that this is actually more than a park—it's a museum of plants.

Cost and Hours: €4, daily 10:00-21:00, shorter hours off-season, entrance is opposite the Prado's Murillo/south entry, Plaza de Murillo 2, tel. 914-203-017.

▲Naval Museum (Museo Naval)

This museum tells the story of Spain's navy, from 1492 to today, in a plush and fascinating-to-boat-lovers exhibit. Given Spain's importance in maritime history, there's quite a story to tell. Because this is a military facility, you'll need to show your passport or driver's license to get in. A good English brochure is available. Access to the Wi-Fi-based English audioguide can be unreliable, but give it a try.

Cost and Hours: €3, Tue-Sun 10:00-19:00, until 15:00 in Aug, closed Mon, a block north of the Prado, across boulevard from Thyssen-Bornemisza Museum, Paseo del Prado 5, tel. 915-238-789.

CaixaForum

Across the street from the Prado and Royal Botanical Garden, this impressive exhibit hall has sleek architecture and an outdoor hanging garden—a bushy wall festooned with greens designed by a French landscape artist. The forum, funded by La Caixa Bank, features world-class art exhibits—generally 20th-century art, well-described in English and changing three times a year. Ride the elevator to the top, where you'll find a café with a daily €13 fixed-price meal and sperm-like lamps swarming down from the ceiling; from here, explore your way down.

Cost and Hours: €4, daily 10:00-20:00, audioguide-€2-4, Paseo del Prado 36, tel. 913-307-300.

Palacio de Cibeles

This former post-office headquarters was recently converted to a cultural center—featuring mostly empty exhibition halls, an auditorium, and public hang-out spaces—and renamed CentroCentro Cibeles for Culture and Citizenship. (Say that five times fast!) The temporary exhibits can be skipped. The real attraction lies in the gorgeous 360-degree rooftop views from the eighth-floor observation deck (ticket office outside to the right of the main entrance). Visit the recommended sixth-floor Restaurante Palacio de Cibeles and bar for similar views from its two terraces.

Cost and Hours: €2 elevator ride to observation deck, visiting the Palacio itself is free—take advantage of its air-conditioning and free Wi-Fi; building open Tue-Sun 10:00-20:00, limited terrace visits possible every half-hour 10:30-13:30 & 16:00-19:00, closed Mon, ticket office opens 30 minutes early, advance tickets available on their website, Plaza de Cibeles 1, tel. 914-800-008, www. centrocentro.org.

▲▲National Archaeological Museum (Museo Arqueológico Nacional/MAN)

This museum is like a little British Museum—a museum of early history. You'll follow a chronological walk through the story of Iberia. With a well-curated, rich collection of artifacts and tasteful multimedia displays (well-described in English), the museum shows off the wonders of each age: Celtic pre-Roman, Roman, a fine and rare Visigothic section, Moorish, Romanesque, and beyond. A highlight is the Lady of Elche (Room 13), a prehistoric Iberian female bust and a symbol of Spanish archaeology. You may also find underwhelming replica artwork from northern Spain's Altamira Caves (big on bison), giving you a faded peek at the skill of the cave artists who created the originals 14,000 years ago.

Cost and Hours: €3, free on Sat 14:00-20:00 and all day Sun; open Tue-Sat 9:30-20:00, Sun 9:30-15:00, closed Mon; €2 multimedia guide; 20-minute walk north of the Prado at Calle Serrano 13, Metro: Serrano or Colón, tel. 915-777-912, www.man.es.

Royal Tapestry Factory (Real Fábrica de Tapices)

Take this factory tour for a look at traditional tapestry-making. You'll also have the chance to order a tailor-made tapestry (starting at $10,000).

Cost and Hours: €5, by tour only, English tour at 12:00, Spanish at 10:00, 11:00, and 13:00; open Mon-Fri 10:00-14:00, closed Sat-Sun and Aug; south of Retiro Park at Calle Fuenterrabia 2, Metro: Menendez Pelayo, take Gutenberg exit, tel. 914-340-550, www.realfabricadetapices.com.

AWAY FROM THE CENTER
▲Museum of the Americas (Museo de América)

Thousands of pre-Columbian and colonial artworks and artifacts make up the bulk of this worthwhile museum, though it offers few English explanations. Covering the cultures of the Americas (North and South), its exhibits focus on language, religion, and art, and provide a new perspective on the cultures of our own hemisphere. Highlights include one of only four surviving Mayan codices (ancient books) and a section about the voyages of the Spanish explorers, with their fantastical imaginings of mythical creatures awaiting them in the New World.

MADRID

Cost and Hours: €3, free on Sun; open Tue-Sat 9:30-15:00, Thu until 19:00, Sun 10:00-15:00, closed Mon; Avenida de los Reyes Católicos 6, Metro: Moncloa, tel. 915-492-641, http://museodeamerica.mcu.es.

Getting There: The museum is a 15-minute walk from the Moncloa Metro stop: Take the Calle de Isaac Peral exit, cross Plaza de Moncloa, and veer right to Calle de Fernández de los Ríos. Follow that street (toward the shiny Faro de Moncloa tower), and turn left on Avenida de los Reyes Católicos. Head around the base of the tower, which stands at the museum's entrance.

Clothing Museum (Museo del Traje)

This museum shows the history of clothing from the 18th century until today. In a cool and air-conditioned chronological sweep, the museum's one floor of exhibits includes regional ethnic costumes, a look at how bullfighting and the French influenced styles, accessories through the ages, and Spanish flappers. The only downside of this marvelous, modern museum is that it's a long way from anything else of interest.

Cost and Hours: €3, free on Sat 14:30-19:00 and all day Sun; open Tue-Sat 9:30-19:00, Thu until 22:30 in July-Aug, Sun 10:00-15:00, closed Mon; Avenida de Juan Herrera 2; Metro: Moncloa and a longish walk, bus #46, or taxi; tel. 915-497-150, http://museodeltraje.mcu.es.

▲Hermitage of San Antonio de la Florida (Ermita de San Antonio de la Florida)

In this simple little Neoclassical chapel from the 1790s, Francisco de Goya's tomb stares up at a splendid cupola filled with his own proto-Impressionist frescoes. He used the same unique technique that he employed for his "black paintings" (described earlier, under the Prado Museum listing). Use the mirrors to enjoy the drama and energy he infused into this marvelously restored masterpiece.

Cost and Hours: Free, Tue-Sun 9:30-20:00, closed Mon, Glorieta de San Antonio de la Florida 5; Metro: Príncipe Pío, then eight-minute walk down Paseo de San Antonio de la Florida; tel. 915-420-722, www.madrid.es/ermita.

Temple of Debod (Templo de Debod)

In 1968, Egypt gave Spain its own ancient temple. It was a gift of the Egyptian government, which was grateful for the Spanish dictator Franco's help in rescuing monuments that had been threatened by the rising Nile waters above the Aswan Dam. Consequently, Madrid is the only place I can think of in Europe where you can actually wander through an intact original Egyptian temple—complete with fine carved reliefs from 200 B.C. Set in a romantic park that locals love for its great city views (especially at sunset), the temple—as well as its art—is well-described.

Cost and Hours: Free; Tue-Fri 10:00-20:00 in summer, Sat-Sun from 9:30, shorter hours off-season, closed Mon year-round; in Parque de Montaña, north of the Royal Palace, tel. 913-667-415, www.madrid.es (search for "Templo de Debod").

▲▲Sorolla Museum (Museo Sorolla)

The delightful, art-filled home of painter Joaquín Sorolla (1863-1923) is one of the most enjoyable museums in Spain. Sorolla is known for his portraits, landscapes, and use of light. Imagine the mansion, back in 1910, when it stood alone—without the surrounding high-rise buildings. With the aid of the essential audioguide, you stroll through his home and studio, randomly settling on whichever painting grabs you. Sorolla captured wonderful slices of life—his wife/muse, his family, and lazy beach scenes of his hometown Valencia. He was a late Impressionist—a period called Luminism in Spain. And it was all about nature: water, light, reflection. The collection is intimate rather than exhausting, and you can cap it with a few restful minutes in Sorolla's Andalusian gardens. Visit in the morning to experience the works with the best natural light.

Cost and Hours: €3, free on Sat 14:00-20:00 and all day Sun; open Tue-Sat 9:30-20:00, Sun 10:00-15:00, closed Mon; audioguide-€2.50; General Martínez Campos 37, Metro: Iglesia, tel. 913-101-584.

▲Madrid History Museum (Museo de Historia de Madrid)

This building, a hospital from 1716 to 1910, has housed a city history museum since 1929. The entrance features a fine Baroque door by the architect Pedro de Ribera, with a depiction of St. James the Moor-Slayer. Start in the basement (where you can study a detailed model of the city made in 1830) and work your way up through the four-floor collection. The history of Madrid is explained through old paintings that show the city in action, maps, historic fans, jeweled snuffboxes, etchings of early bullfighting, and fascinating late-19th-century photographs.

Don't miss Goya's *Allegory of the City of Madrid* (c. 1810), an angelic tribute to the rebellion against the French on May 2, 1808. The museum is in the trendy Malasaña district, near the Plaza Dos de Mayo, where some of the rebellion that Goya painted occurred.

Cost and Hours: Free, Tue-Sun 10:00-20:00, closed Mon, Calle de Fuencarral 78, Metro: Tribunal, tel. 917-011-863.

Experiences in Madrid

▲▲Self-Guided Bus Tour: Paseo de la Castellana

Tourists risk leaving Madrid without ever seeing the modern "Manhattan" side of town. But it's easy to find. From the museum neighborhood, bus #27 makes the trip straight north along Paseo del Prado and then Paseo de la Castellana, through the no-nonsense skyscraper part of this city of more than three million. The line ends at the leaning towers of Puerta de Europa (Gate of Europe). This trip is simple and cheap. If starting from the Prado, catch the bus from the museum side to head north; from the Reina Sofía, the stop is a couple of blocks away at the Royal Botanical Garden, at the end of the garden fence (€1.50, buses run every 10 minutes). You just joyride for 30-45 minutes to the last stop, get out at the end of the line when everyone else does, ogle the skyscrapers, and catch the Metro for a 20-minute ride back to the city's center. At twilight, when fountains and facades are floodlit, the ride is particularly enjoyable. Possible stops of interest along the way are Plaza de Colon (for the National Archaeological Museum) and Bernabéu (for the massive soccer stadium).

Historic District: Bus #27 rumbles from the end of the Paseo del Prado at the Royal Botanical Garden (opposite McDonald's) and the Velázquez entrance to the Prado. Immediately after the Prado you pass a number of grand landmarks: a square with a fountain of Neptune (left); an obelisk and war memorial to those who have died for Spain (right, with the stock market behind it); the Naval Museum (right); and Plaza de Cibeles—with the fancy City Hall and cultural center. From Plaza de Cibeles, you can see the 18th-century Gate of Alcalá (the old east entry to Madrid), the Bank of Spain, and the start of the Gran Vía (left). Then you can relax for a moment while driving along Paseo de Recoletos.

Modern District: Just past the National Library (right) is a roundabout and square **(Plaza de Colon)** with a statue of Columbus in the middle and a giant Spanish flag. This marks the end of the historic town and the beginning of the modern city. (Hop out here for the National Archaeological Museum.)

At this point the boulevard changes its name (and the sights I mention are much more spread out). This street used to be named for Franco; now it's named for the people he no longer rules—*la Castellana* (Castilians). Next, you pass high-end apartments and embassies. Immediately after an underpass with several modern sculptures comes the **American Embassy** (right, hard to see behind its fortified wall) and some circa-1940s buildings that once housed Franco's ministries (left, typical fascist architecture, with large colonnades). Continuing up the boulevard, look left and ahead to see the **Picasso Tower,** resembling one of New York's former World

Trade Center towers with its vertical black-and-white stripes (it was designed by the same architect). Passing under a second underpass you enter 1980s business sprawl on the left. Just after the Picasso Tower (left) is the huge **Bernabéu Stadium** (right, home of Real Madrid, Europe's most successful soccer team; bus stops on both sides of the stadium).

Your trip ends at **Plaza de Castilla,** where you can't miss the avant-garde Puerta de Europa, consisting of the twin "Torres Kios," office towers that lean at a 15-degree angle (look for the big green sign BANKIA, for the Bank of Madrid). In the distance, you can see the four tallest buildings in Spain. The plaza sports a futuristic golden obelisk by contemporary Spanish architect Santiago Calatrava.

It's the end of the line for the bus—and for you. You can return directly to Puerta del Sol on the Metro, or cross the street and ride bus #27 along the same route back to the Prado Museum or Atocha train station.

▲Electric Minibus Joyride through the Lavapiés District

For a relaxing ride through the characteristic old center of Madrid, hop the little electric **minibus #M1** (€1.50, 5/hour, 20-minute trip, Mon-Sat 8:20-20:00, none on Sun). These are designed especially for the difficult-to-access streets in the historic heart of the city, and they're handy for seniors who could use a lift (offer your seat if you see a senior standing).

The Route: Catch the minibus near the Sevilla Metro stop at the top of Calle Sevilla, and simply ride it to the end (Metro: Embajadores). Enjoy this gritty slice of workaday Madrid—both people and architecture—as you roll slowly through Plaza Santa Ana, down a bit of the pedestrianized Calle de las Huertas, past gentrified Plaza Tirso de Molina (its junkies now replaced by a faded family-friendly flower market), and through Plaza de Lavapiés and a barrio of African and Bangladeshi immigrants. Jump out along the way to explore Lavapiés on foot (see description on next page), or stay on until you get to Embajadores just a few blocks away. From there, you can catch the next #M1 minibus back to the Sevilla Metro stop (it returns along a different route) or descend into the subway system (it's just two stops back to Sol).

The Lavapiés District: In the Lavapiés neighborhood, the multiethnic tapestry of Madrid enjoys seedy-yet-fun-loving life on the streets. Neighborhoods like this typically experience the same familiar evolution: Initially they're so cheap that only immigrants, the downtrodden, and counter-culture types live there. The diversity and color they bring attracts those with more money. Businesses erupt to cater to those bohemian/trendy tastes. Rents go up. Those who gave the area its colorful energy in the first place can no longer afford to live there. They move out...and here comes Starbucks.

For now, Lavapiés is still edgy, yet comfortable enough for most. To help rejuvenate the area, the city built the big Centro Dramático Nacional Theater just downhill from Lavapiés' main square.

The district has almost no tourists. (Some think it's too scary.) Old ladies with their tired bodies and busy fans hang out on their tiny balconies as they have for 40 years, watching the scene. Shady types lurk on side streets (don't venture off the main drag, don't show your wallet or money, and don't linger late on Plaza de Lavapiés).

If you're walking, start from Plaza de Antón Martín (Metro: Antón Martín) or Plaza Santa Ana. Find your way to Calle del Ave María (on its way to becoming Calle del Ave Allah) and on to Plaza de Lavapiés (Metro: Lavapiés), where elderly Madrileños hang out with the swarthy drunks and drug dealers; a mosaic of cultures treat this square as a communal living room. Then head up Calle de Lavapiés to the Plaza Tirso de Molina (Metro stop). This square was once plagued by druggies, but is now home to flower kiosks and a playground. This is a good example of Madrid's vision for reinvigorating its public spaces.

For food, you'll find plenty of tapas bars plus gritty Indian (almost all run by Bangladeshis) and Moroccan eateries lining Calle de Lavapiés. For Spanish fare try **$ Bar Melos,** a thriving dive jammed with a hungry and nubile crowd. It's famous for its giant €11 patty melts called *zapatillas de lacón y queso* (because they're the size and shape of a *zapatilla,* or slipper; feeds at least two, closed Sun-Mon, Calle del Ave María 44).

▲Bullfight

Madrid's Plaza de Toros hosts Spain's top bullfights on most Sundays and holidays from March through mid-October, and nearly

every day during the San Isidro festival (May-early June—often sold out long in advance). Fights start between 17:00 and 21:00 (early in spring and fall, late in summer). The bullring is at the Ventas Metro stop (a 25-minute Metro ride from Puerta del Sol, tel. 913-562-200, www.las-ventas.com).

Getting Tickets: Bullfight tickets range from €5 to €150. There are no bad seats at Plaza de Toros; paying more gets you in the shade and/or closer to the gore. (The action often intentionally occurs in the shade to reward the expensive-ticket holders.) To be close to the bullring, choose areas 8, 9, or 10; for shade: 1, 2, 9, or 10; for shade/sun: 3 or 8; for the sun and cheapest seats: 4, 5, 6, or 7. Note these key words: *corrida*—a real fight with professionals; *novillada*—rookie matadors, younger bulls, and cheaper tickets. Getting tickets through your hotel or a booking office is convenient, but they add 20 percent or more and don't sell the cheapest seats. There are two booking offices, both of which sell tickets online and in person. When buying online, read conditions carefully: The purchase voucher usually must be exchanged for a ticket at the booking office. The easiest place is Bullfight Tickets Madrid at Plaza del Carmen 1 (Mon-Sat 9:00-13:00 & 16:30-19:00, Sun 9:30-14:00, tel. 915-319-131, www.bullfightticketsmadrid.com; run by José and his English-speaking son, also José, who also sells soccer tickets; will deliver tickets to your hotel). A second option is Toros La Central at Calle Victoria 3 (Mon-Fri 10:00-14:00 & 17:00-19:00, Sat-Sun 10:00-13:00, tel. 915-211-213, www.toroslacentral.es).

To save money, you can stand in the ticket line at the bullring. Except for important bullfights—or during the San Isidro festival—there are generally plenty of seats available. About a thousand tickets are held back to be sold in the five days leading up to and on the day of a fight. Scalpers hang out before the popular fights at the Calle Victoria booking office. Beware: Those buying scalped tickets are breaking the law and can lose the ticket with no recourse.

For a dose of the experience, you can buy a cheap ticket and just stay to see a couple of bullfights. Each fight takes about 20 minutes, and the event consists of six bulls over two hours. Or, to keep your distance but get a sense of the ritual and gore, tour the bull bar on Plaza Mayor.

Bullfighting Museum (Museo Taurino): This museum, located at the back of the bullring, is not as good as the ones in Sevilla or Ronda (free, Sun 10:00-13:00, Mon-Fri 9:30-14:30, closed Sat, closes early on fight days, tel. 917-251-857).

"Football" and Bernabéu Stadium

Madrid, like most of Europe, is enthusiastic about soccer (which they call *fútbol*). The Real ("Royal") Madrid team plays to a spirited crowd Saturdays and Sundays from September through May (tickets from €50—sold at bullfight box offices listed earlier). One of the most popular sightseeing activities among European visitors to Madrid is touring the 80,000-seat stadium. The €24 unguided visit includes the box seats, dressing rooms, technical zone, playing field, trophy room, and a big panoramic stadium view (Mon-Sat 10:00-19:00, Sun 10:30-18:30, shorter hours on game days, bus #27 or Metro: Santiago Bernabéu, tel. 913-984-300, www.

realmadrid.com). Even if you can't catch a game, you'll see plenty of Real Madrid's all-white jerseys and paraphernalia around town.

Shopping in Madrid

Madrileños have a passion for shopping. It's a social event, often incorporated into their afternoon paseo, which eventually turns into drinks and dinner. Most shoppers focus on the colorful pedestrian area between and around Gran Vía and Puerta del Sol. Here you'll find shops like H&M and Zara clothing, Imaginarium toys, FNAC books and music, and a handful of small local shops. The fanciest big-name shops (Gucci, Prada, and the like) tempt strollers along Calle Serrano, northwest of Retiro Park. For trendier chain shops and local fashion, head to pedestrian Calle Fuencarral, Calle Augusto Figueroa, and the streets surrounding Plaza de Chueca (north of Gran Vía, Metro: Chueca). Here are some other places to check out:

El Corte Inglés Department Store
The giant El Corte Inglés, with several buildings strung between Puerta del Sol and Plaza del Callou, is a handy place to pick up just about anything you need (Mon-Sat 10:00-22:00, Sun 11:00-21:00).

▲El Rastro Flea Market
Europe's biggest flea market is a field day for shoppers, people-watchers, and pickpockets (Sun only, 9:00-15:00). It's best before 11:00, though bargain shoppers like to go around 14:00, when vendors are more willing to strike end-of-day deals. Thousands of stalls titillate more than a million browsers with mostly new junk. Locals have lamented the tackiness of El Rastro lately—on the main drag, you'll find cheap underwear and bootleg CDs, but no real treasures.

For an interesting market day (Sun only), start at Plaza Mayor, where Europe's biggest stamp and coin market thrives. Enjoy this genteel delight as you watch old-timers paging lovingly through each other's albums, looking for win-win trades. When you're done, head south or take the Metro to Tirso de Molina. Walk downhill, wandering off on the side streets to browse antiques, old furniture, and garage-sale-style sellers who often simply throw everything out on a sheet. Find a fantastic scene on Plaza del Campillo del Mundo Nuevo where kids and adults leaf through each other's albums of soccer cards and negotiate over trades.

A typical Madrileño's Sunday could involve a meander through the Rastro streets with several stops for *cañas* (small beers) at the gritty bars along the way, then a walk to the Cava Baja area for more beer and tapas. El Rastro offers a fascinating chance to see gangs of young thieves overwhelming and ripping off naive tourists while plainclothes police officers circulate and do their best. Don't even bring a wallet. The pickpocket action is brutal.

Specialty Shops

These places are fun to browse for Spanish specialties and locally made goods.

Ceramics: Antigua Casa Talavera has sold hand-made ceramics from Spain's family craftsmen since 1904. They can explain the various regional styles and colors of pottery and tiles, based on traditional designs from the 11th to 19th century (Mon-Fri 10:00-13:30 & 17:00-20:00, Sat 10:00-13:30, closed Sun, Calle Isabel La Católica 2, tel. 915-473-417, www.antiguacasatalavera.com).

Leather: Taller Puntera is a workshop and store where the new generation carries on a longtime family tradition of Madrileño leather artisans. They design and create all of their products on-site, from bags to shoes and more (Mon-Sat 10:00-15:00 & 17:00-20:30, closed Sun, Plaza Conde de Barajas 4, tel. 913-642-926, www.puntera.com).

Shoes: For *the* shoe street in Madrid head up Calle Fuencarral and take a right onto Calle Augusto Figueroa. Walk a couple of blocks down to find one local *zapatería* after another. On Gran Vía, Calle Arenal, or Calle Preciados, you'll also find Camper shoes, launched in 1975 on the Spanish island of Mallorca. This popular brand is now relatively easy to find around the world, though here in Madrid you may see more styles (daily, Calle Preciados 23, tel. 915-317-897, www.camper.com).

Souvenirs: Casa de Diego sells *abanicos* (fans), *mantones* (typical Spanish shawls), *castañuelas* (castanets), *peinetas* (hair combs), and umbrellas. Even if you're not in the market, it's fun to watch the women flip open their final fan choices before buying—for them it is not a souvenir, but an important piece of their wardrobe (Mon-Sat 9:30-20:00, closed Sun, Puerta del Sol 12, tel. 915-226-643).

Guitars: Spain makes some of the world's finest classical guitars. Several of the top workshops, within an easy walk of Puerta del Sol, offer inviting little showrooms that give a peek at their craft and an opportunity to strum the final product. Consider the workshops of José Romero (Calle de Espoz y Mina 30, tel. 915-214-218) and José Ramirez (Calle de la Paz 8, tel. 915-314-229). Union Musical is a popular guitar shop off Puerta del Sol (Carrera de San Jerónimo 26, tel. 914-293-877). If you're looking to buy, be prepared to spend €1,000.

Nightlife in Madrid

Those into clubbing may have to wait until after midnight for the most popular places to even open, much less start hopping. Spain has a reputation for partying very late and not stopping until offices open in the morning. (Spaniards, who are often awake into the wee hours of the morning, have a special word for this time of day: *la madrugada*.) If you're out early in the morning, it's actually hard to tell who is finishing their day and who's just starting it. Even if you're not a party animal after midnight, make a point to be out with the happy masses, luxuriating in the cool evening air between 22:00 and midnight. The scene is absolutely unforgettable.

▲▲▲Paseo

Just walking the streets of Madrid seems to be the way the Madrileños spend their evenings. Even past midnight on a hot summer night, entire families with little kids are strolling, enjoying tiny beers and tapas in a series of bars, licking ice cream, and greeting their neighbors. Good areas to wander include from Puerta del Sol to Plaza Mayor and down Calle del Arenal until you hit Plaza de Isabel II; the pedestrianized Calle de las Huertas from Plaza Mayor to the Prado; along Gran Vía from about Plaza de Callao to Plaza de España, following the last section of my "Gran Vía Walk" (described earlier); and, to window shop with the young and trendy, up Calle de Fuencarral (keep going until you hit traffic).

▲Zarzuela

For a delightful look at Spanish light opera that even English speakers can enjoy, try zarzuela. Guitar-strumming Napoleons in red capes; buxom women with masks, fans, and castanets; Spanish-speaking pharaohs; melodramatic spotlights; and aficionados clapping and singing along from the cheap seats, where the acoustics are best—this is zarzuela...the people's opera. Originating in Madrid, zarzuela is known for its satiric humor and surprisingly good music. Performances occur evenings at Teatro de la Zarzuela, which alternates between zarzuela, ballet, and opera throughout the year. The TI's monthly guide has a special zarzuela section. Be aware that not all shows at the Teatro de la Zarzuela are zarzuelas.

Getting Tickets: Prices range from €16-40, 50 percent off for Wed shows and anytime for those over 65, Teatro de la Zarzuela box office open Mon-Fri 12:00-18:00 and Sat-Sun 15:00-18:00 for advance tickets or until show time for same-day tickets, near the Prado at Jovellanos 4, Metro: Sevilla or Banco de España, tel. 915-245-400, http://teatrodelazarzuela.mcu.es. To purchase tickets online, go to www.entradasinaem.es and click on *"Espacios"* ("Spaces") to find Teatro de la Zarzuela; you will receive an email with your tickets, which you need to print before you arrive at the theater.

▲▲Flamenco

Although Sevilla is the capital of flamenco, Madrid has a few easy and affordable options. And on summer evenings, Madrid puts on live flamenco events in the Royal Palace gardens (ask TI for details). Among the listings below, Casa Patas is grumpy, while Carboneras is friendlier—but Casa Patas has better-quality artists and a riveting seriousness.

Taberna Casa Patas attracts big-name flamenco artists. You'll quickly understand why this intimate venue (30 tables, 120 seats) is named "House of Feet." Since this is for locals as well as tour groups, the flamenco is contemporary and may be jazzier than your notion—it depends on who's performing (€38 includes cover and first drink, Mon-Thu at 22:30, Fri-Sat at 20:00 and 22:30, closed Sun, 1.25-1.5 hours, reservations smart, no flash cameras, Cañizares 10, tel. 913-690-496, www.casapatas.com). Its restaurant is a logical spot for dinner before the show (€30 dinners, Mon-Sat from 18:30).

Las Carboneras, more downscale, is an easygoing, folksy little place a few steps from Plaza Mayor with a nightly hour-long flamenco show (€36 includes entry and a drink, €69 gets you a table up front with dinner and unlimited cheap drinks if you reserve ahead, manager Enrique promises a €5/person discount if you book directly and show this book in 2018, daily at 20:30, also Mon-Thu at 22:30 and Fri-Sat at 23:00, reservations recommended, Plaza del Conde de Miranda 1, tel. 915-428-677, www.tablaolascarboneras.com). Dinner is served one hour before showtime.

Las Tablas Flamenco offers a less-expensive nightly show respecting the traditional art of flamenco. You'll sit in a plain room with a mix of tourists and cool, young Madrileños in a modern, nondescript office block just over the freeway from Plaza de España (€29 with drink, reasonable drink prices, shows daily at 20:00 and usually also at 22:00, 1.25 hours, corner of Calle de Ferraz and Cuesta de San Vicente at Plaza de España 9, tel. 915-420-520, www.lastablasmadrid.com).

More Flamenco: Regardless of what your hotel receptionist may want to sell you, other flamenco places—such as Arco de Cuchilleros (Calle de los Cuchilleros 7), Café de Chinitas (Calle Torija 7, just off Plaza Mayor), Corral de la Morería (Calle de Morería 17), and Torres Bermejas (off Gran Vía)—are filled with tourists and pushy waiters.

Mesones

These long, skinny, cave-like bars, famous for customers drinking and singing late into the night, line the lane called Cava de San Miguel, just west of Plaza Mayor. If you were to toss lowbrow barflies, Spanish karaoke, electric keyboards, crass tourists, cheap sangria, and greasy calamari into a late-night blender and turn it on, this is what you'd get. They're generally lively only on Friday and Saturday.

Bars and Jazz

If you're just picking up speed at midnight and looking for a place filled with old tiles and a Gen-X crowd, power into **Bar Viva Madrid** (daily 13:00-late, downhill from Plaza Santa Ana at Calle Manuel Fernández y González 7, tel. 914-293-640). The same street has other bars filled with music. Or hike on over to Chocolatería San Ginés for a dessert of *churros con chocolate.*

For live jazz, **Café Central** is the old town favorite. Since 1982 it's been known as the place where rising stars get their start (€16, nightly at 21:00—stop by to reserve your table or come early to score one of the unreserved seats by the bar, food and drinks available, great scene, Plaza del Ángel 10, tel. 913-694-143, www.cafecentralmadrid.com).

Movies

Movies in Spain remain about the most often dubbed in Europe. To see a movie with its original soundtrack, look for "V.O." (meaning "original version"). **Cine Ideal,** with nine screens, is a good place for the latest films in V.O. (assigned seats during most days and showings, good to get tickets early on weekends, 5-minute walk south of Puerta del Sol at Calle del Dr. Cortezo 6, tel. 913-692-518 for info, www.yelmocines.es). For extensive listings, see the *Guía del Ocio* entertainment guide or a local newspaper.

Sleeping in Madrid

Madrid has plenty of centrally located budget hotels and *pensiones.* Most of the accommodations I've listed are within a few minutes' walk of Puerta del Sol.

Most of the year you should be able to find a sleepable double for €70, a good double for €100, and a modern, air-conditioned double with all the comforts for €150. Prices vary dramatically throughout the year at bigger hotels, but remain about the same for the smaller hotels and *hostales.* It's almost always easy to find a place. Anticipate full hotels only in May (the San Isidro festival, celebrating Madrid's patron saint with bullfights and zarzuelas—especially around his feast day on May 15), around Easter, during LGBT Pride Week at the end of June, and in September (when conventions can clog the city). During the hot months of July and August, prices can be soft—ask for a discount.

With all of Madrid's street noise, I'd request the highest floor possible. Also, twin-bedded rooms are generally a bit larger than double-bedded rooms for the same price. During slow times, drop-ins can often score a room in business-class hotels for just a few euros more than the budget hotels (which don't have prices that fluctuate as wildly with demand). Breakfast is generally not offered—when it is, it's often expensive (about €15; see page 85 for breakfast options).

Smoking bans have changed the atmosphere in hotel reception areas and hallways, but things aren't completely smoke-free, as hotels are still allowed to designate up to 10 percent of their rooms for smokers.

MIDRANGE AND FANCIER PLACES

These mostly business-class hotels are good values (especially Hotel Europa) for those willing to spend a little more. Their formal prices may be inflated, but most offer weekend and summer discounts when it's slow. Drivers pay about €24 a day in garages.

Near Puerta del Sol and Gran Vía

These hotels are located in and around the pedestrian zone north and west of Puerta del Sol. Use Metro: Sol for these listings unless noted otherwise.

$$$$ Hotel Intur Palacio San Martín is perfectly tucked away from the hustle of the center next to the Descalzas Monastery. It has bright, spacious public areas and comfortable, traditionally decorated rooms (air-con, elevator, Plaza San Martín 5, tel. 917-015-000, www.hotel-inturpalaciosanmartin.com, sanmartin@intur.com).

$$$$ Hotel Ópera, a serious and contemporary hotel with 79 classy rooms, is located just off Plaza Isabel II, a four-block walk from Puerta del Sol toward the Royal Palace (RS%, includes breakfast, air-con, elevator, sauna and gym, ask for a higher floor—there are nine—to avoid street noise, Cuesta de Santo Domingo 2, Metro: Ópera, tel. 915-412-800, www.hotelopera.com, reservas@hotelopera.com). Hotel Ópera's cafeteria is deservedly popular. Consider their "singing dinners"—great operetta music with a delightful dinner—offered nightly (around €60, reservations smart, call 915-426-382 or reserve at hotel).

$$$ Hotel H10 Reina Victoria is a tidy, upgraded, early-20th-century boutique hotel in the heart of the pulsing Gran Vía (air-con, elevator, Gran Vía 22, tel. 915-239-101, www.h10hotels.com, H10.villa.delareina@H10hotels.com).

$$$ Hotel Preciados, a four-star business hotel, has 100 wel-

MADRID

Madrid Center Hotels

- ❶ Hotel H10 Reina Victoria
- ❷ Hotel Preciados
- ❸ Hotel Liabeny
- ❹ Hotel Francisco I
- ❺ Hotel Intur Palacio San Martín
- ❻ Hotel Ópera
- ❼ Hotel Europa
- ❽ Hotel Moderno
- ❾ Ateneo Hotel
- ❿ Petit Palace Posada del Peine

⑪ Hotel Plaza Mayor

⑫ Hostales Acapulco & Triana; Pensión Arcos

⑬ Hostal Santa Cruz

⑭ Hostales Mayrit & Ivor

⑮ Hotel Praktik Metropol; Hostales Residencia Luis XV & Jerez

⑯ Hostal Don Juan

⑰ Launderette (2)

⑱ Baggage Storage

coming, sleek, and modern rooms as well as elegant lounges. It's well-located and reasonably priced for the luxury it provides (free mini-bar, air-con, elevator, pay parking, just off Plaza de Santo Domingo at Calle Preciados 37, Metro: Callao, tel. 914-544-400, www.preciadoshotel.com, preciadoshotel@preciadoshotel.com).

$$$ Hotel Liabeny rents 213 plush, spacious, business-class rooms offering all the comforts (air-con, elevator, sauna, gym, off Plaza del Carmen at Salud 3, tel. 915-319-000, www.liabeny.es, reservas@hotelliabeny.com).

$$$ Hotel Francisco I is a big, quiet, and well-run place with 60 rooms, nicely situated midway between the Royal Theater and Puerta del Sol; they also have an annex just two doors away (air-con, showers only, elevator, Calle del Arenal 15, tel. 915-480-204, www.hotelfrancisco.com, info@hotelfrancisco.com).

$$$ Ateneo Hotel, just steps off Puerta del Sol, lacks public spaces and character, but its 38 rooms are close to business-class (RS%, air-con, elevator, Calle de la Montera 22, tel. 915-212-012, www.hotel-ateneo.com, info@hotel-ateneo.com).

$$ Hotel Europa, with sleek marble, red carpet runners along the halls, happy Muzak charm, and an attentive staff, is a tremendous value. It rents 100 squeaky-clean rooms, many with balconies overlooking the pedestrian zone or an inner courtyard. The hotel has an honest ethos and offers a straight price (family rooms, air-con, elevator, Calle del Carmen 4, tel. 915-212-900, www.hoteleuropa.eu, info@hoteleuropa.eu, run by Antonio and Fernando Garaban and their helpful and jovial staff, Javi, Jim, and Tomás. The recommended **$$** Restaurante-Cafeteria Europa is a lively and convivial scene—fun for breakfast.

$$ Hotel Moderno, renting 97 rooms, has a quiet, profes-sional, and friendly atmosphere. There's a comfy first-floor lounge and a convenient location close to Puerta del Sol (air-con, Calle del Arenal 2, tel. 915-310-900, www.hotel-moderno.com, info@hotel-moderno.com).

Near Plaza Mayor
Both of these are a block off Plaza Mayor.

$$$$ Petit Palace Posada del Peine feels like part of a big, modern chain (which it is), but fills its well-located old building with fresh, efficient character. Behind the ornate Old World facade is a comfortable and modern business-class hotel with 67 rooms (air-con, Calle Postas 17, tel. 915-238-151, www.petitpalace.com, posadadelpeine@petitpalace.com).

$ Hotel Plaza Mayor, with 41 solidly outfitted rooms, is taste-fully decorated and beautifully situated a block off Plaza Mayor (breakfast included for Rick Steves readers who book by email or

Breakfast in Madrid

Many hotels don't include (or even offer) breakfast, so you may be out on the streets first thing looking for a place to eat. Non-touristy cafés only offer a hot drink and a pastry, with perhaps a potato omelet and sandwiches (toasted cheese, ham, or both). I like Restaurante-Cafeteria Europa just off Puerta del Sol for its classic breakfast scene, with a long bar, plenty of locals, and an easy-access menu (described on page 96). Touristy places will have a *desayuno* menu with various ham-and-eggs deals. Try *churros* at least once (see the listings on page 98 for my favorite places); if you're not in the mood for heavy chocolate in the morning, go local and dip your *churros* in a *café con leche*. If all else fails, a Starbucks is often nearby (just like home). Get advice from your hotel staff for their favorite breakfast place. My typical breakfast, found at any corner bar: *café con leche*, *tortilla española* (a slice of potato omelet), and *zumo de naranja natural* (fresh-squeezed orange juice).

phone, air-con, elevator, Calle de Atocha 2, tel. 913-600-606, www.h-plazamayor.com, info@h-plazamayor.com).

Near the Prado

$$$$ Mercure Madrid Centro Hotel Lope de Vega offers good business-class hotel value near the Prado. It is a "cultural-themed" hotel inspired by the 17th-century writer Lope de Vega. With 59 rooms, it feels cozy and friendly for a formal hotel (family rooms, air-con, elevator, very limited pay parking—reserve ahead, Calle Lope de Vega 49, tel. 913-600-011, www.accor.com, H9618@ accor.com).

CHEAP SLEEPS
Near Plaza del Carmen

These three are all in the same building at Calle de la Salud 13, north of Puerta del Sol. The building overlooks Plaza del Carmen—a little square with a sleepy, almost Parisian ambience.

$ Hostal Acapulco rents 16 bright rooms with air-conditioning and all the big hotel gear. The neighborhood is quiet enough that it's smart to request a room with a balcony (family room, elevator, fourth floor, reasonable laundry service, overnight luggage storage, parking—reserve ahead, tel. 915-311-945, www.hostalacapulco. com, hostal_acapulco@yahoo.es, Ana, Marco, and Javier).

$ Hostal Triana, also a good deal, is bigger—with 40 rooms—and offers a little less charm for a little less money (some rooms have air-con, others have fans; elevator and some stairs, first floor, tel. 915-326-812, www.hostaltriana.com, triana@hostaltriana. com, Victor González).

MADRID

¢ **Pensión Arcos** is tiny, granny-run, and old-fashioned—it's been in the Hernández family since 1936. You can reserve by phone (in Spanish), and you must pay in cash—but its five rooms are clean, extra quiet, and served by an elevator. You also have access to a tiny roof terrace and a nice little lounge. For cheap beds in a great locale, assuming you can communicate, this place is unbeatable (cheaper rooms with shared bath, air-con, closed Aug, fifth floor, tel. 915-324-994, Anuncia and Sabino).

Near Puerta del Sol
$ **Hostal Santa Cruz,** simple and well-located, has 16 rooms at a good price (air-con, elevator, Plaza de Santa Cruz 6, second floor, tel. 915-222-441, www.hostalsantacruz.com, info@hostalsantacruz.com).

$ **Hostal Mayrit** and **Hostal Ivor** rent 28 rooms with thoughtful touches on pedestrianized Calle del Arenal (air-con, elevator, near Metro: Ópera at Calle del Arenal 24, reception on third floor, tel. 915-480-403, www.hostalivor.com, reservas@hostalivor.com).

At the Top of Calle de la Montera
These places are a few minutes' walk from Puerta del Sol and a stone's throw from Gran Vía at the top of Calle de la Montera, which some dislike because of the prostitutes who hang out here. They're legal, and the zone is otherwise safe and comfortable.

$$$$ **Hotel Praktik Metropol** sports plaid-and-striped hipster decor in its 70 fresh, modern rooms. Many rooms are tiny and on the building's interior—ask for a corner room or pay extra for the bigger superior double. The spectacular views from the top-floor "skyline" rooms are worth the extra money, too. All guests have access to a rooftop terrace with views (air-con, elevator, reception on first floor, Calle de la Montera 47, tel. 915-212-935, www.hotelpraktikmetropol.com, reservas@hotelpraktikmetropol.com).

$ **Hostal Residencia Luis XV** is a big, plain, well-run, and clean place offering a good value. It's on a quiet eighth floor (air-con, elevator, Calle de la Montera 47, tel. 915-221-021, www.hostalluisxvmadrid.com, info@hostalaliste.net). They also run the 44-room $ **Hostal Jerez**—similar in every way—on the sixth floor (tel. 915-327-565, www.hostaljerezmadrid.com/en, reservas@hrjerez.net). Both properties are completely nonsmoking.

$ **Hostal Don Juan** sits on a quiet-by-day, busy-by-night square just off the Gran Vía in the beginning of the Chueca neighborhood. Its 44 rooms are clean and modern, contrasting with the Baroque explosion of varnish and gold in the common areas (air-con, elevator, Plaza Pedro Zerolo 1—former Plaza Vázquez de Mella, second floor, tel. 915-223-101, hshostaldonjuan@gmail.com).

MADRID

Near the Prado

Two fine budget *hostales* are at Cervantes 34 (Metro: Antón Mar-tín—but not handy to Metro). Both are homey, with inviting lounge areas; neither serves breakfast. **$ Hostal Gonzalo** has 15 spotless, comfortable rooms on the third floor and is well-run by friendly and helpful Javier. It's deservedly in all the guidebooks, so reserve in advance (air-con, elevator, tel. 914-292-714, www.hostalgonzalo.com, hostal@hostalgonzalo.com). Downstairs, the nearly-as-polished **$ Hostal Cervantes** also has 15 rooms (some rooms with air-con, tel. 914-298-365, www.hostal-cervantes.com, correo@hostal-cervantes.com, Fabio).

$ Urban Sea Hotel Atocha 113 is a basic but contemporary option that is nicely located between the Prado and the Reina Sofía, near Atocha station (includes self-service snacks, small rooftop ter-race, Calle de Atocha 113, tel. 913-692-895, www.urbanseahotels.com, recepcionatocha@blueseahotels.es).

Hostel

¢ Madrid Municipal Youth Hostel (Albergue Juvenil Madrid) is fairly new and decidedly big, with 132 beds. A Metro ride north of downtown, it has four to six beds per room, modern bathrooms, and lots of extras, such as billiards and movies (includes breakfast, coed rooms, 24-hour reception; Metro: Tribunal, then walk 2 min-utes down Calle de Barceló to Calle de Mejia Lequerica 21; tel. 915-939-688).

Eating in Madrid

In Spain, only Barcelona rivals Madrid for taste-bud thrills. You have three dining choices: a memorable, atmospheric sit-down meal in a well-chosen restaurant; a forgettable, basic sit-down meal; or a meal of tapas at a bar or two...or four. Unless other-wise noted, restaurants start serving lunch at 13:00 or 13:30 and dinner around 20:30. Depending on what time you show up, the same place may seem forlorn, touristy, or thriving with local eaters. Many restaurants close in August. Madrid has famously good tap water, and waiters willingly serve it free—just ask for *agua del grifo*. Restaurants and bars in Spain are smoke-free inside, but lighting up is allowed in outdoor seating areas.

I've broken my recommended choices into groups: serious din-ing establishments, tapas places, and simple, economical venues. For suggestions on where to eat near the Royal Palace, Prado, and Reina Sofía, see their individual sight listings.

FINE DINING

$$$$ Restaurante Casa Paco is a Madrid tradition. Check out its old walls plastered with autographed photos of Spanish celebrities who have enjoyed their signature dish—ox grilled over a coal fire. Though popular with tourists, the place is authentic, confident, and uncompromising. It's a worthwhile splurge if you want to dine out well and carnivorously (closed Mon, Plaza de la Puerta Cerrada 11, tel. 913-663-166, www.casapaco1933.es).

$$$$ Sobrino del Botín is a hit with many Americans because "Hemingway ate here." It's grotesquely touristy, pricey, and the last place "Papa" would go now...but still, people love it and go for the roast suckling pig, their specialty. I'd eat upstairs for a still-traditional but airier atmosphere (daily 13:00-16:00 & 20:00-24:00, a block downhill from Plaza Mayor at Cuchilleros 17, tel. 913-664-217, www.botin.es).

$$$$ Casa Lucio is a favorite splurge for traditional specialties among power-dressing Madrileños. Juan Carlos and Sofía, the former king and queen of Spain, eat in this formal place, but it's accessible to commoners. This is a good restaurant for a special night out and a full-blown meal, but you pay extra for this place's fame (daily 13:00-16:00 & 20:30-24:00, closed Aug, Calle Cava Baja 35; unless you're the king or queen, reserve several days in advance—and don't even bother on weekends; tel. 913-653-252, www.casalucio.es).

$$$$ Restaurante Palacio de Cibeles, with a dress-up interior on the sixth floor of the Palacio de Cibeles (City Hall), features an outdoor terrace with spectacular views, an extensive wine list, and a creative, seasonal Spanish menu (daily 13:00-16:00 & 20:00-24:00, Plaza de Cibeles 1, tel. 915-231-454, www.adolfo-palaciodecibeles.com). The neighboring and swanky **$$ Terrace Cibeles** serves drinks and light bites late into the night on its outdoor terrace (open only in good weather, daily 13:00-24:00). The first-floor **$$ Colección Cibeles** offers a simplified and less expensive version of Restaurante Palacio's fare (daily 10:00-24:00).

$$$ El Caldero ("The Pot") is a romantic spot and a good place for paella and other rice dishes. A classy, in-the-know crowd appreciates its subdued elegance and crisp service. The house specialty, *arroz caldero* (a variation on paella), is served with panache from a cauldron hanging from a tripod. Most of the formal rice dishes come in pots for two (closed Sun-Mon, Calle de las Huertas 15, tel. 914-295-044). Wash it all down with the house sangria.

$$$ TriCiclo Restaurant is a classy choice for romantic foodies. It serves creative fare with a traditional base from a fun and accessible menu. While the rustically elegant restaurant takes reservations, the bar in front has several small tables for two that are generally open if you arrive at 20:30 (open Mon-Sat 13:30-16:00 &

20:30-24:00, closed Sun, reserve for restaurant, Calle Santa Maria 28, tel. 910-244-798, www.eltriciclo.es).

$$$$ La Bola Taberna, touristy but friendly and tastefully elegant, specializes in *cocido Madrileño*—Madrid stew. The stew, made of various meats, carrots, and garbanzo beans in earthen jugs, is a winter dish, prepared here for the tourists all year. It's served as two courses: First enjoy the broth as a soup, then dig into the meat and veggies. Curious about how it's made? Ask to take a peek in the kitchen (cash only, daily lunch seatings at 13:30 and 15:30, dinner 20:30-23:00, closed Sun in July-Aug, midway between Royal Palace and Gran Vía at Calle Bola 5, tel. 915-476-930, http://labola. es).

Treating Tapas Bars as Restaurants: Of the many recommended *tabernas* and tapas bars listed below, several have tables and menus that lend themselves to fine dining. If you don't mind the commotion of the nearby bar action, you can order high on the menu in these places and, I'd say, eat better and more economically than in the more formal restaurants listed above.

TAPAS-HOPPING FROM BAR TO BAR

For maximum fun, people, and atmosphere, go mobile for dinner: Do the *tapeo,* a local tradition of going from one bar to the next, munching, drinking, and socializing. If done properly, a pub crawl can be a highlight of your trip. Your ability to speak a little Spanish will get you a much better (and less expensive) experience. While tiny tapas plates are standard in Andalucía, these days most of Madrid's bars offer bigger plates for around €6 (vegetables) to €15 (fish). Called *raciones,* these are ideal for a small group to share. The real action begins late (around 21:00). While the energy is fun and local later in the evening, you may find it easier to get service and a spot by dining earlier—which is still late by American standards.

In Madrid, you'll occasionally find a bar that gives a **free tapa** to anyone ordering a drink, a dying tradition. But if you order any food with your drink, you won't get the free dish. If you care (and you should), always order the drink alone first and expect a tapa. If you don't get one, ask, *"Tapa?"* as if expecting the little bonus. Once you get it, order additional food as you like.

There are tapas bars almost everywhere, but two areas in the city center are particularly rewarding for a bar-crawl meal: **Calle de Jesús** (near the Prado) is the easiest, with several wonderful and diverse places in a two-block row, while trendy **Calle Cava Baja** has fancier offerings and feels most energetic. A third area, between **Puerta del Sol** and **Plaza Santa Ana,** is more central but overrun with tourists.

MADRID

Madrid Center Restaurants

1. Restaurante Casa Paco
2. Sobrino del Botín
3. Casa Lucio
4. El Caldero
5. TriCiclo Restaurant
6. La Bola Taberna
7. El Madroño
8. Txakolina Pintxoteca Madrileña
9. Taberna Los Huevos de Lucio
10. Taberna Tempranillo
11. To Juana la Loca Pintxos Bar
12. Museo del Jamón & Lhardy Pastelería
13. La Taurina
14. La Casa del Abuelo
15. La Oreja de Jaime
16. Casa Toni
17. Casa Gonzalez Wine & Cheese Shop
18. Cervecería Pulpito
19. Casa Rúa
20. Mercado de San Miguel
21. La Torre del Oro Bar Andalú
22. La Mallorquina
23. Restaurante Puerto Rico
24. Restaurante-Cafeteria Europa
25. Chiringuito de El Señor Martín

MADRID

26 El Corte Inglés Cafeteria
27 Casa Labra Taberna Restaurante
28 Artemisia Veggie Restaurante
29 To Chueca Area Eateries
30 Angelita Wine Bar
31 Café de Oriente
32 Chocolatería San Ginés
33 Chocolaterías Valor

34 Taberna Casa Patas (Flamenco)
35 Las Carboneras (Flamenco)
36 To Las Tablas (Flamenco)
37 Mesones ("Cave Bars")
38 Bar Viva Madrid
39 Café Central Jazz Bar
40 Supermarket

The Great Tapas Row on Calle de Jesús

This two-block stretch of tapas bars offers a variety of fun places. While the offerings are pretty similar, each has its own personality. Most have chaotic bars in front and small and inviting sections with tables in back. Make the circuit and eyeball each place to see which appeals—you'll see that there's no reason to spend all your time and appetite at your first stop. Calle de Jesús stretches between Calle de Cervantes and Calle de las Huertas, behind the Palace Hotel (across the boulevard from the Prado). In the middle is the Plaza de Jesús, so named because this is the location of the Basilica of Jesús de Medinaceli (home to a relic that attracts huge crowds of pilgrims on special days). Start near the church at the first recommended bar, Cervecería Cervantes. These places are generally open every day for long hours.

$$ **Cervecería Cervantes** serves hearty *raciones,* specializes in octopus, and has both a fine bar and good restaurant seating (intersection of Plaza de Jesús and Calle de Cervantes, tel. 914-296-093).

$$ **Taberna de la Daniela Medinaceli,** part of a local chain, is popular for its specialty *cocido madrileño*—a rich chickpea-based soup. It has a lovely dining area if you want to settle in for a while (Plaza de Jesús 7, tel. 913-896-238).

$$ **La Dolores,** with a rustic little dining area, has been a hit since 1908 and is still extremely popular. Its canapés (little sandwiches) are listed on the wall (Plaza de Jesús 4, tel. 914-292-243).

$$ **Cervezas La Fabrica** packs in seafood lovers at the bar; a quieter back room is available for those preferring a table. Prices are the same in both spots (Calle de Jesús 2, tel. 913-690-671). They serve a nice *cava* (Spanish sparkling wine), which goes well with seafood.

$$ **Cervecería Los Gatos** is a kaleidoscope of Spanish culture, with chandeliers swinging above wine barrels in the intense bar area and characteristic tables in the more peaceful zone behind (Calle de Jesús 2, tel. 914-293-067).

$$ **La Anchoíta** is named "the little anchovy" for its *anchoas* (cured anchovies—salty) and *boquerones* (cured-in-vinegar anchovies, ask for bread if necessary). The three taps serve regular beer, "sin" (nonalcoholic) beer, and *vermut* (vermouth) from a tap shaped like a shrimp. If drinking white wine, get it in a frozen glass—ask for *"copa fría"* (Calle de Jesús 4, tel. 913-601-674).

$$$ **Taberna Maceira,** perhaps the best of the bunch, feels like Northern Spain. It's a Galician place with a wonderfully woody and rustic energy. A sit-down restaurant (not a bar), it specializes in octopus, cod, *pimientos de Padrón* (green peppers), and *caldo gallego* (white bean soup)—all classic Galician specialties of northwest Spain. Every day, the sign reads, *"no hay Coca-Cola"*— "no Coke" (13:00-16:00 & 20:30-24:00, closed Sun, Calle de Jesús 7, tel. 914-291-584).

Tapas on Calle Cava Baja

A few minutes' walk south of Plaza Mayor, Calle Cava Baja fills each evening with a young, professional crowd prowling for chic tapas and social fun. Come at night only and treat the entire street as a destination. I've listed a few standards, but excellent new eateries are always opening up. For a good, authentic Madrid dinner experience, survey the many options here and then choose your favorites. Remember, it's easier and touristy early, jammed with locals later. (If you want a formal dining experience on this street, come early and pick one you like with tables in the back, or see the places recommended under "Fine Dining," earlier. Taberna Tempranillo or Juana la Loca would be my first choices.) These tapas bars, listed in the order you'll reach them as you walk from Plaza Mayor up Calle Cava Baja, are worth special consideration.

$$ El Madroño ("The Berry Tree," a symbol of Madrid), more of a cowboy bar, serves all the clichés. If Knott's Berry Farm was Spanish, this would be its restaurant. Preserving a bit of old Madrid, a tile copy of Velázquez's famous *Drinkers* grins from its facade. Inside, look above the stairs for photos of 1902 Madrid. Study the coats of arms of Madrid through the centuries as you try a *vermut* (vermouth) on tap. Or ask for a small glass *(chupito)* of the *licor de madroño.* Indoor seating is bright and colorful; the sidewalk tables come with good people-watching. Munch *raciones* at the bar or front tables to be in the fun scene, or have a quieter sit-down meal at the tables in the back (daily, a block off the top of Calle Cava Baja at Plaza de la Puerta Cerrada 7, tel. 913-645-629).

$$ Txakolina Pintxoteca Madrileña is a thriving bar serving Basque-style *pinchos* (fancy open-faced sandwiches—*pintxo* in Basque) to a young crowd (Calle Cava Baja 26, tel. 913-664-877).

$$ Taberna Los Huevos de Lucio, owned by the same family as the reputable Casa Lucio (described earlier, under "Fine Dining"), is a jam-packed bar serving good tapas, salads, *huevos estrellados* (fried eggs over fried potatoes), and wine. If you'd like to make it a sit-down meal, head to the tables in the back (avoid the basement, Calle Cava Baja 30, tel. 913-662-984).

$$ Taberna Tempranillo, ideal for hungry wine lovers, offers fancy tapas and fine wine by the glass (see listing on the board or ask for their English menu). While there are a few tables, the bar is just right for hanging out. With a spirit of adventure, use their fascinating menu to assemble your dream meal. When I order high on their menu, I'm generally very happy. The crowds here can be overwhelming. Arrive by 20:00 or plan to wait (closed Aug, Calle Cava Baja 38, tel. 913-641-532).

$$ Juana la Loca Pintxos Bar ("Crazy Juana") packs in the locals and offers elegant *raciones,* refined-yet-tight seating, gorgeously presented dishes from a foodie menu, and reasonable prices considering the quality. Their classic is the runny *tortilla de patatas* with slightly caramelized onions. While it's a bar, you could arrive early to snare a table, and treat it as a nice restaurant outing (Plaza Puerta de Moros 4, tel. 913-665-500).

Central Pub-Crawl Tapas Route

The little streets between Puerta del Sol, San Jerónimo, and Plaza Santa Ana are submerged in a flood of numbskull tourism. But they're also very central...and hold some tasty surprises.

• *Start at the intersection of Carrera de San Jerónimo and Calle Victoria.*

$$ Museo del Jamón (Museum of Ham), festooned with ham hocks, is a fun place to see—unless you're a pig (or a vegetarian). Its frenetic, cheap, stand-up bar (with famously rude service) is an assembly line of fast-and-simple *bocadillos* and *raciones.* If you order anything, get only a cheap sandwich, because the staff is not honest. Take advantage of the easy photo-illustrated menus that show various dishes and their prices. The best ham is the pricey *jamón ibérico*—from pigs who led stress-free lives in acorn-strewn valleys. Point clearly to what you want, and be very specific to avoid being served a pricier meal than you intended. For a small sandwich, ask for a *chiquito* (daily 9:00-24:00, air-con).

• *Across the street is the touristy and overpriced bull bar,* **La Taurina.** *(I wouldn't eat here, but you're welcome to ponder the graphic photos that celebrate the gory art of bullfighting.) And next door, take a detour from your pub crawl with something more suited to grandmothers.*

$$ Lhardy Pastelería offers a genteel taste of Old World charm in this district of rowdy pubs. This peaceful time warp has been a fixture since 1839 for Madrileños wanting to duck in for a cup of consommé or a light snack. Step right in, and pretend you're an aristocrat back between the wars. Serve yourself. Pay as you leave (on the honor system). Help yourself to the silver water dispenser (free), a line of elegant bottles (each a different Iberian fortified wine: sherry, port, and so on), a revolving case of meaty little pastries, and a fancy soup dispenser (chicken broth consommé, try it with a splash of sherry...local style—bottles in the corner, help yourself; Mon-Sat 10:00-22:00, Sun until 15:00; Carrera de San Jerónimo 8, tel. 915-222-207). A very classy **$$$$** dinner-only restaurant hides upstairs.

• *Next, forage up Calle Victoria. The bars on this street and nearby lanes offer bloated prices and all the clichés.*

$$ La Casa del Abuelo serves sizzling plates of tasty little *gambas* (shrimp) and *langostinos* (prawns), with bread to sop up the delightful juices. Try *gambas a la plancha* (grilled shrimp) or *gambas al ajillo* (ah-HEE-yoh, a small clay dish of shrimp cooked in oil and garlic); wash it down with a glass of sweet red house wine (Calle Victoria 12).

• *Head down to Calle de la Cruz.*

$$ La Oreja de Jaime is known for its sautéed pigs' ears *(oreja)*. While pig ears are a Madrid dish (fun to try, hard to swallow), this place is Galician—they serve *pimientos de Padrón* (sautéed miniature green peppers) and the distinctive *ribeiro* (ree-BAY-roh) wine, served Galician-style, in characteristic little ceramic bowls to disguise its lack of clarity (Calle de la Cruz 12).

• *For a finale, continue up Calle de la Cruz.*

$$ Casa Toni is good for classic dishes like *patatas bravas* (fried potatoes in a spicy sauce), *berenjena* (deep-fried slices of eggplant), *champiñones* (sautéed mushrooms), and gazpacho—the cold tomato-and-garlic soup that is generally served only during the hot season, but available here year-round just for tourists like you (Calle de la Cruz 14).

• *If you're still hungry, three blocks past nearby Plaza Santa Ana is...*

$$$ Casa Gonzalez, a venerable gourmet cheese-and-wine shop with a circa-1930s interior. Away from the tourist scene, it offers a genteel opportunity to enjoy a plate of first-class cheese and a fine glass of wine with friendly service and a fun setting recalling the happy days of the Republic of Spain—after the monarchy but before Franco. Their €17.50 assortment of five Spanish cheeses—more than enough for two—is a cheese lover's treat (40 wines by the glass, long hours daily except closed Sun evening, Calle de León 12, tel. 914-295-618, Francisco and Luciano).

EATING REASONABLY
On or near Plaza Mayor

Madrileños enjoy a bite to eat on Plaza Mayor (without its high costs) by grabbing food to go from a nearby bar and just planting themselves somewhere on the square to eat (squid sandwiches are popular). But for many tourists, dinner at a sidewalk café right on Plaza Mayor is worth the premium price (consider Cervecería Pulpito, southwest corner of the square at #10).

Squid Sandwiches: Plaza Mayor is famous for its *bocadillos de calamares*. For a tasty squid-ring sandwich, line up at **$ Casa Rúa** at Plaza Mayor's northwest corner, a few steps up Calle Ciudad Rodrigo (daily 11:00-23:00). Hanging up behind the bar is a photo-advertisement of Plaza Mayor from the 1950s, when the square contained a park.

$$ Mercado de San Miguel: This early-20th-century market sparkles after a recent renovation and bustles with a trendy food circus of eateries (daily 10:00-24:00). While it's expensive and touristy, it's also fun and accessible. You can stroll while you munch, hang out at bars, or take a break at one of the market's food-court-style tables.

Near Puerta del Sol

$$ La Mallorquina ("The Girl from Mallorca"), on the downhill end of Puerta del Sol, is a venerable pastry shop serving the masses at the bar (€1.30 *Napolitana* pastries, €1 *rosquillas*—doughnuts) and takeout on the ground floor. But upstairs is a refined little 19th-century café—popular for generations. It offers an accessible menu and a relative oasis of quiet (daily 9:00-21:00, closed mid-July-Aug).

$$ Restaurante Puerto Rico, a simple, no-nonsense place, serves good meals for great prices to smart Madrileños in a long, congested hall (long hours daily, Chinchilla 2, between Puerta del Sol and Gran Vía, tel. 915-219-834).

Restaurante-Cafeteria Europa is a fun, high-energy scene with a mile-long bar, old-school waiters, local cuisine, and a fine €11 fixed-price lunch special (inside only). The menu lists three price levels: **$ bar** (inexpensive), **$$$ table** (generally pricey), or **$$$$ terrace** (sky-high but with good people-watching). Your best value is to stick to the lunch menu if you're sitting inside, or order off the plastic *barra* menu if you sit at the bar—the ham-and-egg toast or the homemade *churros* make a nice breakfast (daily 7:00-24:00, next to Hotel Europa, 50 yards off Puerta del Sol at Calle del Carmen 4, tel. 915-212-900).

$$$ Chiringuito de El Señor Martín serves fresh seafood from the fishmonger at the Mercado de San Miguel. The chefs are fishermen who cook a changing menu based on the seasonal catches. Don't be surprised to get good fish in this landlocked city—Madrid has an excellent selection flown in daily (daily 13:00-23:30, Calle Mayor 31, tel. 917-957-170).

$$$ El Corte Inglés' "Gourmet Experience," a ninth-floor cafeteria, houses a specialty grocery mart and 10 different mini-restaurants with cuisines ranging from Mexican to Chinese. This snazzy and wildly popular complex is fresh, modern, and not particularly cheap. Take a seat at any of the indoor tables, or out on the open terrace (daily 10:00-24:00, at the top of Calle del Carmen half a block below Plaza del Callao). While here, enjoy great views of Gran Vía and Plaza de España.

Casa Labra Taberna Restaurante is famous as the birth-place of the Spanish Socialist Party in 1879...and as a spot for great cod. Their tasty little *tajada de bacalao* dishes put them on the map. Packed with Madrileños, it manages to be both dainty and rustic. It's a wonderful scene with three distinct sections: the stand-up **$ bar** (line up for cod and croquettes, power up to the bar for drinks); a peaceful little **$ sit-down area** in back (a little more expensive but still cheap), and a fancy **$$$ restaurant.** Consider the outdoor tables self-serve. The waiters are fun to joke around with (daily 11:00-15:30 & 18:00-23:00, a block off Puerta del Sol at Calle Tetuán 12, tel. 915-310-081).

Vegetarian: $$ Artemisia is a hit with vegetarians and vegans who like good, healthy food without the typical hippie ambience that comes with most veggie places (weekday lunch specials, open daily 13:30-16:00 & 20:30-23:30, north of Puerta del Sol at Tres Cruces 4, a few steps off Plaza del Carmen, tel. 915-218-721).

In the Chueca District

Chueca, just a short walk north of Gran Vía, in the past decade has gone from a sleazy no-go zone to a trendy and inviting neighbor-hood. Riding the Metro to the Chueca stop, you'll emerge right on Plaza de Chueca. The square feels like today's Madrid...without the tourism. A handful of places offer relaxing tables on the square, the neighborhood's San Antón market hall (Mercado de San Antón, just a block away) is now a fun food circus, and nearby streets hold plenty of hardworking, creative new eateries. Here are some good options:

$$ Cafetería Verdoy, facing the Metro station right on Plaza de Chueca, is a basic diner with friendly service and an easy, cheap menu, dish-of-the-day, and great tables right on the square (closed Sun).

$$ Antigua Casa Angel Sierra Vermouth Bar offers a thirst-quenching old-time ambience that almost takes you back to 1917, when it opened. Belly up to the bar in its tight front room facing the square or, for more space, enter (through a side entrance) a back room filled with giant barrels of vermouth and more spacious tables for dining (on Plaza de Chueca, Calle Gravina 11, tel. 915-310-126).

$$ Mercado de San Antón, with three bustling floors of ed-ible temptations, is flat-out fun for anyone who likes food (daily 10:00-late). The ground floor remains a produce and fish mar-ket. The first floor is a circle of tempting tapas joints—ranging from Canary Islands to Japanese to healthy veggie—with shared tables looking down on the market action and sample dishes on display for easy ordering. The top floor is a more formal restau-rant—**$$$ La Cocina de San Antón** ("Kitchen of San Antón").

It's part of a modern chain whose forte is ham, and it has a nice rooftop terrace (Augusto Figueroa 24, tel. 913-300-294).

$$ Vinoteca Vides is passionately run by Vicente, who offers a simple one-page list of small plates (finger food, ham, cheese) to go with a long list of quality wines sold by the €3-or-so glass (closed Mon, Calle Libertad 12, tel. 915-318-444). If you're looking for a convivial bar, this is a great bet. And there are many enticing alternatives nearby.

$$$ Angelita Wine Bar is a dressy little restaurant with spacious seating, a short food menu designed to go with the wines, and a long list of wines by the glass. An elegant place for a fine meal, you'll be surrounded by a smart local crowd (Mon-Sat 13:30-17:00 & 20:30-24:00, closed Sun, 100 yards from Gran Vía Metro station at Calle de la Reina 4, tel. 915-216-678).

Other Budget Options

$$ Café de Oriente is recommended mostly for its location, facing the Royal Palace, next to the National Theater and overlooking Plaza de Oriente. It's a venerable and elegant opera-type café with fine tables on the square. Stick to the good and reasonable lunch special—three courses for €15—as the restaurant and terrace menus are pricey (Plaza de Oriente 2, tel. 915-413-974, www.cafedeoriente.es, more interesting menu after 20:00).

Sandwich Joints: For an easy, light, and cheap meal, look for the Spanish answers to Subway: **$ Rodilla** and **$ Pans & Company** (open daily 9:00-23:00). You'll see them on Puerta del Sol and nearly every square, offering all the ambience of a McDonald's and a good selection of fresh sandwiches and prepackaged salads.

Picnic: The department store **El Corte Inglés** has well-stocked meat-and-cheese counters in Building 2's immense subterranean supermarket (Mon-Sat 10:00-22:00, Sun 11:00-21:00, a block off Puerta del Sol at Calle Preciados 3).

Churros con Chocolate

Those not watching their cholesterol will want to try the deep-fried doughy treats called *churros* (or the thicker *porras*), best enjoyed by dipping them in pudding-like hot chocolate. Though many *chocolaterías* offer the dunkable fritters, *churros* are most delicious when consumed fresh out of the greasy cauldron at a place that actually fries them. Two Madrid favorites are near Puerta del Sol.

Chocolatería San Ginés is a classy institution, beloved for a century by Madrileños for its *churros con chocolate*. While busy all day, it's packed after midnight; the popular dance club Joy Eslava is next door (open 24 hours; from Puerta del Sol, take Calle del Arenal 2 blocks west, turn left on bookstore-lined Pasadizo de San Ginés, and you'll see the café at #5; tel. 913-656-546).

Chocolaterías Valor, a modern chain and Spanish chocolate maker, does *churros* with pride and gusto. A few minutes' walk from nearly all my hotel recommendations, it's a fine place for breakfast. With a website like www.amigosdelchocolate.com, you know where their heart is (daily 8:00-22:30, Fri-Sat until 24:00, a half-block below Plaza del Callao and Gran Vía at Postigo de San Martín 7, tel. 915-229-288). You can also buy powdered Valor chocolate at supermarkets (like the one at El Corte Inglés) to make the drink at home.

Madrid Connections

BY TRAIN

Madrid has two main train stations: Chamartín and Atocha. Both stations offer long-distance trains *(largo recorridos)* as well as smaller local trains (*regionales* and *cercanías*) to nearby destinations. You can **buy tickets** at the stations, at travel agencies, or online. (For details, see the Practicalities chapter.) While travel agencies add a small fee, they can be a good place to buy tickets, especially during the high season or holidays, when the station's ticket counters have long lines. Convenient locations include the El Corte Inglés travel agency at Atocha (Mon-Fri 8:00-22:00, Sat-Sun 10:00-18:00, on ground floor of AVE side at the far end) and the El Corte Inglés department store.

Chamartín Station

The TI is near track 20. The impressively large information, tickets, and customer-service office is at track 11. You can relax in the Sala VIP Club if you have a first-class rail pass and first-class seat or sleeper reservations (between tracks 13 and 14, cooler of free drinks). Baggage storage *(consigna)* is across the street, opposite track 17. The station's Metro stop is also called Chamartín (not "Pinar de Chamartín"). Train connections from here are listed later.

Atocha Station

The station is split in two: an AVE side (mostly long-distance trains) and a *cercanías* side (mostly local trains to the suburbs—known as *cercanías*—and the Metro for connecting into downtown). These two parts are connected by a corridor of shops. Each side has separate schedules and customer-service offices. The TI, which is on the AVE arrivals side, offers tourist info, but no train info (Mon-Sat 8:00-20:00, Sun 9:00-14:00, tel. 915-284-630). To get to Atocha, use the "Atocha RENFE" Metro stop (not "Atocha").

Ticket Offices: The *cercanías* side has two offices—a small one for local trains and a big one for major trains (such as AVE). The AVE side has a pleasant, airy office that sells tickets for AVE and other long-distance trains (two lines: "Tickets in Advance" or "Selling Out Today"/"Departures Today"). A ticket counter will sometimes open up to sell tickets for trains departing soon—if you need to make a last-minute purchase, look for your destination and departure time, and get in line at that counter. If the line at one office is long, check the other offices. To secure your place in line, grab a number from a machine, usually located in the middle of the office by a sign with an image of a ticket. Ticket machines outside and around the office require a chip-and-PIN credit card.

AVE Side: Located in the towering old-station building, this half of the station boasts a lush, tropical garden filling its grand

hall. It has the AVE trains, other fast trains (Grandes Líneas), a pharmacy (daily 8:00-22:00, facing garden), a handful of cafés and restaurants, and a pay WC. Baggage storage *(consigna)* is at the far end of the tropical garden (daily 6:00-22:20). In the departure lounge on the upper floor, TV monitors announce track numbers. (A few trains, such as those for Toledo, Alicante, and Valencia, depart from the lower floor.) For information, try the *Información* counter (daily 6:30-22:30), next to Centro Servicios AVE (which handles only AVE changes and problems). The *Atención al Cliente* office deals with problems on Grandes Líneas (daily 6:30-23:30). Also on the AVE side is the Club AVE/Sala VIP, a lounge reserved solely for AVE business-class travelers and for first-class ticket-holders or Eurailers with a first-class reservation (upstairs, past the security check on right; free drinks, newspapers, showers, and info service).

Cercanías Side: This is where you'll find the local *cercanías* trains, *regionales* trains, some eastbound faster trains, and the "Atocha RENFE" Metro stop. The *Atención al Cliente* office in the *cercanías* section has information only on trains to destinations near Madrid. Most AVE trains will pull in on this side—clearly marked signs lead you to a direct route to the *cercanías* train that goes to the airport, or to the Metro, taxi stand, or back to the AVE side.

Terrorism Memorial: The terrorist bombings of March 11, 2004, took place in Atocha and on local lines going into and out of the station. Security is understandably tight here. A moving memorial is in the *cercanías* part of the station near the Atocha

RENFE Metro stop. Walk inside and under the cylinder to read the thousands of condolence messages in many languages (sporadic closings, but generally daily 11:00-14:00 & 17:00-19:00). The 36-foot-tall cylindrical glass memorial towers are visible from outside on the street.

AVE Trains

Spain's bullet train opens up good itinerary options. You can get from Madrid's Atocha station to **Barcelona** nonstop in 2.5 hours (at nearly 200 mph), with trains running almost hourly. The AVE train is faster and easier than flying, but not necessarily cheaper. Second-class tickets are about €110-130 one-way; first-class tickets are €180. Advance purchase and online discounts are available through the national rail company (RENFE), but sell out quickly. Save by not traveling on holidays. Your ticket includes one commuter-train transfer in Madrid or Barcelona.

The AVE is also handy for visiting **Sevilla** (and, on the way, **Córdoba**). Consider this exciting day trip: 7:00-depart Madrid, 8:45-12:40-in Córdoba, 13:30-20:45-in Sevilla, 23:15-back in Madrid.

Other AVE destinations include **Toledo, Segovia, Valencia, Alicante,** and **Malaga.** Prices vary with times, class, and date of purchase—they're usually cheapest up to two months ahead. Eurail Pass holders pay a seat reservation fee (for example, Madrid to Sevilla is €13 second-class, but only at RENFE ticket windows—discount not available at ticket machines). Reserve each AVE segment ahead (tel. 902-320-320 for Atocha AVE info). For the latest, pick up the AVE brochure at the station, or check www.renfe.com.

Train Connections

Below I've listed both non-AVE and (where available) AVE trains. General train info: Tel. 902-320-320; international journeys: Tel. 902-243-402; www.renfe.com.

From Madrid by Train to: Toledo (AVE or cheaper Avant: nearly hourly, 30 minutes, from Atocha), **El Escorial** (*cercanías,* 2/hour, from Atocha and Chamartín, but bus is better), **Segovia** (AVE, Alvia, Avant: 8-10/day, 30 minutes plus 20-minute shuttle bus into Segovia center, from Chamartín, take train going toward Valladolid), **Ávila** (nearly hourly until 22:30, 1.5-2 hours, more frequent departures from Chamartín than Atocha), **Salamanca** (7/day, 1.5-3 hours, from Chamartín), **Valencia** (AVE: nearly hourly, 2 hours, from Atocha; in Valencia, AVE passengers arrive at Joaquín Sorolla station), **Santiago de Compostela** (5/day, 5-5.5 hours, longer trips transfer in Ourense), **Barcelona** (AVE: at least hourly, 2.5-3 hours from Atocha), **San Sebastián** (7/day, 5.5-7.5 hours, from Chamartín), **Bilbao** (2-4/day, 5-7 hours, some transfer in Zaragoza, from Chamartín), **Pamplona** (6/day direct, 3.5 hours, more with transfer in Zaragoza, from Atocha), **Burgos** (6/day, 2.5-4.5 hours, from Chamartín), **León** (8/day, 2.5-5 hours, from Chamartín), **Granada** (2/day on Altaria, 4.5 hours; also 2/day with transfer to AVE in Málaga, 4 hours), **Sevilla** (AVE: hourly, 2.5 hours, departures from 16:00-19:00 can sell out far in advance, from Atocha), **Córdoba** (AVE: almost hourly, 2 hours; Altaria trains: 4/day, 2 hours; all from Atocha), **Málaga** (AVE: 9/day, 2.5-4 hours, from Atocha), **Algeciras** (4/day, half with transfer in Antequera, 5.5-6 hours, from Atocha), **Lisbon, Portugal** (1/night, 10.5 hours, from Chamartín), **Marseille, France** (1/day direct, 8 hours, from Atocha; also stops at Montpellier, Nîmes, Avignon, and Aix-en-Provence).

BY BUS

Madrid has several major bus stations with good Metro connections. There are also several routes serving Barajas Airport's Terminal 4. Multiple bus companies operate from these stations, including Alsa (tel. 902-422-242, www.alsa.es), Avanza and Auto-Res (tel. 902-020-052, www.avanzabus.com), and La Sepulvedana (tel. 901-119-699, www.lasepulvedana.es). If you take a taxi from any bus station, you'll be charged a legitimate €3 supplement (not levied for trips to the station).

Plaza Elíptica Station: Served by Alsa. Buses to Toledo leave from here (2/hour, 1-1.5 hours, *directo* faster than *ruta*, Metro: Plaza Elíptica).

Estación Sur de Autobuses (South Station): Served by Alsa, Socibus, and Avanza. From here, buses go to **Ávila** (9/day, 6/day on weekends, 1.5 hours, Avanza), **Burgos** (2/day, 3.5 hours, Alsa), **Salamanca** (hourly express, 2.5-3 hours, Avanza), **León** (10/day, 4 hours, Alsa), **Santiago de Compostela** (4/day, 9 hours, includes 1 night bus, Alsa), **Granada** (nearly hourly, 5-6 hours, Alsa), and **Lisbon** (2/day, 9 hours, Alsa). The station sits squarely on top of the Méndez Álvaro Metro (has TI, tel. 914-684-200, www.estacionautobusesmadrid.com).

Moncloa Station: This station, in the Moncloa Metro station, serves **Leon** (6/day, 3.5-4.5 hours, Alsa), **Santiago de Compostela** (3/day, 9 hours, Alsa), **El Escorial** (4/hour, fewer on weekends, 1 hour), and **Segovia** (about 2/hour). To reach the **Valley of the Fallen,** it's best to connect via El Escorial.

Avenida de América Station: Served by Alsa. Located at the Avenida de América Metro, buses go to **Lisbon** (2/day, night bus 8.5 hours), **Burgos** (hourly, 3 hours), **Granada** (3/day, 6 hours), and **Pamplona** (nearly hourly, 6 hours).

BY PLANE
Madrid's Adolfo Suárez Barajas Airport

Ten miles east of downtown, Madrid's modern airport has four terminals. Terminals 1, 2, and 3 are connected by long indoor walkways (about an 8-minute walk apart) and serve airlines including Delta, United, US Airways, Lufthansa, and Air Canada. The newer Terminal 4 serves airlines including Iberia, Vueling, Ryanair, British, and American, and also has a separate satellite terminal called T4S. To transfer between Terminals 1-3 and Terminal 4, you can take a 10-minute shuttle bus (free, leaves every 10 minutes from departures level), or take the Metro (stops at Terminals 2 and 4). Make sure to allow enough time if you need to travel between terminals (and then for the long walk within Terminal 4 to the gates). For more information about navigating this massive airport, go to www.aena-aeropuertos.es (airport code: MAD).

International flights typically use Terminals 1 and 4. At the Terminal 1 arrivals area, you'll find a helpful, though privately run, English-speaking Turismo Madrid **TI** (marked *Oficina de Información Turística,* Mon-Sat 8:00-20:00, Sun 9:00-14:00, tel. 913-058-656), **ATMs,** a **flight info office** (marked simply *Information* in airport lobby, open daily 24 hours, tel. 902-353-570), a **post-office** window, a pharmacy, lots of phones (buy a phone card from the nearby machine), a few scattered **Internet** terminals (small fee), **eateries,** a **RENFE office** (where you can get train info and buy long-distance train tickets, long hours daily, tel. 902-320-320), and on-the-spot **car-rental agencies.** The super-modern Terminal 4 offers essentially the same services. **Luggage storage** *(consigna)* is in Terminal 2, near the Metro exit. Some buses leave from the airport to far-flung destinations, such as Pamplona (see www.alsa.es; buy ticket online or from the driver).

Consider flying between Madrid and other cities in Spain (see "By Plane" in the Practicalities chapter). Domestic airline Vueling (www.vueling.com) is popular for its discounts (e.g., Madrid-Barcelona flight as cheap as €30 if booked in advance).

Getting Between the Airport and Downtown

By Public Bus: The yellow **Exprés Aeropuerto** runs between the airport (all terminals) and Atocha station (€5, pay driver in cash, departing from arrivals level every 15-20 minutes, ride takes about 40 minutes, runs 24 hours a day; from 23:30-6:00, the bus only goes to Plaza de Cibeles, not all the way to Atocha). From Atocha, you can take a taxi or the Metro to your hotel. The bus back to the airport leaves Atocha from near the taxi stand on the *cercanías* side (from 23:30-6:00, it departs downtown from Plaza de Cibeles).

Bus #200 (from all terminals) is less handy than the express bus because it leaves you farther from downtown (at the Metro stop at Avenida de América, northeast of the historical center). This bus departs from the arrivals level about every 10 minutes and takes about 20 minutes to reach Avenida de América (runs 6:00-24:00, buy €1.50 ticket from driver; or get a shareable 10-ride Metrobus ticket at a tobacco shop, Metro station, or newsstand).

By *Cercanías* Train: From Terminal 4, passengers can ride a *cercanías* train to either of Madrid's stations (€2.60, 2/hour, 25 minutes to Atocha, 12 minutes to Chamartín). Those returning to Madrid's airport by AVE train from elsewhere in Spain can transfer for free to the *cercanías* at Atocha: Scan your AVE ticket at the *cercanías* ticket machine to receive a ticket for the airport train. Be sure to board a train labeled T-4.

The bus is still a more convenient choice for arriving or departing from the other airport terminals.

By Metro: Considering the ease of riding the Exprés Aeropuerto bus in from the airport, I wouldn't recommend taking the Metro. The subway involves two transfers to reach the city; it's not difficult, but usually involves climbing some stairs (€4.50-6; or add a €3 supplement to your 10-ride Metrobus ticket).

By Minibus Shuttle: The AeroCity shuttle bus provides door-to-door transport in a seven-seat minibus with up to three hotel stops en route. It's promoted by hotels, but if you want door-to-door service, simply taking a taxi generally offers a better value (www.aerocity.com).

By Taxi: With cheap and easy alternatives available, there's not much reason to take a taxi unless you have lots of luggage or just want to go straight to your hotel. If you do take a taxi between the airport and downtown, the flat rate is €30. There is no charge for luggage. Plan on getting stalled in traffic.

BY CAR

Avoid driving in Madrid. If you're planning to rent a car, do it when you depart the city.

Renting a Car: It's cheapest to make car-rental arrangements before you leave home. In Madrid, consider **Europcar** (central reservations tel. 902-105-030, San Leonardo 8 office tel. 915-418-892, Atocha tel. 902-105-055, Chamartín tel. 912-035-070, airport tel. 902-105-055), **Hertz** (central reservations tel. 902-402-405, Plaza de España 18 tel. 915-425-805, Atocha tel. 902-023-932, airport tel. 902-305-230), **Avis** (central reservations tel. 933-443-700, Gran Vía 60 tel. 915-484-204, Chamartín tel.

902-090-343, Atocha tel. 902-110-291, airport tel. 902-200-162), and **Enterprise Atesa** (central reservations tel. 902-100-101). Ask about delivery to your hotel. At the airport, most rental cars are returned at Terminal 1.

Route Tips for Drivers: To leave Madrid from Gran Vía, simply follow signs for *A-6* (direction *Villalba* or *A Coruña*) for Segovia, El Escorial, or the Valley of the Fallen (see next chapter for details). The Madrid-Toledo toll road costs €8.70.

NORTHWEST OF MADRID

El Escorial • Valley of the Fallen • Segovia • Ávila

Before slipping out of Madrid, consider several fine side-trips northwest of Spain's capital city, all conveniently reached by car, bus, or train.

Spain's lavish, brutal, and complicated history is revealed throughout Old Castile. This region, where the Spanish language originated, is named for its many castles—battle scars from the long-fought Reconquista.

An hour from Madrid, tour the imposing and fascinating palace at El Escorial, headquarters of the Spanish Inquisition. Nearby, at the awe-inspiring Valley of the Fallen, pay tribute to the countless victims of Spain's bloody civil war.

Segovia, with its remarkable Roman aqueduct (pictured at top of page) and romantic castle, is another worthwhile side-trip. At Ávila you can walk the perfectly preserved medieval walls.

PLANNING YOUR TIME

You can see El Escorial and the Valley of the Fallen in less than a day, but don't go on a Monday, when both sights are closed. By car, see them en route to Segovia; by bus, make them a day trip from Madrid.

Segovia, worth a half-day of sightseeing, is easy to reach from Madrid. If you have time, spend the night—the city is a joy in the evenings. Ávila, while charming, merits only a quick stop to marvel at its medieval walls and, perhaps, check out St. Teresa's finger.

To see both Segovia and Ávila en route from Madrid to Sala-

Northwest of Madrid

To Burgos & Bilbao
To Valladollid
To León & Santiago
N-110
A-6
A-601
A-6
N
Segovia
La Granja
A-1
E-5
AP-6
N-603
N-110
AP-61
Navacerrado pass
To Salamanca
AP-51
Villacastín
A-50
Ávila
A-51
VALLEY OF THE FALLEN
C-505
El Escorial
M-505
A-6
M-40
Barajas
SILLA DE FELIPE
RING FREEWAY
M-40
To Barcelona
Madrid
N-403
A-3
10 Kilometers
10 Miles
High-Speed Rail Line
E-90
A-42
To Valencia
A-5
AP-41
A-4
E-5
SPAIN
Aranjuez
A-40
A-40
A-4
E-5
100 Miles
Toledo
To Consuegra
AVE high-speed line to Sevilla
To Andalucía

manca, consider taking the fast train (or bus) to Segovia, then bus-
ing from Segovia to Ávila, and finally continuing to Salamanca by
bus or train.

In total, these sights are worth two days if you're in Spain for
less than a month. If you're a history buff in Spain for just a week,
squeeze in a quick side-trip from Madrid to El Escorial and the
Valley of the Fallen.

El Escorial

The Monasterio de San Lorenzo de El Escorial, worth ▲▲▲, is a symbol of power rather than elegance. This 16th-century palace, 30 miles northwest of Madrid, was built at a time when Catholic Spain felt threatened by Protestant "heretics," and its construction dominated the Spanish economy for a generation (1562-1584). Because of this bully in the national budget, Spain has almost nothing else to show from this most powerful period of her history.

El Escorial gives us a better feel for the Counter-Reformation and the Inquisition than any other building.

GETTING THERE

Most people visit El Escorial from Madrid. By public transportation, the bus is most convenient (since it gets you closer to the palace than the train does). Remember that it makes sense to combine El Escorial with a visit to the nearby Valley of the Fallen.

By Bus: Buses leave from the Moncloa bus station. For El Escorial, follow signs to Terminal 1 (blue), go up to the platforms in the blue hallway and find platform 11—this is where buses #664 and #661 depart (4/hour, fewer on weekends, 1 hour, €4.20 one-way, buy ticket from driver, Herranz Bus, tel. 918-969-028). The bus drops you downtown in San Lorenzo de El Escorial, a pleasant 10-minute stroll from the palace (see map): Exit the bus station from the back ramp that leads over the parked buses (noting that return buses to Madrid leave from platform 3 or 4 below; schedule posted by info counter inside station), turn left, and follow the cobbled pedestrian lane, Calle San Juan. This street veers to the right and becomes Calle Juan de Leyva. In a few short blocks, it dead-ends at Duque de Medinaceli, where you'll turn left and see the palace. Stairs lead past several decent eateries, through a delightful square, past the TI (Mon-Sat 9:30-14:00 & 15:00-18:00, Sun 10:00-14:00; tel. 918-905-313), and directly to the tourist entry of the immense palace/monastery.

By Train: Local trains (*cercanías* line C-8A) run at least twice an hour from Madrid's Atocha and Chamartín stations to El Escorial. From the station, walk 20 minutes uphill through Casita del Príncipe park, straight up from the station. Or you can take a shuttle bus (L1) from the station (2/hour, usually timed with train arrival, €1.30) or a taxi (€7.50) to the San Lorenzo de El Escorial town center and the palace.

By Car: It's quite simple. Pick up or have your rental car de-livered by 8:30, and ask for directions to highway A-6. From Gran Vía in central Madrid, follow signs to *A-6* (direction *Villalba* or *A Coruña*). The freeway leads directly out of town. Stay on A-6 past the first El Escorial exit. At kilometer 37 you'll see the cross mark-ing the Valley of the Fallen ahead on the left. Exit 47 takes you to both the Valley of the Fallen (after a half-mile, a granite gate on right marks Valle de los Caídos turnoff) and El Escorial (follow *San Lorenzo de El Escorial* signs).

The nearby **Silla de Felipe** (Philip's Seat) is a rocky viewpoint where the king would come to admire his palace as it was being built. From El Escorial, follow directions to Ávila, then M-505 to Valdemorillo; look for a sign on your right after about a mile.

When you leave El Escorial for Madrid, Toledo, or Segovia, follow signs to *A-6 Guadarrama*. After about six miles you pass the Valley of the Fallen and hit the freeway.

ORIENTATION TO EL ESCORIAL

Cost and Hours: €10, Tue-Sun 10:00-20:00, Oct-March until 18:00, closed Mon year-round, last entry one hour before closing.

Information: Tel. 918-905-904, www.patrimonionacional.es.

Tours: For an extra €4, a 1.5-hour **guided tour** takes you through the complex and covers other buildings on the grounds, including the House of the Infante (Casita del Infante) and House of the Prince (Casita del Príncipe). There are few tours in English; if nothing's running soon, go on your own: Follow my self-guided tour, rent the €3 **audioguide** with photos, or download the smartphone **app** Royal Monastery of San Lorenzo of El Escorial ($1 fee).

Eating: The **Mercado Público,** a four-minute walk from the palace, is the place to shop for a picnic (Mon-Wed and Fri 9:30-13:30 & 17:00-20:00, Thu and Sat 9:30-14:00, closed Sun, Calle del Rey 9). On **Plaza Jacinto Benavente** and **Plaza de la Constitución,** just two blocks north of the palace complex, you'll find a handful of nondescript but decent restaurants serving fixed-price lunches or tapas, often at shady outdoor tables (best on weekdays).

❷ SELF-GUIDED TOUR

The *monasterio* looks confusing at first—mostly because of the pure magnitude of this stone structure—but the *visita* arrows and signs help guide you through one continuous path. English descriptions are scattered within the palace. (For more information, get the *Guide: Monastery of San Lorenzo El Real de El Escorial,* which follows the general route you'll take—€9, available at any of several shops in the palace.)

Here is the general order you'll follow.

• *Pass through security and buy your ticket at the ticket window (straight ahead from the scanner) or at the machine (requires a chip-and-PIN credit card, to the left of the scanner after you go through the first door and into the first patio).*

From the patio, follow the signs to the beginning of the tour. You will go through a series of courtyards and stone halls that lead you into...

The Courtyard of the Kings (El Patio de los Reyes)

This is the main entrance to the building designed by architects Juan Bautista de Toledo and Juan de Herrera. The style of architecture, *herreriana,* is known for its use of stone and slate, and is composed of straight lines and little decoration. Look up to see the shiny crowns of the six Kings of the Tribe of Judah reigning over the immensity of this courtyard.

El Escorial – Ground Floor

To Train Station

PALACE OF
PHILIP II

G a r d e n s   WALKING
                       GALLERY   G a r d e n s

                                        ROYAL PANTHEON
                                        (STAIRS LEAD
                                        DOWN TO CRYPT)

ENTRANCE TO
BOURBON PALACE   ALTAR   PANTHEON OF
(UPPER FLOOR)   ROYAL CHILDREN   C
        HALL OF   DOME   H
        BATTLES   A
To Town,   (UPPER FLOOR)   CLOISTER   P
T.I. & Bus   S   BASILICA   T
Station   H   E
             O   TICKET   R
             P   MACHINE WC   CELLINI'S   R
                              CHRIST   O
ENTRANCE   TICKETS   OLD   O
                                        CHURCH   M
TOUR BEGINS   S

                COLLEGE   COURTYARD   MONASTERY
                (CLOSED TO   OF THE   (CLOSED TO
                THE PUBLIC) KINGS   THE PUBLIC)

                                    EXIT

                LIBRARY
                (UPPER FLOOR)   TOUR ENDS

                P l a z a   50 Meters
                                   50 Yards

• *Cross the courtyard as if to exit the main door, but go up the stairs in the corner to the...*

Library (Biblioteca)

As you enter, look above the wooden door. The plaque warns *"Excomunión..."*—you'll be excommunicated if you take a book without checking it out, or if you don't show the guard your ticket. Who needs late fees when you hold the keys to hell? It's clear that education was a priority for the Spanish royalty. Savor this room: The armillary sphere in front of you—an elaborate model of the solar system—

looks like a giant gyroscope, revolving unmistakably around Earth, with a misshapen, underexplored North America. As you walk to the other end of the room, look up. The ceiling (by Tibaldi, depicting various disciplines labeled in Latin, the lingua franca of the multinational Habsburg Empire) is a burst of color.

• *Go downstairs to exit the library. You will walk through a souvenir shop and pass a WC and lockers for bags before walking back across the Courtyard of the Kings. Go through the central arch under the six kings into the...*

Basilica (Basílica)

Find the flame-engulfed grill in the center of the altar wall that features San Lorenzo (the same St. Lawrence depicted in paintings you'll see later) meeting his famous death—and taking "turn the other cheek" to new extremes. Lorenzo was so cool, he reportedly told his Roman executioners, "You can turn me over now—I'm done on this side." With your back to the altar, go to the right corner for the artistic highlight of the basilica: Benvenuto Cellini's marble sculpture, *The Crucifixion.* Jesus' features are supposedly modeled after the Shroud of Turin. Cellini carved this from Carrara marble for his own tomb in 1562 (according to the letters under Christ's feet).

• *Exit to your left and continue to the...*

Gate House (Portería) and Cloister (Claustro)

The Gate House served as a waiting room for people visiting the monks. Continue to the cloister, which glows with bright paintings by Pellegrino Tibaldi. Pass the main staircase, and marvel at the frescos. Lucca Giordano depicted *The Glory of the Spanish Monarch* here, as well as painting 12 other frescoes in the monastery in 22 months— speedy Lucca!

Off the cloister is the **Old Church** (Iglesia Vieja), which was used from 1571 to 1586 while the basilica was finished. During that time, the bodies of several kings, including Charles V, were interred here, and Philip II also had a temporary bedroom here. Among the many paintings, look for the powerful *Martyrdom of St. Lawrence* (Titian) above the main altar.

• *Continue through the cloister to the...*

Chapter Rooms (Salas Capitulares)

These rooms are where the monks met to do church business. They were (and continue to be) a small, disorganized art gallery lined with a few big names alongside many paintings with no labels.

History of El Escorial

The giant, gloomy building made of gray-black stone looks more like a prison than a palace. About 650 feet long and 500 feet wide, it has 2,600 windows, 1,200 doors, more than 100 miles of passages, and 1,600 over-whelmed tourists.

Four hundred years ago, the enigmatic, introverted, and extremely Catholic King Philip II (1527-1598) ruled his bulky empire from here, including giving direction to the Inquisition. To Philip, the building embodied the wonders of Catholic learning, spirituality, and arts. To 16th-century followers of Martin Luther, it epitomized the evil of closed-minded Catholicism. To architects, the building—built on the cusp between styles—exudes both Counter-Reformation grandeur and understated Renaissance simplicity. Today it's a time capsule of Spain's Golden Age, packed with history, art, and Inquisition ghosts. (And at an elevation of nearly 3,500 feet, it can be friggin' cold.)

The building was conceived by Philip II to serve several purposes: as a grand mausoleum for Spain's royal family, starting with his father, Holy Roman Emperor Charles V; as a monastery to pray (a lot) for the royal souls; as a small palace to use as a Camp David of sorts for Spain's royalty; and as a school to embrace humanism in a way that promoted the Catholic faith.

Spanish architect Juan Bautista de Toledo, who had studied in Italy, was called by Philip II to carry out the El Escorial project, but he died before it was finished. His successor, Juan de Herrera, made extensive changes to Toledo's original design and completed the palace in 1584.

Highlights are El Greco's *Martyrdom of St. Lawrence* (1580) and Titian's *Last Supper*.
• *Go downstairs and through a gift shop into the...*

Pantheon of the Princes (Panteón de los Principes)

The rooms here are filled with the tombs of lesser royals. Each bears that person's name (in Latin), relationship to the king, and slogan or epitaph. The wedding-cake **Pantheon of Royal Children** (Panteón de los Infantes) holds the remains of various royal children who died before the age of seven (and their first Communion).
• *At the end of this pantheon, walk up a handful of steps, then go downstairs to the...*

Royal Pantheon (Panteón Real)

This is the gilded resting place of 26 kings and queens...four centuries' worth of Spanish monarchy. All the kings are here—but the only queens allowed are mothers of kings.

A post-mortem filing system is at work in the Pantheon. From the entrance, kings are on the left, queens on the right. (The only exception is Isabel II, since she was a ruling queen and her husband was a consort.) The first and greatest, Charles V and his Queen Isabel, flank the altar on the top shelf. Her son, Philip II, rests below Charles and opposite (only) one of Philip's four wives, and so on. There is a waiting process, too. Before a royal corpse can rest in this room, it needs to decompose for at least 25 years. The bones of the current king's (Felipe VI) great-grandmother, Victoria Eugenia (who died in 1964), were transferred into the crypt in late 2011. The two empty niches are already booked: Felipe's grandfather, Don Juan (who died in 1993), is on the waiting list...controversially. Technically, he was never crowned king of Spain—Generalísimo Francisco Franco took control of Spain before Don Juan could ascend to the throne, and he was passed over for the job when Franco reinstituted the monarchy. Felipe's grandmother is the most recent guest in the rotting room. So where does that leave Felipe's parents, Juan Carlos and Sofía, and monarchs still to come (and go)? This hotel is *completo*.

• Head back up the stairs, and continue up to the...

Palace of Philip II (Palacio de Felipe II)

You'll begin in **Philip II's bedroom.** Look at the king's humble bed...barely queen-size. He could view Mass at the basilica's high altar without leaving his bed. The red box next to his pillow holds the royal bedpan. But don't laugh—the king's looking down from the wall to your left. At age 71, Philip II, the gout-ridden king of a dying empire, died in this bed (1598). As you enter the **King's Antechamber,** study the fine inlaid-wood door, one of a set of five (a gift from the German emperor that celebrates the exciting humanism of the age). The slate strip on the floor is a sundial from 1755. It lined up with a (now plugged) hole in the wall so that at noon a tiny beam hit the middle of the three lines. Palace clocks were set by this. Where the ray crossed the strip indicated the date and sign of the zodiac.

A second sundial is in the **Walking Gallery** that follows. Here the royals got their exercise privately, with no risk of darkening their high-class skins with a tan. Study the 16th-century maps along the walls, and look for Charles V's 16th-century portable altar.

The **Audience Chamber** is now a gallery filled with portraits of Habsburg royals painted by popular local artists. The portraits of unattractive people that line the walls provide an instructive peek at the consequences of mixing blue blood with more of the same blue blood (inbreeding among royals was a common problem throughout Europe in those days). Holy Roman Emperor Charles V (1500-1558, who is known as King Charles I in Spain) is over the fireplace mantel. Charles, Philip II's dad, was the most powerful man in Europe, having inherited not only the Spanish crown, but also control over Germany, Austria, the Low Countries (Belgium and the Netherlands), and much of Italy. When he announced his abdication in 1555, his son Philip II inherited much of this territory...plus the responsibility of managing it. Philip's draining wars with France, Portugal, Holland, and England—including the disastrous defeat of Spain's navy, the Spanish Armada, by England's Queen Elizabeth I (1588)—knocked Spain from its peak of power and began centuries of decline. The guy with the red tights and good-looking legs to the right of Charles is his illegitimate son, Don Juan de Austria—famous for his handsome looks, thanks to a little fresh blood. Other royal offspring weren't so lucky: When one king married his niece, the result was Charles II (1665-1700, opposite Charles V). His severe underbite (an inbred royal family trait) was the least of his problems. An epileptic before that disease was understood, poor "Charles the Mad" would be the last of the Spanish Habsburgs. He died without an heir in 1700, ushering in the continent-wide War of the Spanish Succession and the dismantling of Spain's empire.

Go through the **Guard's Room** to the **King's Apartments** and find the small portrait of Philip II flanked by two large paintings of his daughters. The palace was like Philip: austere. Notice the simple floors, plain white walls, and bare-bones chandelier. This was the bedroom of one of his daughters. The sheet warmer beside her bed was often necessary during the winter. If the bed curtains are drawn, bend down to see the view from her bed...of the high altar in the basilica next door. The entire complex of palace and monastery buildings was built around that altar.

Leaving Philip's Palace, notice the reclinable sedan chair that Philip II, thick with gout, was carried in (for seven days) on his last trip from Madrid to El Escorial. He wanted to be here when he died.

• *Go up several stairs to the...*

Hall of Battles (Sala de Batallas)

Its paintings celebrate Spain's great military victories—including the Battle of San Quentin over France (1557) on St. Lawrence's feast day, which inspired the construction of El Escorial. The sprawling series, painted in 1590, helped teach the new king all the elements of warfare. Stroll the length for a primer on army skills.

• Head back down the same stairs, and then down again to the level where you entered the monument. Follow the series of courtyards back to where you entered (in the hall with the ticket machines), and then go toward the cloakroom (consigna) *to go upstairs to the...*

Bourbon Palace (El Palacio de los Borbones)

This area was modified by Charles III to have a French-style layout. It was occupied by royalty in the fall, so they kept warm by covering the walls with tapestries, mostly with scenes of hunting, the main activity when they retreated here. Most of the tapestries were made in the Royal tapestry factory in Madrid. As you wander through several rooms, look for tapestries made from Goya cartoons, including *Dance on the Banks of the Manzanares Canal* (the cartoon is in Madrid's Municipal Museum). Listen for the ticking of the clock collection, a contribution of Charles IV.

• Your tour is over. Exit the palace through the Hall of Battles, downstairs, through a couple of courtyards to where you began, and out the door with the security scanner.

Valley of the Fallen

Six miles from El Escorial, high in the Guadarrama Mountains, is the Valley of the Fallen (Valle de los Caídos). A 500-foot-tall granite cross marks this immense and powerful underground monument to the victims of Spain's 20th-century nightmare—the Spanish Civil War (1936-1939).

GETTING THERE

Most visitors side-trip to the Valley of the Fallen from El Escorial. If you don't have your own wheels, the easiest way to get between these two sights is to negotiate a deal with a **taxi** (to take you from El Escorial to Valley of the Fallen, wait 30-60 minutes, and then bring you back to El Escorial, €45 total). Or you can use the **bus** service between El Escorial and the Valley of the Fallen, though the timing isn't the most convenient (€11.20 includes entrance fee, 1/day Tue-Sun at 15:15, 15 minutes, return bus to El Escorial doesn't leave until 17:30—a long time to spend at this place).

ORIENTATION TO THE VALLEY OF THE FALLEN

Cost and Hours: €9; April-Sept Tue-Sun 10:00-19:00, Oct-March until 18:00, closed Mon year-round, last entry one hour before closing; ask about audioguide, tel. 918-905-611, www.valledeloscaidos.es.

Mass: You can enter the basilica during Mass, but you can't sightsee or linger afterward. One-hour services run Tue-Sat at 11:00 and Sun at 11:00, 13:00, and 17:30 (17:00 in winter). During services, the entire front of the basilica (altar and tombs) is closed. Mass is usually accompanied by the resident boys' choir, the "White Voices" (Spain's answer to the Vienna Boys' Choir).

VISITING THE VALLEY OF THE FALLEN

Approaching by car or bus, you enter the sprawling park through a granite gate. The best views of the cross are from the bridge (but note that it's illegal for drivers to stop anywhere along this road). To the right, tiny chapels along the ridge mark the stations of the cross, where pilgrims stop on their hike to this memorial.

In 1940, prison workers dug 220,000 tons of granite out of the hill beneath the cross to form an underground basilica, then used the stones to erect the cross (built like a chimney, from the inside). Since it's built directly over the dome of the subterranean basilica, a seismologist keeps a careful eye on things.

The stairs that lead to the imposing **monument** are grouped in sets of tens, meant to symbolize the Ten Commandments (including "Thou shalt not kill"—hmm). The emotional pietà draped over the basilica's entrance is huge—you could sit in the palm of Christ's hand. The statue was sculpted by Juan de Ávalos, the same artist who created the dramatic figures of the four Evangelists at the base of the cross. It must have had a powerful impact on mothers who

came here to remember their fallen sons.

A solemn silence and a stony chill fill the **basilica.** At 300 yards long, it was built to be longer than St. Peter's...but the Vatican had the final say when it blessed only 262 of those yards. Many Spaniards pass under the huge, foreboding angels of fascism to visit the grave of General Franco—an unusual place of pilgrimage, to say the least.

After walking through the two long vestibules, stop at the iron gates of the actual basilica. The line of torch-like lamps adds to the shrine ambience. Franco's prisoners, the enemies of the right, dug

The Spanish Civil War (1936-1939)

Thirty-three months of warfare killed roughly 500,000 Spaniards. Unlike America's Civil War, which split the US north and south, Spain's war was between classes and ideologies, dividing every city and village, and many families. It was especially cruel, with atrocities and reprisals on both sides.

The war began as a military coup to overthrow the democratically elected Republic, a government that the army and other conservative powers considered too liberal and disorganized. The rebel forces, called the Nationalists (Nacionalistas), consisted of the army, monarchy, Catholic Church, big business, and rural estates, with aid from Germany, Italy, and Portugal. Trying to preserve the liberal government were the Republicans (Republicanos), also called Loyalists: the government, urban areas, secularists, small business, and labor unions, with aid from the United States (minimal help) and the "International Brigades" of communists, socialists, and labor organizers.

In the summer of 1936, the army rebelled and took control of its own garrisons, rejecting the Republic and pledging allegiance to Generalísimo Francisco Franco (1892-1975). These Nationalists launched a three-year military offensive to take Spain region by region, town by town. The government ("Republicans") cobbled together an army of volunteers, local militias, and international fighters. The war pitted conservative Catholic priests against socialist factory workers, rich businessmen against radical students, sunburned farmers loyal to the old king against upwardly mobile small businessmen. People suffered. You'll notice that many elderly Spaniards are very short—a product of growing up during these hungry and very difficult civil war years.

Spain's civil war attracted international attention. Adolf Hitler and Benito Mussolini sent troops and supplies to their fellow fascist Franco. It was Hitler's Luftwaffe that helped Franco bomb the town of Guernica (April 1937), an event famously captured on canvas by Pablo Picasso (for more on the bombing, and to read about the painting, see page 64). On the Republican side, hundreds of Americans (including Ernest Hemingway) steamed over to Spain, some to fight for democracy as part of the "Abraham Lincoln Brigade."

By 1938, only Barcelona and Madrid held out. But they were no match for Franco's army. On April 1, 1939, Madrid fell and the war ended, beginning 36 years of iron-fisted rule by Franco.

this memorial out of solid rock from 1940 to 1950. (Though it looks like bare rock still shows on the ceiling, it's just a clever design.) The sides of the monument are lined with copies of 16th-century Brussels tapestries of the Apocalypse, and side chapels contain alabaster copies of Spain's most famous statues of the Virgin Mary.

Interred behind the high altar and side chapels (marked "RIP, 1936-1939, died for God and country") are the remains of approximately 34,000 people, both Franco's Nationalists and the anti-Franco Republicans (about 12,000), who lost their lives in the war. Regrettably, the urns are not visible, so it is Franco who takes center stage. His grave, strewn with flowers, lies behind the high altar. In front of the altar is the grave of José Antonio Primo de Rivera (1903-1936), the founder of Spanish fascism, who was killed by Republicans during the civil war. Between these fascists' graves, the statue of a crucified Christ is lashed to a timber Franco himself is said to have felled. The seeping stones seem to weep for the victims. Today, families of the buried Republicans remain upset that their kin are lying with Franco and his Nationalists.

As you leave, stare into the eyes of those angels with swords and two right wings and think about all the "heroes" who keep dying "for God and country," at the request of the latter. The expansive view from the monument's terrace includes the peaceful, forested valley and sometimes snow-streaked mountains.

While the **cross** is undergoing a lengthy restoration, access to it by funicular or by foot along the trail (marked *Sendero de la Cruz*) is closed.

Segovia

Fifty miles from Madrid, this town of 55,000 boasts a thrilling Roman aqueduct, a grand cathedral, and a historic castle. Since the city is more than 3,000 feet above sea level and just northwest of a mountain range, it is exposed to cool northern breezes, and people come here from Madrid for a break from the summer heat.

Day-Tripping from Madrid: Considering the easy train and bus connections, Segovia makes a fine day trip from Madrid (30 minutes one-way by AVE train, 1.5 hours by bus; see "Segovia Connections" for details). The disadvantages of this plan are that you spend the coolest hours of the day (early and late) en route, you miss the charming evening scene in Segovia, and you'll pay more for a hotel in Madrid than in Segovia. If you have time, spend the night. But even if you just stay the day, Segovia offers a rewarding and convenient break from the big-city intensity of Madrid.

Orientation to Segovia

Segovia is a medieval "ship" ready for your inspection. Start at the stern—the aqueduct—and stroll up Calle de Cervantes and Calle Juan Bravo to the prickly Gothic masts of the cathedral. Explore the tangle of narrow streets around playful Plaza Mayor and then descend to the Alcázar at the bow.

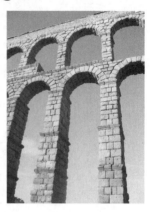

Tourist Information: Segovia has four TIs. The TI on Plaza Mayor covers both Segovia and the surrounding region (at #10; daily July-mid-Sept 9:00-14:00 & 17:00-20:00; mid-Sept-June Mon-Sat 9:30-14:00 & 16:00-19:00, Sun 9:30-17:00; tel. 921-460-334, www.turismocastillayleon.com). The TI at Plaza del Azogüejo, at the base of the aqueduct, specializes in Segovia and has friendly staff, pay WCs, and a gift shop (daily 10:00-19:00, mid-Oct-Easter until 18:30, see wooden model of Segovia, tel. 921-466-720, www.turismodesegovia.com). Smaller TIs are at the bus station (behind a window, Wed-Sun 10:00-14:00, closed Mon-Tue, tel. 921-436-569) and the AVE train station (Mon-Fri 8:15-15:15, Sat-Sun 10:00-14:15 & 16:00-17:45, often closed Mon-Fri in winter, tel. 921-447-262).

ARRIVAL IN SEGOVIA

If day-tripping from Madrid, check the return schedule when you arrive here (or get one at the Segovia TI).

By Train: From the AVE train station (called Guiomar), ride bus #11 for 20 minutes to the base of the aqueduct. There's no luggage storage at the train station. Bus #12 also takes you into town, but it drops you off at the bus station, a 10-minute walk to the aqueduct.

By Bus: You'll find luggage storage near the exit from the bus station (tokens sold daily 9:00-14:00 & 16:00-19:00, gives you access to locker until end of day). It's a 10-minute walk from the bus station to the town center: Exit left out of the station, continue straight across the street, and follow Avenida Fernández Ladreda, passing San Millán church on the left, then San Clemente church on the right, before coming to the aqueduct.

HELPFUL HINTS

Free Churches: Segovia has plenty of little Romanesque churches that are free to enter shortly before or after Mass (see TI for a list of times), and many have architecturally interesting exteriors that are worth a look. Keep your eyes peeled for these hidden treasures: San Millán church on Avenida Fernández Ladreda; San Martín church and San Esteban church, on squares of the same names (though you can't go inside San Esteban); and San Andrés church on the way to the Alcázar on Plaza de la Merced.

Shopping: If you buy handicrafts such as tablecloths from street vendors, make sure the item you want is the one you actually get; some unscrupulous vendors substitute inferior goods at the last minute. A flea market is held on Plaza Mayor on Thursdays (roughly 8:00-15:00, food also available).

Local Guide: Elvira Valderrama Rascon, a hardworking young woman, is a good English-speaking guide (€115/3 hours, mobile 636-227-949, elvisvalrras@yahoo.es).

Group Tours: At the TI on Plaza del Azogüejo, at the base of the aqueduct, you can join a two-hour "World Heritage" tour in English (€15, includes entrance to the Alcázar and sometimes the cathedral, runs daily, check schedule and reserve at the TI, tel. 921-466-720).

Segovia Walk

This 15-minute self-guided walk goes uphill from the Roman aqueduct to the city's main square along the pedestrian-only street.

It's most enjoyable just before dinner, when it's cool and filled with strolling Segovians.

Start at Plaza del Azogüejo, at Segovia's emblematic Roman aqueduct (described later, under "Sights in Segovia"). Walk about 100 yards up Calle de Cervantes, which becomes Calle Juan Bravo, until you reach the **"house of a thousand beaks"** (Casa de los Picos) on your right. This building's original Moorish design is still easy to see, despite the wall just past the door that blocks your view from the street. This wall, the architectural equivalent of a veil, hid this home's fine courtyard—Moors didn't flaunt their wealth. You can step inside to see art students at work and perhaps an exhibit on display, but it's most interesting from the exterior. Notice its truncated tower, one of many fortified towers that marked the homes of feuding local noble families. In medieval Spain, clashing loyalties led to mini civil wars. In the 15th century, as Ferdinand and Isabel centralized authority in Spain, nobles were required to lop their towers. You'll see the once-tall, now-stubby towers of 15th-century noble mansions all over Segovia. Another example of a similar once-fortified,

NORTHWEST OF MADRID

VERA CRUZ CHURCH

ZAMARRAMALA

Río Eresma

CALLE SAN MARCOS

CALLE DE LA MONEDA

PASEO SANTO DOMINGO DE GUZMAN

PASEO SAN JUAN DE LA CRUZ

ALCÁZAR

Plaza de la Reina Victoria Eugenia

PASEO SAN JUAN DE LA CRUZ

CALLE DE VELARDE

DOCTORAL

CALLE DE DAOIZ

RONDA DON JUAN II

CITY WALLS

SAN ANDRÉS

SAN ESTEBAN

Plaza San Esteban

ESCUDEROS

C. MARQUES ARCO

14

C. DE

CATHEDRAL

11

WC

S. FRUTOS

C. DE LA PEÑOLERÍA

MARTÍNEZ CAMPOS

PUERTA DE SAN ANDRÉS

100 Meters
100 Yards

CUESTA DE LOS HOYOS

1 Hotel Palacio San Facundo
2 Hotel Infanta Isabel
3 La Hostería Natura
4 Hotel Eurostars Plaza Acueducto
5 Hostal Don Jaime
6 Hospedaje el Gato
7 José María Restaurante
8 Mesón de Candido Rest.
9 Restaurante Duque
10 Café Jeyma
11 La Concepción Restaurante
12 Restaurante Bar José
13 Narizotas Restaurante
14 La Almuzara
15 Café La Colonial
16 Limón y Menta Pastry Shop
17 Bus #11

To N-110 -
Ávila, Salamanca
& Madrid

CALLE 3 DE ABRIL

Segovia

NORTHWEST OF MADRID

Río Eresma

CALLE DEL DOCTOR VELASCO

PASEO DEL OBISPO

SANTA CRUZ CONVENT

CALLE CARDENAL ZÚÑIGA

PASEO SANTO DOMINGO DE GUZMAN

CITY WALLS

SAN NICOLÁS

Plaza San Nicolás

C. SAN QUIRCE

C. SAN NICOLÁS

M. CONSEJO

CALLE SAN BARTOLOMÉ

LA TRINIDAD

CALLE DE LA TRINIDAD

CALLE DEL TARAY

Plaza de Colmenares

Plaza Mayor

CRONISTA LECEA SERAFIN SAN FACUNDO

CALLE DE SAN AGUSTÍN

10

7

16

12

WALK ENDS

C. COLÓN

C. INF. ISABEL

C. CATÓLICA

2

Pl. San Facundo

3

Plaza de los Huertos

1

ANGOSTA

MUSEO ESTEBAN VICENTE

CALLE DE JOSÉ CANALEJAS

Plaza del Seminario

J. P. VILLANUEVA

15

CORPUS CHRISTI CONVENT

CALLE DE JUAN BRAVO

SAN MARTÍN

13

HOUSE OF A THOUSAND BEAKS

C. OBISPO GANDÁSEGUI

CALLE SAN JUAN

To La Granja

AV. DE LA ROMA

17

PADRE CLARET

To AVE Train Stn.

4

PUENTE SANCTI-SPIRITU

CALLE DE SAN MILLÁN

CALLE DE CERVANTES

9

Plaza del Azoguejo

8

WALK BEGINS

Padre Claret

SANTOS JUSTO Y PASTOR

5

To **6**

CALLE CARMEN

SAN CLEMENTE

SAN FRANCISCO

ROMAN AQUEDUCT

CALLE TENIENTE OCHOA

CALLE DE LAS CARRETAS

AV. FERNÁNDEZ LADREDA

SAN MILLÁN

C. INDEPENDENCIA

PASEO DE EZEQUIEL GONZÁLEZ

BUS STATION

Acueducto Parking

CALLE DE LOS COCHES

To Cercanías Train Station

now-softened house with a cropped tower is about 50 yards farther down the street, on the left, on tiny Plaza del Platero Oquendo.

Continue uphill until you come to the complicated **Plaza de San Martín,** a commotion of history surrounding a striking statue of Juan Bravo. When Charles V, a Habsburg who didn't even speak Spanish, took power, he imposed his rule over Castile. This threatened the local nobles, who, inspired and led by Juan Bravo, revolted in 1521. Although Juan Bravo lost the battle—and his head—he's still a symbol of Castilian pride. This statue was erected in 1921 on the 400th anniversary of his death.

In front of the Juan Bravo statue stands the bold and bulky **House of Siglo XV.** Its fortified *Isabelino* style was typical of 15th-century Segovian houses. Later, in a more peaceful age, the boldness of these houses was softened with the decorative stucco work called *esgrafiado*—Arabic-style floral and geometrical patterns—that you see today (for example, in the big house across the street). The 14th-century Tower of Lozoya, behind the statue, is another example of the lopped-off towers.

On the same square, the 12th-century Church of St. Martín is Segovian Romanesque in style (a mix of Christian Romanesque—clustered columns with narrative capitals—and Moorish styles—minaret-like towers built with bricks).

If you continue up the street another 100 yards, you'll see the **Corpus Christi Convent** on the left. For €1, you can pop in to see the Franciscan church, which was once a synagogue, which was once a mosque. It is sweet and peaceful, with lots of art featuring St. Francis, and allows you to see the layers of religious history here.

Veer right at the fork directly after the convent, and keep going until you reach Segovia's inviting **Plaza Mayor**—once the scene of executions, religious theater, and bullfights with spectators jamming the balconies. The bullfights ended in the 19th century. When Segovians complained, they were given a more gentle form of entertainment—bands in the gazebo. Today the very best entertainment here is simply enjoying a light meal, snack, or drink in your choice of the many restaurants and cafés lining the square. The Renaissance church opposite the City Hall and behind the TI was built to replace the church where Isabel was proclaimed Queen of Castile in 1474. The symbol of Segovia is the aqueduct where you started—find it in the seals on the Theater Juan Bravo and atop the City Hall. Finally, treat yourself to the town's specialty pastry, *ponche segoviano* (marzipan cake), at the recommended Limón y Menta, the bakery on the corner where you entered Plaza Mayor.

Sights in Segovia

▲Roman Aqueduct

Segovia was a Roman military base and needed water. Emperor Trajan's engineers built a nine-mile aqueduct to channel water

from the Río Frío to the city, culminating at the Roman castle (which is the Alcázar today). The famous and exposed section of the 2,000-year-old *acueducto romano* is 2,500 feet long and 100 feet high, has 118 arches, was made from 20,000 granite blocks without any mortar, and can still carry a stream of water. It actu-

ally functioned until the late 19th century. On Plaza del Azoguejo, a grand stairway leads from the base of the aqueduct to the top—offering close-up looks at the imposing work. As you walk through the streets, keep an eye out for small plaques depicting the arches of the aqueduct, which tell you where the subterranean channel runs through the city.

▲Segovia Cathedral (Catedral de Segovia)

Segovia's cathedral, built from 1525-1768 (the third on this site), was Spain's last major Gothic building. Embellished to the hilt

with pinnacles and flying buttresses, the exterior is a great example of the final, overripe stage of Gothic, called Flamboyant. Yet the Renaissance arrived before it was finished—as evidenced by the fact that the cathedral is crowned by a dome, not a spire.

Cost and Hours: Cathedral—€3, free Sun April-Oct 9:30-10:30, Nov-March until 13:15 (cathedral access only—no cloisters), open daily 9:30-18:30, Oct-March until 18:00; tower—€5, visits by guided tour only daily at 10:30, 12:30, and 16:30 (16:00 in winter); combo-ticket for cathedral and tower—€7; tel. 921-462-205.

Visiting the Cathedral: The spacious and elegantly simple interior provides a delightful contrast to the frilly exterior. The **choir** features finely carved wooden stalls from the previous church (1400s). The *cátedra* (bishop's chair) is in the center rear of the choir.

The many side chapels are mostly 16th-century, and come with big locking gates—a reminder that they were the private sacred domain of the rich families and guilds that "owned" them. They could enjoy private Masses here with their names actually spoken in the blessings and a fine burial spot close to the altar.

Find the **Capilla La Concepción** (the last chapel in the rear that looks like a mini art gallery). Its many 17th-century paintings

hang behind a mahogany wood gate imported from colonial America. The painting, *Tree of Life*, by Ignacio Ries (left of the altar), shows hedonistic mortals dancing atop the Tree of Life. As a skeletal Grim Reaper prepares to receive them into hell (by literally chopping down the tree...timberrrr), Jesus rings a bell imploring them to wake up before it's too late. The center statue is Mary of the Apocalypse (as described in Revelations, standing on a devil and half-moon, which looks like bull's horns). Mary's pregnant, and the devil licks his evil chops, waiting to devour the baby Messiah.

Opposite from where you entered, a fine door (which leads into the cloister) is crowned by a painted Flamboyant Gothic pietà in its tympanum (the statue of Jesus with a skirt, on the left, is a reminder of how prudishness from the past looks silly in the present).

The **cloisters** hold a nice little museum containing French tapestries, paintings, and silver reliquaries. The gilded chapter room is draped with precious Flemish tapestries. Notice the gilded wagon. The Holy Communion wafer is placed in the top of this temple-like cart and paraded through town each year during the Corpus Christi festival. Hanging just outside these rooms is a glass case displaying keys to the 17th-century private chapel gates. From the cloister courtyard, you can see the Renaissance dome rising above the otherwise Gothic rooftop.

The 290-foot **tower** offers stunning views of the city and the surrounding area. You can climb 190 steps to the top on a guided tour three times a day.

▲Alcázar

In the Middle Ages, this fortified palace was one of the favorite residences of the monarchs of Castile, a key fortress for controlling the region. The Alcázar grew through the ages, and its function changed many times: After its stint as a palace, it was a prison for 200 years, and then a Royal Artillery School. It burned in 1862. Since the fire, it's basically been a museum.

Cost and Hours: Palace—€5.50, daily 10:00-19:00, Oct-March until 18:00, €3 audioguide describes each room (45 minutes, €5 deposit); tower—€2, same hours as palace except closed third Tue of month and in windy, rainy weather; tel. 921-460-759, www.alcazardesegovia.com.

Getting In: Buy your tickets at Real Laboratorio de Chimia, facing the palace on your left. Pick up a free English leaflet at the desk across from the ticket counter. At the entrance, pass your ticket through the turnstiles on the right for the palace, or the turnstiles on the left for the tower.

Visiting the Alcázar: You'll enjoy a one-way route through 11 rooms, including a fine view terrace. Visit the tower afterward; its 152 steps up a tight spiral staircase reward you with the only 360-degree city view in town. What you see today in the Alcázar is rebuilt—a Disney-esque exaggeration of the original. Still, its fine Moorish decor and historic furnishings are fascinating. The sumptuous ceilings are accurately restored in Mudejar style, and the throne-room ceiling is the artistic highlight of the palace.

Look for a big mural of Queen Isabel the Catholic being proclaimed Queen of Castile and León in Segovia's main square in 1474. The **Hall of the Monarchs** is lined with the busts of the 52 rulers of Castile and León who presided during the long and ultimately successful Reconquista (711-1492): from Pelayo (the first), clockwise to Juana VII (the last). There were only seven queens during the period (the numbered ones). In this current age of Islamic extremists decapitating Christians, study the painting of St. James the Moor-Slayer—with Muslim heads literally rolling at his feet (poignantly...in the chapel). James is the patron saint of Spain. His name was the rallying cry in the centuries-long Christian crusade to push the Muslim Moors back into Africa.

Stepping onto the terrace (the site of the original Roman military camp, circa A.D. 100) with its vast views, marvel at the natural fortification provided by this promontory cut by the confluence of two rivers. The terrace is closed in the winter and sometimes on windy days. The Alcázar marks the end (and physical low point) of the gradual downhill course of the nine-mile-long Roman aqueduct. Can you find the mountain nicknamed *Mujer Muerta* ("dead woman")?

In the **armory** (just after the terrace), find the king's 16th-century ornately carved ivory crossbow, with the hunting scene shown in the adjacent painting. The final rooms are the Museum of Artillery, recalling the period (1764-1862) when this was the Royal Artillery School. It shows the evolution of explosive weaponry, with old photos and prints of the Alcázar.

Church of Santos Justo y Pastor

This simple yet stately old church has fascinating 12th- and 13th-century frescoes filled with Gothic symbolism, plus a stork's nest atop its tower. From the base of the aqueduct, it's a short climb uphill into the newer part of town. Kind old Rafael, the volunteer caretaker, welcomes you.

Cost and Hours: Free, Tue-Sat 11:00-14:00 & 17:00-19:00, Sun 11:00-14:00, closed Mon and when Rafael needs to run an errand; located a couple of blocks from Plaza del Azogüejo, tel. 921-422-413.

Museo de Arte Contemporáneo Esteban Vicente

A collection of local artist Esteban Vicente's abstract art is housed in two rooms of the remodeled remains of Henry IV's 1455 palace. Wilder than Rothko but more restrained than Pollock, Vicente's vibrant work influenced post-WWII American art. The temporary exhibits can be more interesting than the permanent collection.

Cost and Hours: €3, free on Thu; open Thu-Fri 11:00-14:00 & 16:00-19:00, Sat 11:00-20:00, Sun 11:00-15:00, closed Mon-Wed; tel. 921-426-010, www.museoestebanvicente.es.

NEAR SEGOVIA

Vera Cruz Church

This 12-sided, 13th-century Romanesque church, built by the Knights Templar, once housed a piece of the "true cross." You can enjoy a postcard view of the city from the church, and more views follow as you continue around Segovia on the small road below the castle, labeled *Ruta Turística Panorámica.*

Cost and Hours: €2, Wed-Sun 10:30-13:30 & 16:00-19:00, until 18:00 in winter, closed Mon-Tue and when caretaker takes his autumn holiday; outside town beyond the castle, 25-minute walk from main square; tel. 921-431-475.

▲La Granja de San Ildefonso Palace

This "little Versailles," six miles south of Segovia, is much smaller and happier than nearby El Escorial. The palace and gardens were built by the homesick French-born King Philip V, grandson of Louis XIV. Today it's restored to its original 18th-century splendor, with its royal collection of tapestries, clocks, and crystal (actually made at the palace's royal crystal factory). Plumbers and gardeners imported from France and Italy made Philip a garden that rivaled Versailles'. The fanciful fountains feature mythological stories (explained in the palace audioguide). The Bourbon Philip chose to be buried here rather than with his Habsburg predecessors at El Escorial. His tomb is in the adjacent church, included with your ticket.

Cost and Hours: Palace—€9, open Tue-Sun 10:00-20:00, Oct-March until 18:00, closed Mon year-round, last entry one hour before closing, audioguide—€4, guided tour—€4 (ask for one in English—you might need to wait); park—free, daily 10:00-20:00, off-season until 19:00; tel. 921-470-019, www.patrimonionacional.es.

Getting There: La Sepulvedana buses make the 25-minute trip from Segovia (catch at the bus station) to San Ildefonso-La Granja (about 2/hour 7:30-21:30, fewer on weekends, tel. 902-119-699, www.lasepulvedana.es).

Sleeping in Segovia

The best places are on or near the central Plaza Mayor. This is where the city action is—the best bars, most tourist-friendly and *típico* eateries, and the TI. During busy times—on weekends and in July and August—reserve in advance.

NEAR PLAZA MAYOR

$$$ Hotel Palacio San Facundo, on a quiet square a few blocks off Plaza Mayor, is luxuriously modern in its amenities but has preserved its Old World charm. This palace-turned-monastery has 29 uniquely decorated rooms surrounding a skylit central patio (includes breakfast, air-con, elevator, pay parking, tel. 921-463-061, Plaza San Facundo 4, www.hotelpalaciosanfacundo.com, info@ hotelpalaciosanfacundo.com, José Luis). From Plaza Mayor, take Cronista Lecea; it's a four-minute walk directly to Plaza San Facundo.

$$ Hotel Infanta Isabel, right on Plaza Mayor, has 38 impeccable and elegant rooms, some with plaza views, and a welcoming staff (elevator, pay parking, tel. 921-461-300, www. hotelinfantaisabel.com, admin@hotelinfantaisabel.com).

$$ La Hostería Natura is a fresh version of a typical *hostal*. Their 12 cared-for rooms are a few blocks away from the Plaza Mayor (air-con, Calle Colón 5, tel. 921-466-710, www. hosterianatura.com, info@naturadesegovia.com).

NEAR THE AQUEDUCT

$$$$ Hotel Eurostars Plaza Acueducto has little character but provides the comforts of a business-class hotel. It's right at the foot of the aqueduct and next to the bus stops for the AVE train station. Some rooms have full or partial views of the aqueduct (air-con, elevator, gym, pay parking; Avenida Padre Claret 2, tel. 921-413-403, www.eurostarshotels.com, reservas@eurostarsplazaacueducto.com).

$ Hostal Don Jaime, opposite the Church of San Justo, is a friendly family-run place with 38 basic, worn, yet well-maintained rooms in two buildings (some single rooms with shared bath, family rooms, breakfast included for Rick Steves readers, Wi-Fi in main building only, pay parking; Ochoa Ondategui 8—from TI at Plaza del Azoguejo, cross under the aqueduct, go right, angle left, then snake uphill for 2 blocks; tel. 921-444-787, hostaldonjaime@ hotmail.com).

¢ Hospedaje el Gato, a family-run place on a quiet nondescript square just outside the old town, has 10 modern, comfortable rooms and no formal reception desk (air-con, bar serves breakfast and good tapas, uphill from Hostal Don Jaime and aqueduct at Plaza del Salvador 10, tel. 921-423-244, mobile 678-405-079, www.hostalsegovia.es, hbarelgato@yahoo.es).

Eating in Segovia

Look for Segovia's culinary claim to fame, roast suckling pig (*cochinillo asado:* 21 days of mother's milk, into the oven, and onto your plate—oh, Babe). It's worth a splurge here, or in Toledo or Salamanca.

For slightly lighter fare, try *sopa castellana*—soup mixed with eggs, ham, garlic, and bread—or warm yourself up with the *judiones de La Granja,* a popular soup made with flat white beans from the region. Segovia also has a busy tapas bar scene, featuring small bites served up with every drink you order.

Ponche segoviano, a dessert made with an almond-and-honey *mazapán* base, is heavenly after an earthy dinner or with a coffee in the afternoon (at the recommended Limón y Menta).

PLACES TO EAT ROAST SUCKLING PIG

$$$$ José María is *the* place to pig out in the old town, a block off Plaza Mayor. And though it doesn't have the history or fanfare of Cándido (see next), Segovians claim this high-energy place serves the best roast suckling pig in town. It thrives with a hungry mix of tourists and locals. The bar leading into the restaurant is a scene in itself. Muscle up to the bar and get your drink and tapa before going into the dining room (daily 13:00-16:00 & 20:00-23:30, reservations recommended, air-con, Cronista Lecea 11, tel. 921-466-017, www. restaurantejosemaria.com).

$$$$ Mesón de Cándido, one of the top restaurants in Castile, is famous for its memorable dinners. Even though it's filled with tourists, it's a grand experience. Take time to wander around and survey the photos of celebs—from Juan Carlos I to Antonio Banderas and Melanie Griffith—who've suckled here. Try to get a table in a room with an aqueduct view (daily 13:00-16:30 & 20:00-23:00, reservations recommended, Plaza del Azogüejo 5, air-con, under aqueduct, tel. 921-428-103, www.mesondecandido.es). Three gracious generations of the Cándido family still run the show.

$$$$ Restaurante Duque claims to be the oldest eatery in Segovia, open since 1895. The venerable institution is currently run by fourth-generation Marisa, who offers a menu of tapas alongside the rustic, traditional dishes of her ancestors. You'll find boisterous people bellied up to the bar, while both locals and tourists enjoy the comfortable dining room (daily 12:30-23:30, sometimes closes in afternoon, a few blocks from Plaza Mayor downhill from "house of a thousand beaks" at Calle de Cervantes 12, tel. 921-462-486, www.restauranteduque.es).

MOSTLY PIG-FREE PLACES IN THE OLD CENTER

Plaza Mayor, the main square, provides a great backdrop for a light lunch, dinner, or drink. Prices at the cafés are generally reasonable, and many offer a good selection of tapas and *raciones*. Grab a table at the place of your choice and savor the scene. **$$$ Café Jeyma** has a fine setting and cathedral view. **$$$ La Concepción Restaurante,** closer to the cathedral, is also good. For a filling lunch on the plaza, try **$$ Restaurante Bar José,** which has a three-course fixed-price meal for €16 (includes wine, bread, and excellent cathedral views, tel. 921-460-919).

$$$$ Narizotas serves more imaginative and non-Castilian alternatives to the gamey traditions. Dine outside on a delightful square or inside with modern art under medieval timbers. For a wonderful dining experience, try their chef's-choice mystery samplers, either the "Right Hand" (€35, about nine courses) or the "Left Hand" (€31, about six courses); both include wine, water, dessert, and coffee. They offer a less elaborate three-course €13-18 fixed-priced meal, and their à la carte menu is also a treat (daily 13:00-16:00 & 20:30-24:00, midway down Calle Juan Bravo at Plaza de Medina del Campo 1, tel. 921-462-679, www.narizotas.net).

$$ La Almuzara is a garden of veggie and organic delights: whole-wheat pizzas, tofu, seitan, and even a few dishes with meat (Tue 20:00-23:00, Wed-Sun 12:00-16:00 & 20:00-23:00, closed Mon, between cathedral and Alcázar at Marques del Arco 3, tel. 921-460-622).

Breakfast: In the morning, I like to eat on Plaza Mayor (many choices) while enjoying the cool air and the people scene. Or, 100 yards down the main drag toward the aqueduct, **$$ Café La Colonial** serves good breakfasts (with seating on a tiny square or inside, Plaza del Corpus).

Nightlife: Inexpensive bars and eateries line Calle de Infanta Isabel, just off Plaza Mayor. For nightlife, the bars on Plaza Mayor, Calle de Infanta Isabel, and Calle de Isabel la Católica are packed. There are a number of late-night dance clubs along the aqueduct.

Dessert: Limón y Menta offers a good, rich *ponche segoviano* (marzipan) cake by the slice—or try the lighter honey-and-almond *crocantinos* (generally daily 9:00-20:00, seating inside, Calle de Isabel la Católica 2, tel. 921-462-141).

Market: An outdoor produce market thrives on Plaza Mayor on Thursday (roughly 8:00-15:00). Nearby, on Calle del Cronista Ildefonso Rodríguez, a few stalls are open daily except Sunday. **Carrefour Express,** a small supermarket, is across from the Casa de los Picos (Mon-Sat 9:00-21:00, Sun 10:00-14:00, Calle Juan Bravo 54).

Segovia Connections

BY PUBLIC TRANSPORTATION

From Segovia to Madrid: Choose between the fast AVE train and the bus. Even though the 30-minute AVE train takes less than half as long as the bus, the train stations in Segovia and Madrid are less convenient, so the total time spent in transit is about the same. (Skip the *cercanías* commuter trains, as they take two hours and don't save you much money.)

The **AVE train** goes between Segovia's Guiomar station (labeled "Segovia AV" on booking sites) and Madrid's Chamartín station (8-10/day, 30 minutes). To get to Guiomar station, take city bus #11 from the base of the aqueduct (20 minutes, buses usually timed to match arrivals).

Buses run from Segovia to Madrid's Moncloa station. If arriving at the station in Madrid by Metro, follow the signs for the color-coded terminals to Terminal 1 (blue). From there, signs marked *Taquillas Segovia* lead you to the ticket office, or look for the ticket machines, which accept cash or chip-and-PIN credit cards (2/hour, 1.5 hours; tel. 902-119-699, www.lasepulvedana.es).

If you're riding the bus from Madrid to Segovia, about 30 minutes after leaving Madrid you'll see—breaking the horizon on the left—the dramatic concrete cross of the Valley of the Fallen. Its grand facade marks the entry to the mammoth underground memorial.

From Segovia by Bus to: La Granja Palace (about 2/hour, fewer on weekends, 25 minutes), **Ávila** (5/day, 2/day on weekends,

1 hour), **Salamanca** (2/day, more with transfer in Labajos, 3-3.5 hours, Auto-Res bus, tel. 902-020-999, www.avanzabus.com).

ROUTE TIPS FOR DRIVERS

From Madrid to Segovia: Leave Madrid on A-6. Exit 39 gets you to Segovia via a slow, winding route over the scenic mountain. Exit at 60 (after a long toll tunnel—about €3 depending on time of day), or get there quicker by staying on the toll road all the way to Segovia (add roughly €2 weekdays or €3 on weekends). At the Segovia aqueduct, follow *casco histórico* signs to the old town (on the side where the aqueduct adjoins the crenellated fortress walls).

Parking in Segovia: Free parking is available in the Alcázar's lot, but you must move your car by 19:00 (18:00 Oct-March), when the gates close. Or try the lot northwest of the bus station by the statue of Cándido, along the street called Paseo de Ezequiel González. Outside the old city, there's an Acueducto Parking underground garage kitty-corner from the bus station. Although it can be a hard slog up the hill to the Alcázar on a hot day, it beats trying to maneuver your car uphill through tight bends. There's also the huge and convenient Padre Claret garage near the aqueduct.

The city center has lots of parking spaces, but they're not free. To park in the old town, be legal or risk an expensive fine. Buy a ticket from a nearby machine to park in areas marked by blue stripes, and place the ticket on your dashboard (pay meter every 2 hours 9:00-14:00 & 16:30-20:00; free parking 20:00-9:00, Sat afternoon, and all day Sun).

From Segovia to Salamanca (100 miles): Leave Segovia by driving around the town's circular road, which offers good views from below the Alcázar. Then follow signs for *Ávila* (road N-110). Notice the fine Segovia view from the three crosses at the crest of the first hill. The Salamanca road leads around the famous Ávila walls to the right. The best wall view is from the signposted *Cuatro Postes*, a mile northwest of town. Salamanca (N-501) is clearly marked, about an hour's drive away.

About 20 miles before Salamanca, you might want to stop at the huge bull on the left side of the road. There's a little dirt lane leading right up to it. As you get closer, it becomes more and more obvious it isn't alive. Bad boys climb it for a goofy photo. For a great photo op of Salamanca, complete with river reflection, stop at the edge of the city (at the light before the first bridge).

Ávila

Another popular side-trip from Madrid, Ávila is famous for its perfectly preserved medieval walls, as the birthplace of St. Teresa, and for its yummy *yema* treats. For more than 300 years, Ávila was on the battlefront between the Muslims and Christians, changing hands several times. Today perfectly peaceful Ávila has a charming old town. With several fine churches and monasteries, it makes for an enjoyable quick stop between Segovia and Salamanca (each about an hour away by car).

Orientation to Ávila

On a quick stop, everything in Ávila that matters is within a few blocks of the cathedral (which actually forms part of the east end of the city wall).

Tourist Information: The TI is just outside the wall gate near the cathedral (Mon-Sat 9:30-14:00 & 16:00-19:00, Sun 9:30-17:00, on Calle San Segundo, tel. 920-211-387). Another TI, with a friendlier staff, is located outside the wall, opposite the Basilica of San Vicente. They sell handy maps and mini guidebooks in English, which provide details on the palaces and churches. If you want to see more than the highlights, consider the general *Descubre Ávila*, which outlines 10 walking-tour itineraries in the old town (daily April-Oct 9:00-20:00, Nov-March 9:00-18:00, public WCs, tel. 920-354-000 ext. 370, www.avilaturismo.com).

Sightseeing Pass: The **VisitÁvila** pass is €15 and valid for 48 hours. It includes the wall, cathedral, museum of St. Teresa, the Mysticism Interpretation Center, and a handful of other sights. If you plan on seeing them all you can save a few euros.

ARRIVAL IN ÁVILA

Approaching by bus, train, or car, you'll need to make your way through the nondescript modern part of town to find the walled old town.

By Bus or Train: There are lockers at Ávila's bus station (use the newer-looking locks), but not at the train station.

The cathedral and wall are 15 minutes by foot from the bus station and 20 minutes from the train station. City buses #4 and #1 run from the train station to the Basilica of San Vicente (to find the bus stop, exit the station, walk one block, and turn right at the first street). When you arrive at the basilica, check the posted return bus schedule to ensure you make your train connection.

By Car: Drivers can use the public parking east of Puerta del Alcázar, just south of the cathedral, or at Parking Dornier.

Sights in Ávila

▲Walking the Wall

Built from around 1100 on even-more-ancient remains, Ávila's fortified wall is the oldest, most complete, and best-preserved in

Spain. It has four gates and three entrances, allowing visitors the chance to walk almost three-quarters of the wall: One entrance is just off Plaza de Santa Teresa (Puerta del Alcázar). The best one, which leads to a longer walk, starts from inside the TI on Calle San Segundo, by the gate closest to the cathedral (Puerta del Peso de la Harina) and takes you to the third and fourth gates: Puerta del Carmen (exit only) and Puerta Puente Adaja (on the end farthest from the cathedral—look for the door marked *subida a la muralla*).

An interesting paseo scene takes place along the wall each night—make your way along the southern wall (Paseo del Rastro) to Plaza de Santa Teresa for spectacular vistas across the plains.

Cost and Hours: €5, free Tue 14:00-16:00; open Tue-Sun 10:00-20:00, July-Aug until 21:00, Nov-March until 18:00, closed Mon except mid-June–mid-Oct; last entry 45 minutes before closing, ticket includes English audioguide.

Viewing the Wall: The best views of the wall itself are actually from street level. If you're wandering the city and see arched gates leading out of the old center, pop out to the other side and take in the impressive wall from the ground. Drivers can see the especially impressive north side as they circle to the right from Puerta de San Vicente to catch the highway to Salamanca.

Viewing Ávila from Cuatro Postes

The best overall view of the walled town of Ávila is about a mile away on the Salamanca road (N-501), at a clearly marked turnout for the Cuatro Postes (four posts). You can reach the Cuatro Postes by catching city bus #7 (€1) at the stop in front of the Basilica of San Vicente—it goes through the old town, then out to the Cuatro Postes viewpoint, back to San Vicente, and on to the RENFE train station. Bus #7 doesn't run on weekends; ask at the TI for walking directions (about 30 minutes each way), or take bus #1 to the stop nearest the Hermitage of San Segundo and walk five minutes to the viewpoint.

Ávila Cathedral (Catedral de Ávila)

While it started as Romanesque, Ávila's cathedral, finished in the 16th century, is considered the first Gothic cathedral in Spain. Its

Ávila

To
Salamanca
& **6**
via N-501

**CONVENT OF
ST. TERESA**

8

Puerta de
Santa Teresa

MYSTICISM
INTERPRETATION
CENTER

Parque
del Rastro

Adaja River

1 Hotel Palacio de los Velada

2 Hostal-Restaurante
Puerta del Alcázar

3 Hotel Arco San Vicente

4 La Bodeguita de
San Segundo Restaurante

5 Yemas Pastries

6 To Cuatro Postes Viewpoint

7 Wall Entrances (2 shown)

8 St. Teresa's Finger

CALLE DE LOS CASTILLA

PASAJE DE PRADO SANCHO

C. DE LOS CASTILLA

CALLE DE LA ENCARNACIÓN

PADRE BALBINO

CALLE DE VALLADOLID

CALLE DE LOS AJATES

PARILLA

CALLE DE SOLIS

P AVENIDA DE MADRID

Puerta del Mariscal

To Segovia
via N-501

Plaza Fuente El Sol

CALLE DE BRIEVA

C. DE BRACAMONTE

BASILICA OF
SAN VICENTE

MOSÉN RUBI CHAPEL

CALLE DE LÓPEZ NUÑEZ

Puerta de San Vicente

B

HUMILLADERO

M. BENAVITES

ESTEBAN DOMINGO

CALLE DEL TOSTADO

3

AVENIDA DE PORTUGAL

CALLE DE EDUARDO MARQUINA

Plaza Mercado Chico

MARKET

TOMÁS LUIS VICTORIA

1

ALEMANIA

4

2 *Puerta del Peso de la Harina*

To Train &
Bus Stations

REYES CATÓLICOS

7

LEALES

Plaza Italia

LESQUINAS

5

CABALLEROS

PEDRO DE LAGASCA

CARDENAL PLACITA Y DENIEL

DON GERÓNIMO

CATHEDRAL

CALLE DE SAN SEGUNDO

ESTRADA

DUQUE DE ALBA

Puerta del Alcázar

Plaza de Santa Teresa

P

S. JUAN DE LA CRUZ

7

PASEO DEL RASTRO

FRANCISCO GALLEGO

BAJADA DEL PEREGRINO

C. DE GRACIA

PASEO DE SANTO TOMÁS

S. JUAN BOSCO

PIEDRAHITA

CALLE DE CEBREROS

CALLE DE DEAN CASTOR ROBLEDO

CALLE DE SAN JOSÉ

CALLE DE PIEDRAHITA

CALLE JESÚS DEL GRAN PODER

CALLE DEL BARRACO

C. DE NUESTRA SEÑORA DE BONSOLES

CALLE DEL DOCTOR JESÚS GALÁN

100 Meters

100 Yards

position—with its granite apse actually part of the fortified wall—underlines the "medieval alliance between cross and sword." You can tour the cathedral, its sacristy, cloister, and museum—which includes an El Greco painting.

Cost and Hours: €5; Mon-Fri 10:00-17:30, Sat 10:00-19:00, Sun 12:00-15:00, generally closes one hour earlier off-season; last entry 45 minutes before closing, English audioguide-€2, Plaza de la Catedral.

Convent of St. Teresa

Built in the 17th century on the spot where the saint was born, this convent is a big hit with pilgrims (10-minute walk from cathedral). St. Teresa (1515-1582)—reforming nun, mystic, and writer—bought a house in Ávila and converted it into a convent with more stringent rules than the one she belonged to. She faced opposition in her hometown from rival nuns and those convinced her visions of heaven were the work of the devil. However, with her mentor and fellow mystic St. John of the Cross, she established convents of Discalced (shoeless) Carmelites throughout Spain, and her visions and writings led her to sainthood (she was canonized in 1622).

A lavishly gilded side chapel marks the actual place of her birth (left of main altar, door may be closed). A separate room of relics (outside, facing the church on your right, Sala de Reliquias) houses a shop that shows off Teresa's finger, complete with a fancy emerald ring, along with one of her sandals and the bones of St. John of the Cross. A museum dedicated to the saint is in the crypt at the side entrance and is worth a visit for devotees.

Cost and Hours: Convent—free, daily 9:30-13:30 & 15:30-19:30, off-season until 19:00, no photos of finger allowed; museum—€2, April-Oct Tue-Sun 10:00-14:00 & 16:00-20:00, shorter hours off-season, closed Mon year-round.

Mysticism Interpretation Center
(Centro de Interpretación del Misticismo)

If St. Teresa were alive today, she'd love this place, which explores modern mysticism from a Catholic perspective. Pick up the English handout that explains the art and texts, then take the elevator down on a "journey to the inner realms of the Self."

Cost and Hours: €3, Tue-Sun 10:00-13:30 & 16:00-17:30, closed Mon, Paseo del Rastro, tel. 920-212-154, www.avilamistica.es/interpretacion.

Yemas

These pastries, made by local nuns, are more or less soft-boiled egg yolks that have been cooled and sugared (*yema* means yolk). They're sold all over town. The shop **Las Delicias del Convento** is actually a retail outlet for the cooks of the convent (€4 for a small box, Tue-Sat 10:30-14:00 & 17:00-20:00, Sun 10:30-18:00, closed Mon, hours and closed day vary by season, between the TI and convent at Calle de los Reyes Católicos 12, tel. 920-220-293).

Sleeping in Ávila

Ávila is cold in fall, winter, and early spring, so you'll likely need to turn up the heat in these hotels.

$$$ Hotel Palacio de los Velada is antique and classy and faces the cathedral. Located in a five-centuries-old palace, it has 144 elegant rooms surrounding a huge and inviting arcaded courtyard (air-con, elevator, Plaza de la Catedral 10, tel. 920-255-100, www.veladahoteles.com, reserves.avila@veladahoteles.com).

$ Hostal Puerta del Alcázar has 27 basic yet spacious rooms right next to the Puerta del Peso de la Harina just outside the wall (family rooms, includes breakfast, air-con, San Segundo 38, tel. 920-211-074, www.puertadelalcazar.com, info@puertadelalcazar.com). It's home to a recommended restaurant.

$ Hotel Arco San Vicente has a friendly staff and a great location two blocks from the cathedral and one block from the Basilica of San Vicente, with its handy stop for buses to the train station or the Cuatro Postes viewpoint (air-con on second floor, elevator, limited pay parking, restaurant, Calle López Núñez 6, tel. 920-222-498, www.arcosanvicente.com, info@arcosanvicente.com).

Eating in Ávila

Ávila specialties include *chuletón,* a thick steak, and *judías del Barco de Ávila,* big white beans often cooked in a meaty stew. Around Plaza del Mercado Chico, the main square of the old center, are several good spots to try the stew or to have a reasonable fixed-price lunch (many of which include the *judías*).

$$$ La Bodeguita de San Segundo is good for a light lunch. Owned by a locally famous wine connoisseur, it serves fine wine by the glass with tapas such as smoked-cod salad and wild-mushroom scrambled eggs (Wed-Mon 11:00-24:00, closed some afternoons and all day Tue, outside the wall near the cathedral at San Segundo 19, tel. 920-228-634).

$$$ Hostal-Restaurante Puerta del Alcázar, filled with more locals than hotel guests, serves elaborate salads, fixed-price meals, and more. You can sit indoors or, even better, outdoors with cathedral views (Mon-Sat 13:00-16:00 & 21:00-23:30—outside tables open for dinner at 20:30 in summer, Sun 13:00-16:00, San Segundo 38, tel. 920-211-074).

Picnics: The town's market house is a good spot to pick up fruit and water (Mon-Thu 9:00-14:00 & 17:00-20:00, Fri 9:00-20:00, Sat 9:00-14:00, closed Sun, between Plaza del Mercado Chico and the cathedral). On Friday mornings, there's a farmers market on Plaza del Mercado Chico.

Café: For a pleasant break from sightseeing, pop in to the courtyard of the recommended **$$ Hotel Palacio de los Velada** for a coffee or hot chocolate.

Ávila Connections

The bus terminal is closed on Sundays, but you can purchase tickets when boarding the bus.

From Ávila to: Segovia (4 buses/day weekdays, 2/day weekends, 1 hour), **Madrid Chamartín** (trains run nearly hourly until 21:10, 1.5-2 hours), **Madrid Estación Sur** (9 buses/day weekdays, 6/day weekends, 1.5 hours), **Salamanca** (8 trains/day, 1-1.5 hours; 4-5 buses/day, 1.5 hours). Train info: Toll tel. 902-320-320, www.renfe.com. Bus info: Tel. 902-020-052 or 902-020-999 (Avanza and Auto-Res), www.avanzabus.com.

TOLEDO

An hour south of Madrid by car, Toledo teems with tourists, souvenirs, and great art by day, and delicious dinners, echoes of El Greco, and medieval magic by night. Incredibly well-preserved and full of cultural wonder, the entire city has been declared a national monument.

Spain's former capital crowds 2,500 years of tangled history—Roman, Jewish, Visigothic, Moorish, and Christian—onto a high, rocky perch protected on three sides by the Tajo River. To keep the city's historic appearance intact, the Spanish government has forbidden any modern exteriors. The rich mix of Jewish, Moorish, and Christian heritages makes it one of Europe's cultural highlights.

Today, Toledo thrives as a provincial capital—and tourist destination. A high-speed AVE train connection makes it a quick 30-minute ride from Madrid. The city's convention center (Palacio de Congresos Miradero), while of little interest to tourists, has a huge underground parking garage and escalators into town that make arrival by car efficient. The escalators make it easy to walk into town from the train station, too. The plan is for the old city center to be essentially traffic-free (except for residents' cars, public transit, and service vehicles).

Despite its tremendously kitschy tourist vibe, this stony wonderland remains the historic, artistic, and spiritual center of Spain. Toledo sits enthroned on its history, much as it was when Europe's most powerful monarch, the Holy Roman Emperor Charles V (King Charles I in Spain), and its most famous resident artist, El Greco, called it home.

PLANNING YOUR TIME

To properly see Toledo's sights—including its museums (great El Greco) and cathedral (best in Spain)—and to experience its medieval atmosphere (wonderful after dark), you'll need at least a night and a day. If you have time, spend a second day in the city for a more relaxing visit. If you're traveling to Toledo only for the day, keep in mind that early and late trains tend to sell out to commuters and day-trippers. Day-tripping tourists can pack the city during midday.

Here's a good one-day plan: Upon arrival, take the Toledo City Tour bus to the viewpoint overlooking the town's impressive skyline, immortalized by El Greco. Then head to the cathedral. Other top stops are the Army Museum (for history aficionados) and the Santa Cruz Museum (for art lovers). El Greco fans will enjoy seeing his art in chapels and museums around town. Plan carefully for lunchtime closures and take a rest break during Toledo's notorious midday heat in summer. In the evening, dine well—*carcamusas* (pork chili), anyone?—and cap your evening with a stroll.

With a second day, choose from Toledo's historic synagogues, monastery, Visigothic museum, more art museums, and many shops. Wander the back lanes, sample sweet *mazapán*, and people-watch in the main square, Plaza de Zocodover.

Orientation to Toledo

Toledo sits atop a circular hill, with the cathedral roughly dead-center. Lassoed into a tight tangle of streets by the sharp bend of

the Tajo River (called the "Tejo" in Portugal, where it hits the Atlantic at Lisbon), Toledo has Spain's most confusing medieval street plan. But it's a small town within its walls, with only 10,000 inhabitants (84,000 live in greater Toledo, including its modern suburbs). The major sights are well-signposted, and most locals will politely point you in the right direction if you ask. (You are, after all, the town's bread and butter.)

The top sights stretch from the main square, Plaza de Zocodover (zoh-koh-doh-VEHR), southwest along Calle del Comercio (a.k.a. Calle Ancha, "Wide Street") to the cathedral, and beyond that to Santo Tomé and more. The visitor's city lies basically along this small but central street, and most tourists never stray from this axis. Make a point to get lost. The town is compact. When it's time to return to someplace familiar, pull out the map or

Toledo Overview

To Madrid
via A-42

To Ávila
via N-403

BULLRING

BUS STATION

AV. DE LA RECONQUISTA

CARDENAL TAVERA

AV. DE CARLOS III

ROMAN CIRCUS RUINS

PICNIC ZONE

To Train Station & Consuegra

"EL MARTES" FLEA MARKET

CARRERA

PUENTE AZARQUIEL

PASEO ROSA

CITY WALLS

BISAGRA GATE

MIRADERO

AV. DE LA VEGA

CARRETAS

ESCALATORS

ESCALATOR

OLD PR.

MEZQUITA

Plaza de Zocodover

SANTA CRUZ MUSEUM

HOSTEL

PUERTA CAMBRÓN

VISIGOTHIC MUSEUM

POST

COMMERCIO

SAN JUAN DE LOS REYES

C. ÁNGEL S. TOMÉ

MKT.

ALCÁZAR

SINAGOGA DE SANTA MARÍA LA BLANCA

SANTO TOMÉ

CATHEDRAL

MUSEO VICTORIO MACHO

EL GRECO MUSEUM

SINAGOGA DEL TRÁNSITO

Path

CARRETERA PIEDRABUENA

VIEWPOINT

C. ALTA

To CM-40 Motorway

Tajo River

See detail map

CARRETERA CIRCUNVALACIÓN

C. COBISA

C. COBISA

PARADOR

C. AZUELA

300 Meters

300 Yards

TOLEDO

ask, "*¿Para Plaza de Zocodover?*" From the far end of town, handy bus #12 circles back to Plaza de Zocodover.

While the city is very hilly (in Toledo, they say everything's uphill—it certainly feels that way), nothing is more than a short hike away.

TOURIST INFORMATION

Toledo has four TIs, which share a website: www.toledo-turismo. com. At the train station, the official TI is just down the track as you get off the train (daily 9:30-15:00, tel. 925-239-121)—but bypass the first information booth on the concourse, which mostly sells services. Other TIs are at Bisagra Gate, in a freestanding building in the park just outside the gate (Mon-Sat 10:00-18:00, Sun until 14:00, tel. 925-211-005); on Plaza del Ayuntamiento near the cathedral (daily 10:00-18:00, WC, tel. 925-254-030); and on Plaza de Zocodover (Mon-Sat 10:00-18:00, Sun until 14:00).

Sightseeing Passes: Skip Toledo's sightseeing passes. You'd pay more for any of the **Toledo Pass** or **Toledo Card** options than you would buying individual tickets.

The **Pulsera Turística** wristband (€9, sold at participating sights) doesn't cover the city's top three sights but makes sense if you want to see at least four of its covered monuments and churches (Santo Tomé, Sinagoga de Santa María la Blanca, San Juan de los Reyes Monasterio, Mezquita del Cristo de la Luz, Church of El Salvador, Real Colegio de Doncellas Nobles, and Church of San Ildefonso/Jesuitas; sold at participating sights, no time limit as long as it stays on your wrist, nontransferable).

ARRIVAL IN TOLEDO

"Arriving" in Toledo means getting uphill to Plaza de Zocodover. As the bus and train stations are outside the town center and parking can be a challenge, this involves a taxi, a city bus, or a walk plus a ride up a series of escalators.

By Train: Toledo's early-20th-century train station is Neo-Moorish and a national monument itself for its architecture and art, both of which celebrate the three cultures that coexisted here.

Remember that early and late trains can sell out; reserve ahead. If you haven't yet bought a ticket for your departure from Toledo (even if it's for the next day), get it before you leave the Toledo station and choose a specific time rather than leave it open-ended. (If you prefer more flexibility, take the bus instead—see "By Bus" next.)

From the train station to Plaza de Zocodover, it's a €4.50 **taxi** ride (to hotels, the ride is metered), a 25-minute walk with the help of escalators, or an easy ride on various buses. You can take **city bus** #5, #11, #61, or #62; leaving the station, you'll see the bus stop 30 yards to the right (€1.40, pay on bus, confirm by asking, "*¿Para Plaza de Zocodover?*"). The red **Toledo City Tour bus**, which circles the city, also picks up outside the station, and stops briefly at the famous El Greco viewpoint before heading up to Plaza de Zocodover.

To **walk** into town, turn right as you leave the station and follow the fuchsia line on the sidewalk labeled *Up Toledo, Follow the Line.* Track this line (and periodic escalator symbols) past a bus stop, over the bridge, around the roundabout to the left, and into a bus parking area. From here, go up a series of escalators that take you to the center of town: You'll emerge about a block downhill from Plaza de Zocodover.

By Bus: At the bus station, buses park downstairs. Luggage lockers and a small bus-information office—where you can buy

Toledo's History

Perched strategically in the center of Iberia, for centuries Toledo was a Roman transportation hub with a thriving Jewish population. After Rome fell, the city became a Visigothic capital (A.D. 554). In 711 the Moors (Muslims) made it a regional center. The city was reconquered by Christians in 1085, but many Moors remained in Toledo, tolerated and respected as scholars and craftsmen.

Whereas Jews were commonly persecuted elsewhere in Europe, Toledo's Jewish community—educated, wealthy, and cosmopolitan—thrived from the city's earliest times. Jews of Spanish origin are called Sephardic Jews. The American expression "Holy Toledo" likely originated from the Sephardic Jews who eventually immigrated to America. To them, Toledo was the holiest Jewish city in Europe...Holy Toledo!

During its medieval heyday (c. 1350), Toledo was a city of the humanities, where God was known by many names. In this haven of cultural diversity, people of different faiths lived together in harmony.

Toledo remained Spain's political capital until 1561, when Philip II moved to more-spacious Madrid. Historians fail to agree on the reason for the move; some say that Madrid was the logical place for a capital in the geographic center of newly formed *España,* while others say that Philip wanted to separate politics from religion. (Toledo remained Spain's religious capital.) Whatever the reason, when the king moved out, Toledo was mothballed, only to be rediscovered by 19th-century Romantic travelers. They wrote of it as a mystical place, which it remains today.

locker tokens—are upstairs opposite the cafeteria. From the bus station, Plaza de Zocodover is a 15-minute **hike,** a €4.50 **taxi** ride, or a short **bus** ride (catch #5 or #12 downstairs; €1.40, pay on bus). On foot, exit the bus station, cross a roundabout, and walk up Avenida Castilla la Mancha (with the river on your left) until you reach a bus parking area with escalators that take you up into town near Plaza de Zocodover.

Before leaving the station, confirm your departure time (around 2/hour to Madrid). Buses don't tend to get booked up, and you can put off buying a return ticket until just minutes before you leave Toledo. Specify that you'd like a *directo* bus (the *ruta* trip takes longer—1 hour versus 1.5 hours). But if you miss the *directo* bus (or

TOLEDO

Central Toledo

ROMAN CIRCUS RUINS

"EL MARTES" FLEA MARKET

N

100 Meters
100 Yards

AV. DE LA RECONQUISTA

AV. DE CARLOS III

ALFONSO

Glorieta de la Reconquista

AV. DE LA CAVA

P

ESCALATORS

CITY WALLS

SUBIDA LA GRANJA

PASEO DE RECAREDO

CALLE REAL

CALLE MERCED

S. ILDEFONSO

To CM-40 Ring Road & Parador

CUESTA SANTA LEOCADIA

Plaza de Padilla

TEND.

PACHECO

SAN MARTÍN

C. PINTOR M. MORENO

COL. DONCELLAS

MARÍA

S. ROMAN

BAJADA DE SAN MARTÍN

Plaza San Juan de los Reyes

C. DE BULAS

VISIGOTHIC MUSEUM

B #12

C. GORGO ROJAS

C. DE ALFONSO XII

BAJADA DE SANTA ANA

SAN JUAN DE LOS REYES

CALLE DEL ÁNGEL

C. SANTO TOMÉ

CALLE DE EL SALVADOR

CALLE REYES CATÓLICOS

SINAGOGA DE SANTA MARÍA LA BLANCA

SANTO TOMÉ

PUENTE DE SAN MARTÍN

Cliffs

JUDERÍA

DE DIOS

B #12

TALLER MORO

DE SANTA URSULA

MUSEO VICTORIO MACHO

SAN JUAN

EL GRECO MUSEUM

ZAMORANO KNIFE WORKSHOP

SINAGOGA DEL TRÁNSITO

PASEO TRÁNSITO

CARRETERA DE PIEDRABUENA

Tajo River

Park

CALLE DESCALZOS

PASEO SAN CRISTOBAL

SAN TORCUATO

SAN BARTOLOMÉ

Note: Some street width exaggerated for clarity

S. CIPRIANO

CALLE CARRERAS

Cliffs

TOLEDO

To Bullring & Madrid

CARD. TAV.

CALLE DE LA CARRERA

PERALA

C. CARRERA

To Bus Station & P

PUENTE AZARQUIEL

CITY WALLS

To Train Station, Consuegra & P

VI

BISAGRA GATE

C. REAL DEL ARRABAL

CALLE AZACANES

CALLE DE LAS CARRETAS

CALLE DE GERARDO LOBO

PASEO ROSA

MEZQUITA

C. CRISTO DE LA LUZ

CUESTA CARMELITAS DESCALZAS

C. NUÑEZ DE ARCE

Miradero P

ESCALATOR

SANTA CRUZ MUSEUM

OLD BRIDGE

Plaza de San Agustín

SILLERIA

C. CADENAS

CALLE DE ALFILERITOS

Plaza de Zocodover

NUEVA

C. CERVANTES

AQUEDUCT

EL SABIO

POST

CALLE DE LA PLATA

CALLE COMERCIO

BARRIO REY

B B

ALFERECES

CUESTA DE CARLOS V

C. NUNCIO VIEJO

SINAGOGA

TONERIAS

TRASTAMARA

JUAN LABRADOR

ALCÁZAR (ARMY MUSEUM)

PUENTE NUEVO ALCÁNTARA

LA TRINIDAD

Plaza Mayor

MARKET

J. BIZ

MOSCARDÓ P

Plaza del Consistorio

CATHEDRAL

LA CANDELARIA

Plaza del Ayuntamiento

CARD. CISNEROS

& CITY HALL

SANTA ISABEL

Plaza de San Justo

SAN JUSTO

PASEO DE CABESTREROS

PASEO DE CABESTREROS

CALLE AVE MARÍA

COLEGIO DE INFANTES

CALLE POZO AMARGO

BAJADA DEL BARCO

C. BARCO

CALLE CANDELARIA

Tajo River

S. CATALINA

CALLE DE PLEGADERO

Cliffs

SANTA CATALINA

SAN SEBASTIÁN

One-way streets →

Traffic barriers

To Parador & CM-40 Ring Road

VIEWPOINT

if it's sold out), the *ruta* option offers a peek of off-the-beaten-path Madrid suburbia.

By Car: If you're arriving by car, enjoy a scenic big-picture orientation by following the *Ronda de Toledo* signs on a big circular drive around the city. You'll view the city from many angles along the Circunvalación road across the Tajo Gorge. Stop at a viewpoint or drive to Parador de Toledo, just south of town, for the view (from the balcony) that El Greco made famous in his portrait of Toledo. The best time for this trip is the magic hour before sunset, when the top viewpoints are busy with tired old folks and frisky young lovers.

A car is useless within Toledo's city walls, where the narrow, twisting streets are no fun to navigate. Many hotels offer discounted parking rates at nearby garages; ask when making your reservation.

The most convenient place to park is in the big **Miradero Garage** at the convention center (€16/day; drive through Bisagra Gate, go uphill half a mile, look for sign on the left directing you to *Plaza del Miradero*). There's parking farther into town at the **Alcázar Garage** (just past the Alcázar—€2/hour, €20/day). There are also two big, free, **uncovered parking lots:** the one between the river and the bus station is best if you want to use the escalators to get up to the center; the other lot is between the river and the train station. North of the city walls, you'll find parking and another set of escalators going up near the **Glorieta de la Reconquista roundabout,** but at the top you'll still be far from Plaza de Zocodover.

HELPFUL HINTS

Useful App: Toledo Be Your Guide is a simple but useful free travel app. Ignore the sections on restaurants, shopping, and nightlife; instead select "Attractions" for info on sights around town.

Taxis: There are three taxi stands in the old center: Plaza de Zocodover, Bisagra Gate, and Santo Tomé. Taxis routinely give visitors scenic circles around town with photo stops for around €15.

Local Guidebook: Consider the readable *Toledo: Its Art and Its History* (€4-6, same text and photos in both big and small versions, sold all over town). It explains all the sights (which generally provide no on-site information) and gives you a photo to point at and say, "*¿Dónde está...?*"

Tours in Toledo

▲Tourist Bus

Toledo City Tour offers three tourist bus options for day-trippers. For transportation with a view to the city center, meet the bus at the train station, and ride along the river to the famous "El Greco" lookout point, where you can get off for a five-minute photo stop. Then the bus continues around the city and up to Plaza de Zocodover, where you can get off and visit Toledo. Pay a little more, and you get a hop-on, hop-off version that allows you to stop at the photo viewpoint, Bisagra Gate, and the San Martín medieval bridge—but be prepared to wait an hour for the next bus (€5.50 with one stop, €9 for hop-on, hop-off option, pay at stand in train station; departures timed to train arrivals—first bus leaves train station at 9:50, then almost hourly until about 20:00 in summer, shorter hours off-season; longer rides include recorded English commentary on headphones; tel. 925-950-000, www.toledo-turismo.com/en/tourist-bus_555). Skip the *lanzadera* shuttle bus, which offers the same ride up to Plaza de Zocodover as the city bus described earlier, but costs about €1 more.

TOLEDO

Tourist Train

For a pleasant city overview, hop on the **TrainVision Tourist Train** for a 45-minute putt-putt through Toledo and around the Tajo River Gorge. It's a cheesy but fine way for nondrivers to enjoy views of the city from across the Tajo Gorge (€5.50, buy ticket from kiosk on Plaza de Zocodover, leaves Plaza de Zocodover daily 1-2/hour 10:00-18:30, later in summer, recorded English/Spanish commentary, tel. 625-301-890). For the best views, sit on the right side, not behind the driver. There's a five-minute photo stop at the viewpoint.

Public Buses

For the cheapest tour, use public transportation. Take the "Bus #12 Self-Guided Tour" through town. Or, for a "gorge-ous" loop trip, try bus #71, which leaves from opposite the entrance of the Alcázar (hourly 7:45-21:45) and offers the same classic view across the gorge as the tourist train; its route circles around to El Greco's famous viewpoint, where you can hop off and snap some photos, then wait about an hour at the same stop for the next bus to take you back.

Local Guide

Juan José Espadas (a.k.a. Juanjo) is a good guide who enjoys sharing his hometown in English. He gracefully brings meaning to the complex mix of Toledo's history, art, religion, and culture (€150/3 hours, tel. 667-780-475, juanjo@guiadetoledo.es).

Sights in Toledo

▲▲▲TOLEDO CATHEDRAL

Holy Toledo! Spain's leading Catholic city has a magnificent cathedral. Shoehorned into the old center, its exterior is hard to appreci-

ate. (As is so typical of religious sites in hard-fought Iberia, it was built after the Reconquista on the spot where a mosque once stood.) But the interior is so lofty, rich, and vast that it'll have you wandering around like a Pez dispenser stuck open, whispering "Wow." The sacristy has a collection of paintings that would put any museum on the map.

TOLEDO

Cost and Hours: €10 includes audioguide and Colegio de Infantes (described later); €12.50 also includes trip up bell tower at assigned times; tickets sold in shop opposite church entrance on Calle Cardenal Cisneros; open Mon-Sat 10:00-18:30, Sun 14:00-18:30, open earlier for prayer only; tel. 925-222-241.

➋ Self-Guided Tour

Wander among the pillars, thick and sturdy as a redwood forest. Sit under one and imagine a time when the light bulbs were candles and the tourists were pilgrims—when every window provided spiritual as well as physical light. The cathedral is primarily Gothic. But because it took more than 250 years to build (1226-1493)—with continuous embellishments after that (every archbishop wanted to leave his imprint)—it's a mix of styles, including Gothic, Renaissance, Baroque, and Neoclassical. Enjoy the elaborate wrought-iron work, lavish wood carvings, and window after colorful window of 500-year-old stained glass. Circling the interior are ornate chapels, purchased by the town's most noble families, and the sacristy, with its world-class collection of El Grecos and works by other famous painters.

This confusing collage of great Spanish art deserves a close look. Hire a private guide, discreetly freeload on a tour (they come by every few minutes during peak season), listen to the audioguide, or follow this quick tour.

• *First, walk to the high altar.*

High Altar: Climb two steps and grip the iron grille as you marvel at one of the most stunning altars in Spain. Real gold on wood, by Flemish, French, and local artists, it's one of the country's best pieces of Gothic art. Study the wall of scenes from the life of Christ, frame by frame. All the images seem to celebrate the colorful Assumption of Mary in the center, with Mary escorted by six

Toledo at a Glance

▲▲▲**Toledo Cathedral** One of Europe's best, with a marvelously vast interior and great art. **Hours:** Mon-Sat 10:00-18:30, Sun 14:00-18:30. See page 150.

▲▲**Army Museum** Covers all things military; located in the imposing fortress, the Alcázar. **Hours:** Thu-Tue 10:00-17:00, closed Wed. See page 159.

▲**Santa Cruz Museum** Renaissance building housing wonderful artwork, including eight El Grecos. **Hours:** Mon-Sat 9:45-18:30, Sun 10:00-14:00. See page 157.

▲**Santo Tomé** Simple chapel with El Greco's masterpiece, *The Burial of the Count of Orgaz.* **Hours:** Daily 10:00-18:45, until 17:45 mid-Oct-Feb. See page 162.

▲**El Greco Museum** Small collection of paintings, including the *View and Plan of Toledo,* El Greco's panoramic map of the city. **Hours:** Tue-Sat 9:30-19:30—Nov-Feb until 18:00, Sun 10:00-15:00, closed Mon. See page 163.

▲**Sinagoga del Tránsito** Museum of Toledo's Jewish past. **Hours:** Tue-Sat 9:30-19:30—until 18:00 off-season, Sun 10:00-15:00, closed Mon. See page 164.

▲**Museo Victorio Macho** Collection of 20th-century Toledo sculptor's works, with expansive river-gorge view. **Hours:** Mon-Fri 10:00-14:00 & 17:00-19:00, closed Sat-Sun. See page 165.

▲**San Juan de los Reyes Monasterio** Church/monastery intended as final resting place of Isabel and Ferdinand. **Hours:** Daily 10:00-18:45, until 17:45 mid-Oct-March. See page 166.

Visigothic Museum Romanesque church housing the only Visigothic artifacts in town. **Hours:** Tue-Sat 10:00-14:30 & 16:00-18:15, Sun 10:00-14:00, closed Mon. See page 161.

Sinagoga de Santa María la Blanca Synagogue that harmoniously combines Toledo's three religious influences: Jewish, Christian, and Moorish. **Hours:** Daily 10:00-18:45, until 17:45 in winter. See page 166.

Toledo's Cathedral

SAN BLAS CHAPEL

PUERTA DEL RELOJ

ARCO DE PALACIO

CLOISTER

SACRISTY

NEW KINGS CHAPEL

TREASURY

TRANSPARENTE

PUERTA PERDÓN

Plaza del Ayuntamiento

MOZARABIC CHAPEL

CHOIR

HIGH ALTAR

GRILLE

CHAPTER HOUSE

PUERTA LLANA MAIN ENTRANCE

PUERTA LEONES

To City Hall &

CALLE CARDENAL CISNEROS

To Colegio de Infantes

WC BUY TICKETS HERE AT SHOP

20 Meters

20 Yards

To Plaza de Zocodover

upwardly mobile angels. The crucified Christ on top is nine feet tall—taller than the lower statues—to keep this towering altar approachable. Don't miss the finely worked gold-plated iron grille itself—considered to be the best from the 16th century in Spain.

• *About-face to the...*

Choir: Facing the high altar, the choir is famous for its fine and richly symbolic carving. It all seems to lead to the archbishop's throne in the rear center. First, look carefully at the fine alabaster relief in the center (about where the bishop would rest his head on his throne): It shows a seventh-century Visigothic miracle, when Mary came down to give the local bishop the holy robe, legitimizing Toledo as the spiritual capital (and therefore political capital) of Spain.

Because of its primacy in Iberia, Toledo was the first city in the crosshairs of the Reconquista Christian forces. They recaptured the city in 1085 (over 400 years before they retook Granada). The fall of Toledo marked the beginning of the end of the Muslim domination of Iberia. A local saying goes, "A carpet frays from the edges, but the carpet of Al-Andalus (Muslim Spain) frayed from the very center" (meaning Toledo).

The lower wooden stalls are decorated with scenes showing the steady one-city-at-a-time finale of the Christian Reconquista, when Muslims were slowly pushed back into Africa. Set in the last decade of the Reconquista, these images celebrate the retaking of the towns around Granada: Each idealized castle has the reconquered town's name on it, culminating in the final victory at Granada in 1492 (these two reliefs flank the archbishop's throne). Although the castles are romanticized, the carvings of the clothing, armor, and weaponry are so detailed and accurate that historians have studied them to learn the evolution of weaponry.

The upper stalls feature Old Testament figures—an alabaster genealogy of the church—starting with Adam and Eve and working counterclockwise to Joseph and "S. M. Virgo Mater" (St. Mary the Virgin Mother). Notice how the statues on the Adam and Eve side (left) are more lifelike; they were done by Alonso Berruguete, nicknamed "the Michelangelo of Spain" for his realistic figures. All this imagery is designed to remind viewers of the legitimacy of the bishop's claims to religious power. Check out the seat backs, made of carved walnut and featuring New Testament figures—with Peter (key) and Paul (sword)—alongside the archbishop himself.

And, as is typical of choir decoration, the carvings on the misericords (the tiny seats that allowed tired worshippers to lean while they "stand") represent various sins and feature the frisky, folksy, sexy, profane art of the day. Apparently, since you sat on it, it could never be sacred anyway.

Take a moment to absorb the marvelous complexity, harmony, and cohesiveness of the art around you. Look up. There are two fine pipe organs: one early 18th-century Baroque and the other late 18th-century Neoclassical. As you leave the choir, note the serene beauty of the 13th-century Madonna and child at the front (Virgin Blanca), thought to be a gift from the French king to Spain. Its naturalism and intimacy was proto-Renaissance—radical in its day.

The iron grille of the choir is notable for the dedication of the man who built it. Domingo de Céspedes, a Toledo ironworker, accepted the commission to build the grille for 6,000 ducats. The project, which lasted from 1541 to 1548, was far more costly than he anticipated. The medieval Church didn't accept cost overruns, so to finish it he sold everything he owned and went into debt. He died a poor—but honorable—man. (That's a charming story, but the artistic iron gate before the high altar—described earlier—is the true treasure.)

TOLEDO

• *Face the altar, and go around it to your right to the...*

Chapter House (Sala Capitular): Under its lavish ceiling, a fresco celebrates the humanism of the Italian Renaissance. There's a Deposition (taking crucified Jesus off the cross), a pietà, and a Resurrection on the front wall; they face a fascinating Last Judgment, where the seven sins are actually spelled out in the gang going to hell: arrogance (the guy striking a pose), avarice (holding his bag of coins), lust (the easy woman with the lovely hair and fiery crotch), anger (shouting at lust), gluttony (the fat guy), envy, and laziness. Think about how instructive this was in 1600.

Below the fresco, a pictorial review of 1,900 years of Toledo archbishops circles the room. The upper row of portraits dates from the 16th century. Except for the last two, these were not painted from life (the same face seems to be recycled over and over). The lower portraits were added one at a time from 1515 on and are of more historic than artistic interest. Imagine sitting down to church business surrounded by all this tradition and theology.

The current cardinal—whose portrait will someday grace the next empty panel—is the top religious official in Spain. He's conservative on issues unpopular with Spain's young: divorce, abortion, and contraception. When he speaks, it makes news all over Spain.

As you leave, notice the iron-pumping cupids carved into the pear-tree panels lining the walls.

• *Go behind the high altar to find the...*

Transparente: The Transparente is a unique feature of the cathedral. In the 1700s, a hole was cut into the ceiling to let a sun-beam brighten Mass. The opening faces east, and each morning the rising sun reminds all that God is light. Melding this big hole with the Gothic church presented a challenge: The result was a Baroque masterpiece. Gape up at this riot of angels doing flip-flops, babies breathing thin air, bottoms of feet, and gilded sunbursts. Carved out of marble from Italy, it's bursting with motion and full of energy. Appreciate those tough little cherubs who are supporting the whole thing—they've been waiting for help for about 300 years now.

Step back to study the altar, which looks chaotic, but is actually structured thoughtfully: The good news of salvation springs from Baby Jesus, up past the archangels (including one in the middle who knows how to hold a big fish correctly) to the Last Supper high above, and beyond into the light-filled dome. I like it, as did (I guess) the two long-dead cardinals whose faded red hats hang from the edge of the hole. (A perk that only a cardinal enjoys is to choose a burial place in the cathedral, and hang his hat over that spot until the hat rots.)

• *Now peek into the...*

Chapel of the New Kings (Capilla de Reyes Nuevos): In the 16th century, Emperor Charles V moved the tombs of eight kings who reigned before Ferdinand and Isabel to this spot. As you exit the chapel back into the apse, pass through a short hall and look for a facsimile of a 700-year-old Bible hand-copied and beautifully illustrated by French monks; it was a gift from St. Louis, the 13th-century king of France. Imagine looking at these lavish illustrations with medieval eyes—an exquisite experience. (The precious and fragile lambskin original is preserved out of public view.)

• *Enter into the apse, where the next door on your right takes you into the...*

Sacristy: The cathedral's sacristy is a mini Prado, with 19 El Grecos and masterpieces by Francisco de Goya, Titian, Diego Velázquez, Caravaggio, and Giovanni Bellini. First, notice the fine perspective work on the ceiling. It was painted by Neapolitan artist Lucca Giordano around 1690. (You can see the artist himself—with his circa-1690 spectacles—painted onto the door high above on the left; look for it at the base of the ceiling.) Then walk to the end of the room for the most important painting in the collection, El Greco's *The Spoliation* (a.k.a. *Christ Being Stripped of His Garments*).

Spain's original great painter was Greek, and this is the first masterpiece he created after arriving in Toledo. El Greco's painting from 1579 hangs exactly where he intended it to—in the room where priests prepared themselves for Mass. It shows Jesus surrounded by a sinister mob and suffering the humiliation of being stripped in public before his execution.

The scarlet robe is about to be yanked off, and the women (lower left) avert their eyes, turning to watch a carpenter at work (lower right) who bores the holes for nailing Jesus to the cross. While the carpenter bears down, Jesus—the other carpenter—looks up to heaven. The contrast between the motley crowd gambling for his clothes and Jesus' noble face underscores the quiet dignity with which he endures this ignoble treatment. Jesus' delicate white hand stands out from the flaming red tunic with an odd gesture that's common in El Greco's paintings. Some say this was the way Christians of the day swore they were true believers, not merely Christians-in-name-only, such as former Muslims or Jews who converted to survive.

On the right is a religious painting by Goya, the *Betrayal of Christ,* which shows Judas preparing to kiss Jesus, thus identifying him to the Roman soldiers. Across the room is a scene rarely

TOLEDO

painted: a touching El Greco portrait called *St. Joseph and the Christ Child*. Joseph is walking with Jesus, just as El Greco enjoyed walking around the Toledo countryside with his sons. Notice Joseph's gentle expression—and the Toledo views in the background.

Enjoy the many other El Grecos here, as well as the work of other master artists.

• *As you step out of the sacristy, walk through an open-air courtyard and back into the main naves of the cathedral. Look high up to your right at the oldest stained glass in the church (from the 14th century). Then, passing a chapel reserved for worship, just before the treasury, you come to...*

The Cloister: The cloister is worth a stroll for its finely carved colonnade. Take a peaceful detour to the funerary San Blas Chapel. The ceiling over the alabaster tomb of a bishop is a fresco by a student of Giotto (a 14th-century Italian Renaissance master).

Treasury: The *tesoro* is tiny, but radiant with riches. The highlight is the 10-foot-high, 430-pound monstrance—the tower designed to hold the Holy Communion wafer (the host) during the festival of Corpus Christi ("body of Christ") as it's paraded through the city. Built in 1517 by Enrique de Arfe, it's made of 5,000 individual pieces held together by 12,500 screws. There are diamonds, emeralds, rubies, and 400 pounds of gold-plated silver. The inner part (which is a century older) is 35 pounds of solid gold. Yeow. The base is a later addition from the Baroque period.

Mozarabic Chapel: Before 10:00, the cathedral is open only for prayer (from north entrance). If you're here to worship at the 9:00 Mass (daily except Sunday), you can peek into the otherwise-locked Mozarabic Chapel (Capilla Mozárabe). This Visigothic Mass (in Latin) is the oldest surviving Christian ritual in Western Europe. You're welcome to partake in this stirring example of peaceful coexistence of faiths. Toledo's proud Mozarabic community of 1,500 people traces its roots to Visigothic times.

Bell Tower: If you paid for the bell tower, meet just to the left of the San Blas Chapel at your assigned time. You'll climb up several sections of tight spiral staircases to reach panoramic views of Toledo and the largest (though cracked) bell in Spain.

CENTRAL TOLEDO

In addition to the cathedral, the city's historic core contains these sights:

Plaza de Zocodover

The main square is Toledo's center and your gateway to the old town. The word "Zocodover" derives from the Arabic for "livestock market."

Toledo is the state capital of

Castile-La Mancha, and the regional governmental building over-looks Plaza de Zocodover. Look for the three flags: one for Europe, one for Spain, and one for Castile-La Mancha. And speaking of universal symbols—find the low-key McDonald's. A source of controversy, it was finally allowed...with only one small golden arch. Next came the bigger Burger King, which no one blinked at twice.

The square is a big local hangout and city hub. Once the scene of Inquisition judgments and bullfights, today it's a lot more peaceful. Old people arrive in the morning, and young people come in the evening. The goofy tourist train leaves from here, as well as the Tourist Bus and city buses #5, #11, #61, and #62, which lumber to the train station. Just uphill, near the taxi stand, is the stop for bus #12, which travels around the old town to Santo Tomé (and works as a good self-guided tour) and for bus #71, which heads out to the panoramic viewpoint made famous by El Greco.

Colegio de Infantes

The cathedral displays its fine collection of tapestries and vestments at the nearby Colegio de Infantes. Many of the 17th-century tapestries here are still used to decorate the cathedral during one of the city's biggest events, the festival of Corpus Christi. You'll also find the lavish-but-faded *Astrolabe Tapestry* (c. 1480, Belgian). It shows a new view of the cosmos at the dawn of the Age of Discovery: God (far left) oversees all, as Atlas (with the help of two women and a crank handle) spins the universe, containing the circular Earth. The wisdom gang (far right) heralds the wonders of the coming era. Rather than a map of Earth, this is a chart showing the cosmic order of things as the constellations spin around the stationary North Star (center).

Cost and Hours: €2, €10 includes cathedral; €12.50 includes cathedral and bell tower, daily 10:00-18:00, from the cathedral go down Calle Barco to Plaza Colegio Infantes, tel. 925-258-723.

▲Santa Cruz Museum (Museo de Santa Cruz)

This stately Renaissance building was formerly an orphanage and hospital, funded by money left by the humanist and diplomat Cardinal Mendoza when he died in 1495. The cardinal, confirmed as Chancellor of Castile by Queen Isabel, was so influential that he was called "the third royal." The museum's collections feature Roman and Arabic archaeology; paintings of the 16th and 17th centuries (including eight El Grecos); and traditional decorative arts such as ceramics and glass.

Cost and Hours: Museum—€5, buy ticket at machine in entrance hall (attendants can help); courtyard—free, get ticket at window in entry; open Mon-Sat 9:45-18:30, Sun 10:00-14:00; from Plaza de Zocodover, go through arch to Calle Miguel de Cervantes 3; tel. 925-221-036, www.patrimoniohistoricoclm.es.

Visiting the Museum: The building's facade still wears bullet scars from the Spanish Civil War. The exterior, cloister arches, and stairway leading to the upper cloister are fine examples of the Plateresque style. This ornate strain of Spanish Renaissance is named for the fancy work of silversmiths of the 16th century. During this time (c. 1500-1550), the royal court moved from Toledo to Madrid—when Madrid was a village and Toledo was a world power. (You'll see no Plateresque work in Madrid.) Note the Renaissance-era mathematics, ideal proportions, round arches, square squares, and classic columns.

The museum's **El Greco** paintings are its highlight. Most impressive is *Assumption of Mary,* a spiritual poem on canvas. This altarpiece, finished one year before El Greco's death in 1614, is the culmination of his unique style, combining all his techniques to express an otherworldly event.

Study the *Assumption* (which some believe is misnamed and actually shows the Immaculate Conception—the plaque describing the work entitles it both *Inmaculada Concepción* and *Inmaculada Ovalle,* for the family who commissioned it). Bound to earth, the city of Toledo sleeps, but a vision is taking place overhead. An angel in a billowing robe, as if doing the breaststroke with his wings, flies up, supporting Mary, the mother of Christ. She floats up through warped space, to be serenaded by angels and wrapped in the radiant light of the Holy Spirit. Mary flickers and ripples, charged from within by her spiritual ecstasy, caught up in a vision that takes her breath away. No painter before or since has captured the supernatural world better than El Greco.

Free Courtyard Visit: Even if you skip the museum, it's possible to step into the building's peaceful Renaissance courtyard. Enter the front doorway, and obtain a free ticket from the attendant. On the lower courtyard level, walk around to view exposed ancient artifacts; there are no ropes or motion detectors to stop you from getting close to this history. In the corner opposite the entrance you'll see funerary columns, a third-century Roman mosaic that depicts the four seasons, and a marble well bearing an Arabic inscription. Note the grooves in the sides of the well, made by generations of Muslims pulling their buckets up by rope. This well was

Toledo's Muslim Legacy

You can see the Moorish influence in these sights:

• Mezquita del Cristo de la Luz, the last of the town's mosques
• Sinagoga del Tránsito's Mudejar plasterwork
• Sinagoga de Santa María la Blanca's mosque-like horseshoe arches and pinecone capitals
• Puerta del Sol (Gate of the Sun) and other surviving gates (with horseshoe arches) along the medieval wall
• The city's labyrinthine, medina-like streets

once located in the courtyard of an 11th-century mosque, which stood where the cathedral does today.

The upper level of the courtyard holds the beautiful Carranza collection of tiles and ceramics dating from the end of the Reconquista (1492). Each piece is categorized by the Spanish region where it was made. This may be the only place in Spain where you can compare regional differences in tile work and pottery. From the top level of the courtyard (go up a short flight of stairs) it's possible to access the temporary exhibit area of the main building. From here you can appreciate the architecture and peer down through an interior courtyard that is the axis of the museum.

▲▲Army Museum (Museo del Ejército)

This museum tells the military history of Spain from 1492 to the 20th century, with endless rooms of Spanish military collections of armor, uniforms, cannons, guns, paintings, and models. The museum has one major flaw: its skimpy coverage of the Spanish Civil War (1936-1939). Otherwise, the displays are wonderfully explained in English, and the audioguide is excellent. If you like military history, allow at least three hours for this, one of Europe's top military museums.

Cost and Hours: €5, €8 ticket includes great 2-hour audioguide, free to enter temporary exhibits and archeological ruins—ask for a pass at ticket office, free on Sun; open Thu-Tue 10:00-17:00, closed Wed; café/restaurant where you can bump elbows with Spanish military, tel. 925-238-800, www.museo.ejercito.es.

Visiting the Museum: The museum is located in the Alcázar, the huge former imperial residence that dominates Toledo's skyline. It's built on the site of Roman, Visigothic, Moorish, and early Renaissance fortresses, the ruins of which (displayed just past the turnstile and free to visit) are a poignant reminder of the city's strategic importance through the centuries.

Today's structure (originally built in the 16th century, then destroyed in the civil war and rebuilt) became a kind of right-wing Alamo. During the civil war, Franco's Nationalists (and hundreds of hostages) were besieged here by Republican troops for two months in 1936. The Republicans took the son of the Alcázar's commander—Colonel José Moscardó—hostage and called Colonel Moscardó, threatening to execute his son if he didn't surrender in 10 minutes. Moscardó asked for his son to be put on the line, and told him that he would have to be a hero and die for Spain. Moscardó then informed the Republican leader that he didn't need 10 minutes: the choice was made—he would never give up the Alcázar. (While the Nationalists believed the son was shot immediately, he was actually executed with other prisoners weeks later in a reprisal for an air raid.)

Finally, after many fierce but futile Republican attacks that destroyed much of the Alcázar, Franco sent in an army that took Toledo, a major victory for the Nationalists. After the war, the place was rebuilt and glorified under Franco. Only one room on the sixth floor (labeled as *CM-Despacho del Coronel Moscardó* on the museum map) has been left in a tattered ruin since the siege: the office of Colonel Moscardó.

It's a confusing floor plan, but if you start at the top floor and follow the "historical round" arrows, you'll enjoy a roughly chronological sweep. Since so much of this country's history is military, this museum tells much of the story of Spain.

Look for special theme rooms (e.g., the use of photography in the army, and the evolution of Spain's flag). The main courtyard—Italian-inspired Renaissance in style—comes with a proud statue of Holy Roman Emperor Charles V (a.k.a. King Charles I of Spain), the ultimate military king and Europe's most powerful 16th-century leader. While in the courtyard, consider the restoration of this massive-yet-elegant fortress.

The 20th-century section comes with some fascinating videos, but has just three small rooms of civil-war artifacts, including uniforms from both sides, Franco's cloak and cane, and posters. In addition, there are photographs of the conflict and a small audiovisual slide show. As the museum was preparing to open, controversy broke out on how to handle the civil war. The curators dodged the issue by going light on *the* major event of 20th-century Spanish history; it's not even marked on the museum's map (look for *El Siglo XX*).

Mezquita del Cristo de la Luz

Of Muslim Toledo's 10 mosques, this barren little building (dating from about 1000) is the best survivor. Looking up, you'll notice the Moorish fascination with geometry—each dome is a unique design. The lovely keyhole arch faces Mecca. In 1187, after the Reconquista, the mosque was changed to a church, the Christian apse (with its crude Romanesque art) was added, and the former mosque got its current name. The small garden with its fountains is a reminder of the Quranic image of heaven. From the outside of the building, you can see a Roman road, leading to the city wall, that was discovered and excavated when the mosque was undergoing restoration.

Cost and Hours: €2.80, Mon-Fri 10:00-14:00 & 15:30-18:45, until 17:45 in winter, Sat-Sun 10:00-17:45, Cuesta de las Carmelitas Descalzas 10, tel. 925-254-191.

Visigothic Museum in the Church of San Román (Museo de los Concilios y de la Cultura Visigoda)

This 13th-century Mudejar church (with its rare, strangely modernist 13th-century Romanesque frescoes) provides an exquisite space for a small but interesting collection of Visigothic artifacts. The Visigoths were the Christian barbarian tribe who ruled Spain between the fall of Rome and the rise of the Moors. The only things Visigothic about the actual building are the few capitals topping its columns, recycled from a seventh-century Visigothic church. Though the elaborate crowns are copies (the originals are in Madrid), other glass cases show off metal and stone artifacts from the age when Toledo was the capital of the Visigoths. The items, while featuring almost no human figures, are rich in symbolism. Their portability fits that society's nomadic heritage. Archaeologists have found almost no Visigothic artifacts within Toledo's fortified hill location. They lived in humble settlements along the river—apparently needing no defense system...until the Moors swept through in 711, ending two centuries of Visigothic rule in Iberia. Climb the steep stairs for a view of Toledo's rooftops from the church tower.

Cost and Hours: €1, buy at ticket machine, Tue-Sat 9:45-14:15 & 16:00-18:30, Sun 10:00-14:00, closed Mon, no English information, Plaza San Román, tel. 925-227-872.

TOLEDO

SOUTHWEST TOLEDO

These sights cluster at the southwest end of town. For efficient sightseeing, visit them in this order, then zip back home on bus #12 (listed at the end of this section).

▲Santo Tomé

A simple chapel on Plaza del Conde holds El Greco's most beloved painting. *The Burial of the Count of Orgaz* couples heaven and earth in a way only The Greek could. It feels so right to see a painting in the same church where the artist placed it 400 years ago. It originally filled the space immediately to the right of where it is now, but because the popularity of this masterpiece was disturbing the main church, it was moved. Church officials even created a special entryway for viewing it.

Cost and Hours: €2.80, daily 10:00-18:45, until 17:45 mid-Oct-Feb, audioguide-€1, tel. 925-256-098. This sight often has a line; try going early or late to avoid tour groups.

Visiting Santo Tomé: Take this slow. Stay a while—let it perform. The year is 1323. Count Don Gonzalo Ruiz has died. You're at his burial right here in this chapel. The good count was so holy, even saints Augustine and Stephen have come down from heaven to lower his body into the grave. (The painting's subtitle is "Such is the reward for those who serve God and his saints.")

More than 250 years later, in 1586, a local priest (depicted on the far right, reading the Bible) hired El Greco to make a painting of the burial to hang over the count's tomb. The funeral is attended by Toledo's most distinguished citizens. (El Greco used local nobles as models.) A serene line of noble faces divides the painting into two realms—heaven above and earth below. Above the faces, the count's soul, symbolized by a little baby, rises up through a mystical birth canal to be reborn in heaven, where he's greeted by Jesus, Mary, and all the saints. A spiritual wind blows through as colors change and shapes stretch. This is Counter-Reformation propaganda—notice Jesus pointing to St. Peter, the symbol of the pope in Rome, who controls the keys to the pearly gates. Each face is a detailed portrait.

It's clear that these portraits inspired the next great Spanish painter, Velázquez, a century later. El Greco himself (eyeballing you, seventh figure in from the left) is the only one not involved in the burial. The boy in the foreground—pointing to the two saints as if to say, "One's from the first century, the other's from the

El Greco (1541-1614)

Born on Crete and trained in Venice, Doménikos Theotokópoulos (tongue-tied friends just called him "The Greek") came to

Spain to get a job decorating El Escorial.
He failed there, but succeeded in Toledo, where he spent the last 37 years of
his life. He mixed all three regional influences into his palette. From his Greek
homeland, he absorbed the solemn, abstract style of icons. In Italy, he learned
the bold use of color, elongated figures,
twisting poses, and dramatic style of the
later Renaissance. These elements were
then fused in the fires of fanatic Span-
ish-Catholic devotion.

Not bound by the realism so important to his fellow artists, El Greco
painted dramatic visions of striking col-
ors and figures—bodies unnatural and lengthened as though
stretched between heaven and earth. He painted souls, not
faces. His work is on display at nearly every sight in Toledo.
Thoroughly modern in his disregard for realism, he didn't impress the austere Philip II. But his art still seems as fresh as
contemporary art does today. El Greco was essentially for-
gotten through the 18th and most of the 19th centuries. Then,
with the Romantic movement (and the discovery of Toledo by
Romantic-era travelers, artists, and poets), the paintings of El
Greco became the hits they are today.

fourth...it's a miracle!"—is El Greco's son. On the handkerchief in
the boy's pocket is El Greco's signature, written in Greek.

Don Gonzalo Ruiz's actual granite tombstone is at your feet.
The count's two wishes upon his death were to be buried here and
for his village to make an annual charity donation to feed Toledo's
poor. Finally, more than two centuries later, the people of Orgaz
said, "Enough!" and stopped the payments. The last of the money
was spent to pay El Greco for this painting.

▲El Greco Museum (Museo del Greco)

This small museum, built near the site of El Greco's house, gives a
look at the genius of his art and Toledo in his day. Its small collection of paintings is accompanied by interactive touch screens and
videos.

A comfy little theater shows a fine 10-minute video on both
the life of the artist and the story of this museum. You then proceed through halls that show the evolution of El Greco's art. While
there aren't many great El Grecos here, you'll see a hall lined with
his *Twelve Apostles, San Bernardino of Siena* (in a chapel), and the

highlight of the museum—the *View and Plan of Toledo*. El Greco's panoramic map shows the city in 1614. Study the actual map and list of sights. It was commissioned to promote the city (suddenly a former capital) after the king moved to Madrid.

Cost and Hours: €3, €5 combo-ticket with Sinagoga del Tránsito, free Sat afternoon from 14:00 and all day Sun; open Tue-Sat 9:30-19:30, Nov-Feb until 18:00, Sun 10:00-15:00, closed Mon; next to Sinagoga del Tránsito on Calle Samuel Leví, tel. 925-223-665.

▲Sinagoga del Tránsito (Museo Sefardí)

Built in 1361, this is the best surviving slice of Toledo's Jewish past. Serving as Spain's national Jewish museum, it displays Jewish artifacts, including costumes, menorahs, and books. Your visit comes with three parts: the nave, a ground floor exhibition space with a history of Spain's Jews, and the women's gallery upstairs, which shows lifestyles and holy rituals among Sephardic Jews. While English sheets in each room explain the collection, to get the most out of the exhibits, rent the audioguide.

Cost and Hours: €3, €5 combo-ticket with El Greco Museum, free Sat afternoon from 14:00 and all day Sun; open Tue-Sat 9:30-19:30 (off-season until 18:00), Sun 10:00-15:00, closed Mon; audioguide-€2 (or download for free from www.audioviator.com—search for "Museo Sefardi"; Wi-Fi on-site); near El Greco Museum on Calle de los Reyes Católicos, tel. 925-223-665.

Visiting the Synagogue: This 14th-century synagogue was built at the peak of Toledo's enlightened tolerance—constructed for Jews with Christian approval by Muslim craftsmen. Nowhere else in the city does Toledo's three-culture legacy shine brighter than at this place of worship. But in 1391, just a few decades after it was built, the Church and the Spanish kings began a violent campaign to unite Spain as a Christian nation, forcing Jews and Muslims to convert or leave. In 1492 Ferdinand and Isabel exiled Spain's remaining Jews, and while a third of them left, others remained and converted to Christianity.

Surveying the synagogue from the back, notice that its interior decor looks more Muslim than Jewish. After Christians reconquered the city in 1085, many Moorish workmen stayed on, beautifying the city with their unique style called Mudejar. The synagogue's intricate, geometrical carving in stucco—nearly all original, from 1360—features leaves, vines, and flowers; there are no human shapes, which are forbidden by the Torah—like the Quran—as being potential objects of idolatry. In the frieze (running along the upper wall, just below the ceiling), the Arabic-looking script is actually Hebrew, quoting psalms (respected by all "people of the book"—Muslims, Jews, and Christians alike). The balcony was the traditional separate worship area for women.

Move up to the front. Stand close to the holy wall and study the exquisite workmanship (with reminders of all three religions: the coat of arms of the Christian king, Hebrew script, and Muslim decor). Look down. The small rectangular patch of the original floor survived only because the Christian altar table sat there. In the side room and upstairs, scale models of the development of the Jewish quarter and video displays give a picture of Jewish life in medieval Toledo.

▲Museo Victorio Macho

Overlooking the gorge and Tajo River, this small, attractive museum—once the home and workshop of the early-20th-century sculptor Victorio Macho—offers a delightful collection of his bold Art Deco-inspired work. The museum's theater hosts a gimmicky multimedia show called the Toledo Time Capsule, which isn't worth the extra fee even if it's pouring down rain.

Cost and Hours: €3, Mon-Fri 10:00-14:00 & 17:00-19:00, closed Sat-Sun, between the two *sinagogas* at Plaza de Victorio Macho 2, ring doorbell to enter, tel. 925-284-225. Download free audioguide from www.audioviator.com—search for "Victorio Macho" (Wi-Fi on-site).

Visiting the Museum: The house itself is a cool oasis of calm in the city. Your visit comes in four stages: ticket room with theater, courtyard with view, crypt, and museum.

Macho was Spain's first great modern sculptor. When his left-wing Republican (say that three times) politics made it dangerous for him to stay in Franco's Spain, he fled to the USSR, then Mexico and Peru, where he met his wife, Zoila. They later returned to Toledo, where they lived and worked until he died in 1966. Zoila eventually gave the house and Macho's art to the city.

Enjoy the peaceful and expansive view from the terrace. From here it's clear how the Tajo River served as a formidable moat protecting the city. Imagine trying to attack. The 14th-century bridge (on the right) connected the town with the region's *cigarrales*— mansions of wealthy families, whose orchards of figs and apricots dot the hillside even today. To the left (in the river), look for the stubs of 15th-century watermills; directly below is a riverside trail that's delightful for a stroll or jog.

The door marked *Crypta* leads to *My Brother Marcelo*—the touching tomb Macho made for his brother. Eventually he featured his entire family in his art.

A dozen steps above the terrace, you'll find a single room marked *Museo* filled with Macho's art. A pietà is carved expressively in granite. Next to the pietà, several self-portrait sketches show the artist's genius. The bronze statue is a self-portrait at age 17. In the next section, exquisite pencil-on-paper studies illustrate how a sculptor must understand the body (in this case, Zoila's body). The sketch of Zoila from behind is entitled *Guitar* (Spaniards traditionally think of a woman's body as a guitar). Other statues show the strength of the peoples' spirit as leftist Republicans stood up to Franco's fascist forces, and Spain endured its 20th-century bloodbath. The highlight is *La Madre* (from 1935), Macho's life-size sculpture of his mother sitting in a chair. It illustrates the sadness and simple wisdom of Spanish mothers who witnessed so much suffering. Upon a granite backdrop, her white marble hands and face speak volumes.

Sinagoga de Santa María la Blanca

This synagogue-turned-church has Moorish horseshoe arches and wall carvings. It's a vivid reminder of the religious cultures that shared (and then didn't share) this city.

While it looks like a mosque, it never was one. Built as a Jewish synagogue by Muslim workers around 1200, it became a church in 1492 when Toledo's Jews were required to convert or leave—hence the mix-and-match name. After being used as horse stables by Napoleonic troops, it was further ruined in the 19th century. Today, it's an evocative space, beautiful in its simplicity.

Cost and Hours: €2.80, daily 10:00-18:45, until 17:45 in winter, Calle de los Reyes Católicos 4, tel. 925-227-257.

▲San Juan de los Reyes Monasterio

"St. John of the Monarchs" is a grand Franciscan monastery, impressive church, and delightful "Isabeline" cloistered courtyard. The style is late Gothic, contemporaneous with Portugal's Manueline (c. 1500) and Flamboyant Gothic elsewhere in Europe. It was the intended burial site of the Catholic Monarchs, Isabel and Ferdinand. But after the Moors were expelled in 1492 from Granada, their royal bodies were planted there to show Spain's commitment to maintaining a Moor-free peninsula.

Cost and Hours: €2.80, daily 10:00-18:45, mid-Oct-March until 17:45, San Juan de los Reyes 2, tel. 925-223-802. After buying your ticket, look up. A skinny monk welcomes you (and reminds us of our mortality).

Visiting the Sight: Before entering and getting your ticket, take in the **facade.** It is famously festooned with 500-year-old chains. Moors used these to shackle Christians in Granada until 1492. It's said that the freed Christians brought these chains to the church, making them a symbol of their Catholic faith and a sign of victory. Enter the monastery at the side door.

Even without the royal tombs that would have dominated the space, the glorious **chapel** gives you a sense of Spain when it was Europe's superpower. The monastery was built to celebrate the 1476 Battle of Toro, which made Isabel the queen of Castile. Since her husband, Ferdinand, was king of Aragon, this effectively created the Spain we know today. (You could say 1476 is to Spain what 1776 is to the US.) Now united, Spain was able to quickly finish the Reconquista, ridding Iberia of its Moors within the next decade and a half.

Sitting in the chapel, you're surrounded by propaganda proclaiming the Catholic Monarchs' greatness. The coat of arms is

repeated obsessively. The eagle with the halo disk represents St. John, protector of the royal family. The yoke and arrows are the symbols of Ferdinand and Isabel. The lions remind people of the power of the kingdoms joined together under Ferdinand and Isabel. The coat of arms is complex because of Iberia's many kingdoms (e.g., a lion for León, and a castle for Castile).

As you leave, look up over the door to see the Franciscan coat of arms—with the five wounds of the Crucifixion (the stigmata—which St. Francis earned through his great faith) flanked by angels with dramatic wings.

Enjoy a walk around the **cloister.** Notice details of the fine carvings. Everything had meaning in the 15th century. In the cor-

ner (opposite the entry), just above eye level, find a small monkey—an insulting symbol of Franciscans—on a toilet reading the Bible upside down. Perhaps a stone carver snuck in a not-too-subtle comment on Franciscan pseudo-intellectualism, with their big libraries and small brains.

Napoleon's troops are mostly to blame for the destruction of the church, a result of Napoleon's view that monastic power in Europe was a menace. While Napoleon's biggest error was to invade Russia, his second-dumbest move was to alienate the Catholic faithful by destroying monasteries such as this one. This strategic mistake eroded popular support from people who might have seen Napoleon as a welcome alternative to the tyranny of kings and the Church.

If you're tired, skip going upstairs—if not, you can take a simple walk around the top level of the courtyard under a finely renovated Moorish-style ceiling.

▲Bus #12 Self-Guided Tour (A Sweat-Free Return Trip from Santo Tomé to Plaza de Zocodover)

When you're finished with the sights at the Santo Tomé end of town, you can hike all the way back (not fun)—or simply catch bus #12 (fun!) back to Plaza de Zocodover. The ride offers tired sightseers a quick, interesting 15-minute look at the town walls. You can catch the bus from Plaza del Conde in front of Santo Tomé. This is the end of the line, so buses wait to depart from here twice hourly (at :25 and :55, until 21:25, pay driver €1.40). You can also catch the same bus across the street from the San Juan de los Reyes ticket entrance (at :28 and :58). Here's what you'll see on your way if you catch it from Santo Tomé:

Leaving Santo Tomé, you'll first ride through Toledo's Jewish section. On the right, you'll pass the El Greco Museum, Sinagoga del Tránsito, and Sinagoga de Santa María la Blanca, followed by— on your left—the ornate Flamboyant Gothic facade of San Juan de los Reyes Monasterio. After squeezing through the 16th-century city gate, the bus follows along the outside of the mighty 10th-century wall. (Toledo was never conquered by force...only by siege.)

Just past the big escalator (which brings people from parking lots up into the city) and the Hotel Cardinal, the wall gets fancier, as demonstrated by the little old Bisagra Gate. Soon after, you see the big new Bisagra Gate, the main entry into the old town. While the city walls date from the 10th century, this gate was built as an arch of triumph in the 16th century. The massive coat of arms of Emperor Charles V, with the double eagle, reminded people that he ruled a unified Habsburg empire (successor of ancient Rome), and they were entering the capital of an empire that, in the 1500s, included most of Western Europe and much of America. (We'll enter the town through this gate in a couple of minutes after a stop at the bus station.)

Just outside the big gate is a well-maintained and shaded park—a picnic-perfect spot and one of Toledo's few green areas. After a detour to the bus station basement to pick up people coming from Madrid, you swing back around Bisagra Gate. As an example of how things have changed in the last generation, as recently as

1960, all traffic into the city at this point had to pass through this gate's tiny original entrance.

As you climb back into the old town, you'll pass the fine 14th-century Moorish Puerta del Sol (Gate of the Sun) on your right. Then comes the modern Palacio de Congresos Miradero convention center on your left, which is artfully incorporated into the more historic cityscape. Within moments you pull into the main square, Plaza de Zocodover. You can do this tour in reverse by riding bus #12 from Plaza de Zocodover to Plaza del Conde (departing at :25 and :55, same price and hours).

Shopping in Toledo

Toledo probably sells more souvenirs than any city in Spain. This is *the* place to buy medieval-looking swords, armor, maces, three-legged stools, lethal-looking letter-openers, and other nouveau antiques. It's also Spain's damascene center, where, for centuries, craftspeople have inlaid black steel with gold, silver, and copper wire. Spain's top bullfighters wouldn't have their swords made anywhere else.

Knives: At the workshop of English-speaking **Mariano Zamorano,** you can see swords and knives being made. His family has been putting its seal on hand-crafted knives since 1890. Judging by what's left of Mariano's hand, his knives are among the sharpest (Mon-Fri 10:00-14:00 & 16:00-19:00, Sat-Sun 10:00-14:00—although you may not see work done on weekends, 10 percent discount with this book, behind Ayuntamiento/City Hall at Calle Ciudad 19, tel. 925-222-634, www.marianozamorano.com).

Damascene: You can find artisans all over town pounding gold and silver threads into a steel base to create shiny inlaid plates, decorative wares, and jewelry. The damascene is a real tourist racket, but it's fun to pop into a shop and see the intricate handiwork in action.

El Martes: Toledo's colorful outdoor market is a lively scene on Tuesdays at Paseo de Merchan, better known to locals as "La Vega" (9:00-14:00, outside Bisagra Gate near TI).

Sleeping in Toledo

Madrid day-trippers darken the sunlit cobbles, but few stay to see Toledo's medieval moonrise. Spend the night. Hotels often have a two-tiered price system, with prices 20 percent higher on Friday and Saturday, and some may require a two-night stay on the weekend. Spring and fall are high season; rooms are scarce and prices go up during the Corpus Christi festival as well (usually late May or early June). Most places have an arrangement with parking lots in town that can save you a few euros; ask when you reserve.

NEAR PLAZA DE ZOCODOVER

$$ Hotel Toledo Imperial sits efficiently above Plaza de Zocodover and rents 29 business-class rooms that are a solid value (air-con, elevator, Calle Horno de los Bizcochos 5, tel. 925-280-034, www. hoteltoledoimperial.com, reservas@hoteltoledoimperial.com).

$$ Hotel La Conquista de Toledo, a three-star hotel with 33 rooms, gleams with marble. It's so sleek and slick it almost feels more like a hospital than a hotel (RS%, family rooms, air-con, elevator, near the Alcázar at Juan Labrador 8, tel. 925-210-760, www.hotelconquistadetoledo.com, conquistadetoledo@githoteles. com, Yuki).

$ Hostal Centro rents 28 spacious rooms with sparse, well-worn furniture and a ramshackle feel. It's wonderfully central, with a third of its rooms overlooking the main square. Request a quiet room on the back side to minimize night noise. Book through email or by phone for best price (RS%, 50 yards off Plaza de Zocodover—take the first right off Calle del Comercio to Calle Nueva 13, tel. 925-257-091, www.hostalcentro.net, hostalcentro@telefonica.net, warmly run by Asun and David).

NEAR BISAGRA GATE

$$ Hacienda del Cardenal, a 17th-century cardinal's palace built into Toledo's wall, is quiet and elegant, with a cool garden, a less-than-helpful staff, and a stuffy restaurant. This poor man's parador, at the dusty old gate of Toledo, is close to the station, but below all the old-town action (enter through town wall 100 yards below Bisagra Gate, Paseo de Recaredo 24, tel. 925-224-900, www. haciendadelcardenal.com, hotel@haciendadelcardenal.com).

$$ Hotel Abad sits at the bottom of the old town's hill just a block inside the Bisagra Gate and offers 22 clean, rustic rooms with stone walls, wooden rafters, and contemporary furnishings (air-con, elevator, Calle Real del Arrabal 1, tel. 925-283-500, www. hotelabadtoledo.com, reservas@hotelabad.com).

$ Hospedería de los Reyes has 15 colorful and thoughtfully appointed rooms in an attractive, quiet, yellow building

100 yards downhill from Bisagra Gate, outside the wall. They also offer 11 apartments near the gate, with kitchens and living rooms (air-con, street parking nearby, Calle Perala 37, tel. 925-283-667, www.hospederiadelosreyes.com, hospederiadelosreyes@hospederiadelosreyes.com, Alicia and Carolina).

$ El Hostal Puerta Bisagra is in a sprawling old building that is fresh and modern inside. Located just across from Bisagra Gate, it's convenient for arrivals but a long hike uphill to the action (hop on any bus). Its 38 comfortable rooms are rented at some of the best prices in town (air-con, Calle del Potro 5, tel. 925-285-277, www.puertabisagra.com, elhostal@puertabisagra.com).

$ Hotel Sol, with 15 nicely decorated pastel rooms, is a good value. It's on a quiet, ugly side street between Bisagra Gate and Plaza de Zocodover (RS%, air-con, pay parking; leave the busy main drag at Hotel Imperial and head 50 yards down the lane to Azacanes 8; tel. 925-213-650, www.hotelyhostalsol.com, info@hotelyhostalsol.com, José Carlos). Their 11-room **¢ Hostal Sol** annex across the street is just as comfortable, and a bit cheaper (RS%).

DEEP IN TOLEDO

$$ La Posada de Manolo rents 14 furnished rooms across from the downhill corner of the cathedral. Manolo Junior opened this *hostal* according to his father's vision: a place with each of its three floors themed differently—Moorish, Jewish, and Christian. Book ahead, as they tend to fill up (RS%, air-con, no elevator, two nice view terraces, Calle Sixto Ramón Parro 8, tel. 925-282-250, www.laposadademanolo.com, toledo@laposadademanolo.com).

$ Hotel Eurico cleverly fits 23 sleek rooms into a medieval building buried deep in the old town. The staff is friendly, and the hotel offers a good value (air-con, Calle Santa Isabel 3, tel. 925-284-178, www.hoteleurico.com, reservas@hoteleurico.com).

$ Hotel Santa Isabel, in a 15th-century building two blocks from the cathedral, has 41 clean, modern, and comfortable rooms and squeaky tile hallways (some view rooms, elevator, scenic roof terrace, pay parking, buried deep in old town—take a taxi instead of the bus, drivers enter from Calle Pozo Amargo, Calle Santa Isabel 24, tel. 925-253-120, www.hotelsantaisabel.net, info@hotelsantaisabel.net).

HOSTELS

¢ Albergue Juvenil San Servando youth hostel is lavish but fairly cheap, with 96 beds and small rooms for two or four people (two-bed rooms available, swimming pool, views, cafeteria, good management, located in 10th-century Arab castle of San Servando, 10-minute walk from train station, 15-minute hike from town center, over Puente Viejo outside town, tel. 925-224-554, reservations tel. 925-221-676, alberguesclm@jccm.es, no English spoken).

TOLEDO

Toledo Hotels

ROMAN CIRCUS RUINS

"EL MARTES" FLEA MARKET

AV. DE LA RECONQUISTA

AV. DE CARLOS III

ALFONSO

Glorieta de la Reconquista

AV. DE LA CAVA

P

4 ◆

ESCALATORS

SUBIDA LA GRANJA

CITY WALLS

PASEO DE RECAREDO

CALLE REAL

CALLE MERCED

S. ILDEFONSO

To **14** & CM-40 Ring Road

CUESTA SANTA LEOCADIA

Plaza de Padilla

TEND.

SAN MARTÍN

C. PINTOR M. MORENO

COL. DONCELLAS

MARÍA PACHECO

S. ROMÁN

Plaza San Juan de los Reyes

B #12

C. DE BULAS

VISIGOTHIC MUSEUM

BAJADA DE SAN MARTÍN

SAN JUAN DE LOS REYES

CALLE DEL ÁNGEL

C. GORDO

C. DE ALFONSO XII

BAJADA DE SANTA ANA

CALLE REYES CATÓLICOS

C. SANTO TOMÉ

CALLE DE EL SALVADOR

PUENTE DE SAN MARTÍN

SINAGOGA DE SANTA MARÍA LA BLANCA

SANTO TOMÉ

Cliffs

JUDERÍA

B #12

C. DE SANTA ÚRSULA

MUSEO VICTORIO MACHO

SAN JUAN DE DIOS

EL GRECO MUSEUM

CALLE MORO

ZAMORANO KNIFE WORKSHOP

SINAGOGA DEL TRÁNSITO

PASEO TRÁNSITO

Park

CALLE DESCALZOS

PASEO SAN CRISTÓBAL

SAN BARTOLOMÉ

SAN TORCUATO

CARRETERA DE PIEDRABUENA

Tajo River

S. CIPRIANO

Note: Some street width exaggerated for clarity

CALLE CARRERAS

Cliffs

100 Meters
100 Yards

N

1 Hotel Toledo Imperial
2 Hotel La Conquista de Toledo
3 Hostal Centro
4 Hacienda del Cardenal
5 Hotel Abad
6 Hospedería de los Reyes
7 Hostal Puerta de Bisagra
8 Hotel Sol
9 La Posada de Manolo
10 Hotel Eurico
11 Hotel Santa Isabel
12 To Albergue Juvenil San Servando (Hostel)
13 Oh Oasis Hostel
14 To Parador de Toledo

TOLEDO

To Bullring & Madrid 6

PERALA

To Bus Station & P

CARD. TAV.

CALLE DE LA CARRERA

CITY WALLS

C. CARRERA

PUENTE AZARQUIEL

To Train Station, Consuegra & P

VI

BISAGRA GATE 7

C. REAL DEL ARRABAL

CALLE AZACANES

8

CALLE DE GERARDO LOBO

P

PASEO ROSA

To 12

CALLE DE LAS CARRETAS

Miradero

ARMAS

ESCALATOR

OLD BRIDGE

5 MEZQUITA

CUESTA DE CARMELITAS DESCALZAS

C. CRISTO DE LA LUZ

C. NÚÑEZ DE ARCE

SILLERIA

Plaza de San Agustín

SANTA CRUZ MUSEUM

CALLE DE ALFILERITOS

C. PEÑAS

13

NUEVA

3 Plaza de Zocodover

AQUEDUCT

C. CERVANTES

POST

CALLE DE LA PLATA

EL SABIO

SINAGOGA

CALLE COMERCIO

B B

ALFERECES

C. NUNCIO VIEJO

C. TRINIDAD

TORNERIAS

JUAN LABRADOR

BARRIO REY

TRASTAMARA

H. BIZ.

CUESTA DE CARLOS V

ALCÁZAR (ARMY MUSEUM)

MOSCARDÓ

PUENTE NUEVO ALCÁNTARA

Plaza Mayor

MARKET

Plaza del Consistorio

CATHEDRAL

2 1

P

LA CANDELARIA

Plaza del Ayuntamiento

CARD. CISNEROS

& CITY HALL

C. BARCO

9 Plaza de San Justo

SAN JUSTO

Tajo River

SANTA ISABEL

11 10

CALLE AVE MARÍA

CALLE POLO AMARGO

COLEGIO DE INFANTES

BAJADA DEL BARCO

C. CANDELARIA

PASEO DE CABESTREROS

S. CATALINA

CALLE DE PLEGADERO

PASEO DE CABESTREROS

Cliffs

SANTA CATALINA

SAN SEBASTIÁN

One-way streets →

Traffic barriers

To Parador & CM-40 Ring Road

VIEWPOINT

¢ **Oh Oasis Hostel** is a fresh, 21-room hostel right around the corner from Plaza de Zocodover, with a pleasant rooftop terrace. Weekends may be noisy because there is no curfew (private double and family rooms available, air-con, elevator, Calle Cadenas 5, tel. 925-227-650, www.hosteloasis.com, toledo@hostelsoasis.com).

OUTSIDE TOWN WITH GRAND TOLEDO VIEW

$$$ Parador de Toledo, with 79 rooms, is one of Spain's best-known inns. Its guests enjoy the same Toledo view that El Greco made famous from across the Tajo Gorge (some view rooms, €29 fixed-price meals sans drinks in their fine restaurant overlooking Toledo, 2 windy miles from town at Cerro del Emperador—it may come up as Carretera de Cobisa on GPS systems, tel. 925-221-850, www.parador.es, toledo@parador.es).

Eating in Toledo

DINING IN TRADITIONAL ELEGANCE

A day full of El Greco and the romance of Toledo after dark puts me in the mood for game and other traditional cuisine. Typical Toledo dishes include partridge *(perdiz),* venison *(venado),* wild boar *(jabalí),* roast suckling pig *(cochinillo asado),* or baby lamb (*cordero*—similarly roasted after a few weeks of mother's milk). After dinner, find a *mazapán* place for dessert. Restaurants generally serve lunch from 13:00 to 16:00 and dinner from 20:00 until very late (Spaniards don't start dinner until about 21:00).

$$$ Los Cuatro Tiempos Restaurante ("The Four Seasons") specializes in local game and roasts, proficiently served in a tasteful and elegant setting. They offer spacious dining with an extensive and inviting Spanish wine list. It's a good choice for a quiet, romantic dinner, and a good value for a midday meal (Mon-Sat 13:00-16:00 & 20:30-23:00, Sun 13:00-16:00 only, at downhill corner of cathedral, Calle Sixto Ramón Parro 5, tel. 925-223-782, www.restauranteloscuatrotiempos.es).

$$$ Colección Catedral is the wine bar of local chef Adolfo, who, with his brother Carlos, cooks up a somewhat-pricey but always top-notch list of gourmet plates, including some traditional local dishes like *carcamusas* (pork and seasonal vegetables, sort of a Spanish chili). Some dishes can be modified to suit vegetarians and vegans. A €15 three-course meal, wine included, is a tasty value. Sit next to the kitchen to be near the creative action. If the Starship *Enterprise* had a Spanish wine-and-tapas bar on its holodeck, this would be it. Pick up a bottle of wine to take home or drink it there for €3-8 more than the shop price (daily 12:00-23:30, across from cathedral at Calle Nuncio Viejo 1, tel. 925-224-244, Victoria takes good care of diners).

$$$ El Botero Taberna is a delightful little hideaway. The barman downstairs, who looks like a young Pavarotti, serves mojitos, fine wine, and exquisite tapas. Upstairs, there's an intimate, seven-table restaurant with romantic, white-tablecloth ambience and modern Mediterranean dishes (lunch only Sun-Tue, lunch and dinner Wed-Sat, a block below cathedral at Calle de la Ciudad 5, tel. 925-229-088, www.tabernaelbotero.com).

SIMPLE RESTAURANTS WITH CHARACTER

These places are listed in geographical order from Plaza de Zocodover to Santo Tomé. Plaza de Zocodover is busy with eateries serving edible food at affordable prices, and its people-watching scene is great. But my recommended eateries are just a bit off the main drag on side streets. It's worth a few extra minutes—and the navigating challenge—to find places where you'll be eating with locals as well as tourists. There is a lively midday tapas scene in Toledo, and almost every bar you pop into for a stand-up drink will come with a small plate of something to nibble.

To dine with younger Spaniards, drop into **$$ El Trébol**, tucked peacefully away just a short block off Plaza de Zocodover. Their mixed grill can feed two. Locals enjoy their *pulgas* (sandwiches). The seating inside is basic, but the outdoor tables are nice (daily 9:00-24:00, Calle de Santa Fe 1, tel. 925-281-297).

$$ Restaurante Ludeña is a classic eatery with a bar, a well-worn dining room in back, and a handful of tables on a sunny courtyard. It's very central; locals duck in here to pretend there's no tourism in Toledo (Plaza de la Magdalena 10, tel. 925-223-384).

$$ Madre Tierra Restaurante Vegetariano is Toledo's answer to a vegetarian's prayer. Bright, spacious, classy, air-conditioned, and tuned in to the healthy eater's needs, its appetizing dishes are based on both international and traditional Spanish cuisine (good tea selection, great veggie pizzas, closed Mon night and all day Tue, 20 yards below La Posada de Manolo just before reaching Plaza de San Justo, Bajada de le Tripería 2, tel. 925-223-571).

$$ Restaurante Placido, run by high-energy Anna and *abuela* (grandma) Sagradio, serves traditional family-style cuisine on a shady terrace or in a wonderful Franciscan monastery courtyard (open daily for lunch and dinner in summer, lunch only in winter, about a block uphill from Santo Tomé at Calle Santo Tomé 2, tel. 925-222-603).

$$ Taberna La Flor de la Esquina is a local bar with a simple

TOLEDO

Toledo Restaurants

ROMAN CIRCUS RUINS

"EL MARTES" FLEA MARKET

AV. DE CARLOS III

AV. DE LA RECONQUISTA

Glorieta de la Reconquista

ALFONSO

100 Meters
100 Yards

AV. DE LA CAVA

P

ESCALATORS

SUBIDA LA GRANJA

CITY WALLS

PASEO DE RECAREDO

CALLE REAL

S. ILDEFONSO

CALLE MERCED

To CM-40 Ring Road & Parador

CUESTA SANTA LEOCADIA

Plaza de Padilla

TEND.

PACHECO

SAN MARTÍN

C. PINTOR M. MORENO

COL. DONCELLAS

MARÍA

S. ROMAN

Plaza San Juan de los Reyes

B #12

C. DE BULAS

VISIGOTHIC MUSEUM

BAJADA DE SAN MARTÍN

SAN JUAN DE LOS REYES

CALLE DEL ÁNGEL

C. GORDO ROJAS

C. DE ALFONSO XII

BAJADA DE SANTA ANA

CALLE REYES CATÓLICOS

C. SANTO TOMÉ

CALLE DE

SINAGOGA DE SANTA MARÍA LA BLANCA

SANTO TOMÉ

EL SALVADOR

PUENTE DE SAN MARTÍN

Cliffs

JUDERÍA

B #12

TALLER MORO DE SANTA URSULA

SAN JUAN DE DIOS

MUSEO VICTORIO MACHO

EL GRECO MUSEUM

ZAMORANO KNIFE WORKSHOP

SINAGOGA DEL TRÁNSITO

PASEO TRANSITO

Tajo River

Park

CALLE DESCALZOS

PASEO SAN CRISTÓBAL

SAN TORCUATO

SAN BARTOLOMÉ

CARRETERA DE PIEDRABUENA

S. CIPRIANO

Note: Some street width exaggerated for clarity

CALLE CARRERAS

Cliffs

1 Los Cuatro Tiempos Restaurante
2 Colección Catedral
3 El Botero Taberna
4 El Trébol
5 Restaurante Ludeña
6 Madre Tierra Rest. Vegetariano

7 Restaurante Placido & El Café de las Monjas
8 Taberna La Flor de la Esquina
9 Mercado San Agustín
10 Mercado Municipal
11 Supermarket Suma
12 Santo Tomé (Mazapán)

TOLEDO

To Bullring & Madrid

PERALA

CARD. TAV.

CALLE DE LA CARRERA

CITY WALLS

VI

BISAGRA GATE

C. REAL DEL ARRABAL

Calle Azacanes

To Bus Station & P

PUENTE AZARQUIEL

To Train Station, Consuegra & P

PASEO ROSA

CALLE DE LAS CARRETAS

CALLE DE GERARDO LOBO

Miradero P

MEZQUITA

ESCALATOR

SANTA CRUZ MUSEUM

OLD BRIDGE

CUESTA CARMELITAS DESCALZAS

C. NÚÑEZ DE ARCE

CALLE DE LA LUZ

9 Plaza de San Agustín

Calle de Alfileritos

SILLERIA

CADENAS

NUEVA

C. CERVANTES

Plaza de Zocodover

4

12

B B

ALFERECES

AQUEDUCT

EL SABIO

CALLE DE LA PLATA

Post

CALLE COMERCIO

11

BARRIO REY

CUESTA DE CARLOS V

ALCÁZAR (ARMY MUSEUM)

PUENTE NUEVO ALCÁNTARA

C. NUNCIO VIEJO

SINAGOGA

2

TORNERIAS

5

TRASTAMARA

JUAN LABRADOR

C. BIZ.

LA TRINIDAD

Plaza Mayor

Plaza del Consistorio

MARKET **10**

MOSCARDÓ

P

Plaza del Ayuntamiento

CATHEDRAL **1**

& CITY HALL

CARD. CISNEROS

LA CANDELARIA

SANTA ISABEL

3

C. BARCO

6 Plaza de San Justo

SAN JUSTO

PASEO DE CABESTREROS

CALLE AVE MARIA

CALLE POZO AMARGO

COLEGIO DE INFANTES

BAJADA DEL BARCO

CALLE DE PLEGADERO

PASEO DE CABESTREROS

Cliffs

CALLE CANDELARIA

Tajo River

S. CATALINA

SANTA CATALINA

SAN SEBASTIAN

One-way streets →

Traffic barriers

To Parador & CM-40 Ring Road

VIEWPOINT

basement dining room and wonderful seating on a leafy square under a towering Jesuit church facade. Rustic and part of a fun neighborhood scene, this place is best when you want to eat outside on a square (lunch specials, basic *raciones,* open daily, Plaza Juan de Mariana 2, tel. 925-253-801).

$$ Mercado San Agustín is part of a trend to create a space for several different eateries in one place. It's a good place if you need a modern break in this medieval city. You can choose between gourmet cheeses, organic hamburgers, Spanish tapas, Japanese cuisine, coffee, and sweet delights. Explore the five levels before deciding, then find a table on any of the levels to dig in, or go to the top-floor terrace for a cocktail (Tue-Sun 10:00-24:00, closed Mon, at Calle Cuesta de Águila 1 right off of Plaza San Agustín, tel. 925-215-898, www.mercadodesanagustin.com).

Picnics: Picnics are best assembled at the city market, **Mercado Municipal,** on Plaza Mayor (on the Alcázar side of cathedral, with a supermarket inside open Mon-Sat 9:00-15:00 & 17:00-20:00 and stalls open mostly in the mornings until 14:00, closed Sun). **Supermarket Suma,** on Plaza de la Magdalena, has groceries and lots of other stuff at good prices (Mon-Sat 9:50-15:00 & 16:00-22:00, shorter hours on Sun, just below Plaza de Zocodover). For a picnic with people-watching on an atmospheric square, consider Plaza de Zocodover or Plaza del Ayuntamiento.

AND FOR DESSERT: *MAZAPÁN*

Toledo's famous almond-fruity-sweet *mazapán* is sold all over town. The nuns living in Toledo's convents used to be the main provider of this delight, but their numbers are dwindling. If you can't find a convent still selling sweets in the labyrinth of Holy Toledo, visit **El Café de las Monjas,** a pastry and coffee shop around the corner from the Santo Tomé church that brings in *mazapán* from local convents (daily 9:00-21:00, Calle Santo Tomé 2).

The big *mazapán* producer is **Santo Tomé** (several outlets, including a handy one on Plaza de Zocodover and on Calle Santo Tomé 3, daily 9:00-22:00). Browse their tempting window displays. They sell *mazapán* goodies individually (*sin relleno*—without filling—is for purists, *de piñon* has pine nuts, *imperiales* is with almonds, others have fruit fillings). Boxes are good for gifts, but sampling is much cheaper when buying just a few pieces. Their *Toledana* is a nutty, crumbly, not-too-sweet cookie with a subtle thread of squash filling.

For a sweet and romantic evening moment, pick up a few pastries and head down to the cathedral. Sit on the Plaza del Ayuntamiento's benches (or stretch out on the stone wall to the right of the TI). A fountain is on your right, Spain's best-looking City Hall is behind you, and there before you is her top cathedral—built back when Toledo was Spain's capital—shining brightly against the black night sky.

Toledo Connections

FROM TOLEDO TO MADRID

While the AVE bullet train makes the trip to Madrid in half the time, buses depart twice as frequently. Three or four people traveling together can share a taxi economically. Whichever way you travel, Madrid and Toledo are very easily connected.

By Bus: 2/hour, 1-1.5 hours, *directo* is faster than *ruta*, bus drops you at Madrid's Plaza Elíptica Metro stop, 1/day direct morning bus to Madrid's Barajas Airport Terminal 4, 1.5 hours, Alsa bus company, tel. 902-422-242, www.alsa.es; you can almost always just drop in and buy a ticket minutes before departure.

By Train: Nearly hourly, 30 minutes by AVE or Avant to Madrid's Atocha station, tel. 902-240-202, www.renfe.com; early and late trains can sell out—reserve ahead.

By Taxi: While it may seem extravagant, if you have limited time, lots of luggage, and a small group, simply taking a taxi from your Toledo hotel to your Madrid hotel is breathtakingly efficient (€90, one hour door-to-door, tel. 925-255-050 or 925-227-070). You can ask several cabbies for their best "off the meter" rate. A taxi to the Madrid airport costs €110 (find one who will go "off the meter") and takes an hour.

FROM TOLEDO TO OTHER POINTS

To get to Granada, Sevilla, and elsewhere in Spain from Toledo, assume you'll have to transfer in Madrid. See "Madrid Connections" at the end of that chapter for information on reaching various destinations.

ROUTE TIPS FOR DRIVERS

Granada to Toledo (250 miles, 3.5 hours): The Granada-Toledo drive is long, hot, and boring. Start early to minimize the heat and make the best time you can. Follow signs for *Madrid/Jaén/A-44* into what some call "the Spanish Nebraska"—La Mancha (see next section). After Puerto Lapice, you'll see the Toledo exit.

Toledo to Madrid (40 miles, 1 hour): It's a speedy *autovía* north, past one last billboard to Madrid (on A-42). Expect to pay €9 in tolls (in cash in lanes labeled *"vias manuales"* or by credit or debit card in lanes labeled *"vias automáticas"*). The highways converge into M-30, which encircles Madrid. Follow it to the left (*Nor* or *Oeste*) and take the Plaza de España exit to get back to Gran Vía. If you're airport-bound, keep heading into Madrid until you see the airplane symbol (N-II).

To drive to Atocha station in Madrid, take the exit off M-30 for Plaza de Legazpi, then take Delicias (second on your right off the square). Parking for rental-car return is on the north side of the train station.

La Mancha

La Mancha, which is worth a visit if you're driving between Toledo and Granada, shows a side of Spain that you'll see nowhere else—vast and flat. Named for the Arabic word for "parched earth," it makes you feel small—lost in rough seas of olive-green polka dots. Random buildings look like houses and hotels hurled off some heavenly Monopoly board.

This is the setting of Miguel de Cervantes' *Don Quixote,* published in the early 17th century, after England sank the Armada and the Spanish Empire began its decline. Cervantes' star character fights doggedly for good, for justice, and against the fall of Spain and its traditional old-regime ideals. Ignoring reality, Don Quixote is a hero fighting a hopeless battle. Stark La Mancha is the perfect stage.

The epitome of *Don Quixote* country, the town of **Consuegra** (TI tel. 925-475-731, www.aytoconsuegra.es) must be the La Mancha Cervantes had in mind. Drive up to the ruined 12th-century castle and joust with a windmill. It's hot and buggy here, but the powerful view overlooking the village, with its sun-bleached light-red roofs, modern concrete reality, and harsh, windy silence, makes for a profound picnic (a one-hour drive south of Toledo). The castle belonged to the Knights of St. John (12th and 13th centuries) and is

associated with their trip to Jerusalem during the Crusades. Originally built from the ruins of a nearby Roman circus, it has been recently restored (€4, includes windmill and archaeological museum in town). Sorry, the windmills are post-Cervantes, only 200 to 300 years old—but you can go inside the Molino de Bolero to see how it works (€2, included with €4 castle entry, Mon-Fri 10:00-13:30 & 16:30-18:30, Sat-Sun from 10:30, shorter hours in winter). If your heart is set on fighting the windmills like Don Quixote—and you don't have a car—you can hire a taxi to drive you here from Toledo for about €95 (includes round-trip travel and an hour stop).

The next castle north (above Almonacid, 8 miles from Toledo) is free. Follow the ruined lane past the ruined church up to the ruined castle. The jovial locals hike up with kids and kites.

PRACTICALITIES

This section covers just the basics on traveling in Spain (for much more information, see *Rick Steves Spain*). You'll find free advice on specific topics at www.ricksteves.com/tips.

Money

Spain uses the euro currency: 1 euro (€) = about $1.10. To convert prices in euros to dollars, add about 10 percent: €20 = about $22, €50 = about $55. (Check www.oanda.com for the latest exchange rates.)

The standard way for travelers to get euros is to withdraw money from an ATM (known as a *cajero automático*) using a debit or credit card, ideally with a Visa or MasterCard logo. To keep your cash, cards, and valuables safe, wear a money belt.

Before departing, call your bank or credit-card company: Confirm that your card(s) will work overseas, ask about international transaction fees, and alert them that you'll be making withdrawals in Europe. Also ask for the PIN number for your credit card—you may need it for Europe's "chip-and-PIN" payment machines (see below; allow time for your bank to mail your PIN to you).

Dealing with "Chip and PIN": Most credit and debit cards now have chips that authenticate and secure transactions. European cardholders insert their chip card into the payment slot, then enter a PIN. (For most US cards, you provide a signature.) Any American card, whether with a chip or an old-fashioned magnetic stripe, will work at Europe's hotels, restaurants, and shops. But some self-service chip-and-PIN payment machines—such as those at train stations, toll roads, or unattended gas pumps—may not accept your card, even if you know the PIN. If your card won't work, look for a cashier who can process the transaction manually—or pay in cash.

Dynamic Currency Conversion: If merchants or hoteliers offer to convert your purchase price into dollars (called dynamic currency conversion, or DCC), refuse this "service." You'll pay extra in fees for the expensive convenience of seeing your charge in dollars. If an ATM offers to "lock in" or "guarantee" your conversion rate, choose "proceed without conversion." Other prompts might state, "You can be charged in dollars: Press YES for dollars, NO for euros." Always choose the local currency.

Staying Connected

The simplest solution is to bring your own device—mobile phone, tablet, or laptop—and use it just as you would at home (following the tips below, such as connecting to free Wi-Fi whenever possible).

To call Spain from a US or Canadian number: Whether you're phoning from a landline, your own mobile phone, or a Skype account, you're making an international call. Dial 011-34 and then the nine-digit number. (The 011 is our international access code, and 34 is Spain's country code.) If dialing from a mobile phone, you can enter + in place of the international access code—press and hold the 0 key.

To call Spain from a European country: Dial 00-34 followed by the nine-digit number. (The 00 is Europe's international access code.)

To call within Spain: Just dial the local nine-digit number.

To call from Spain to another country: Dial 00 followed by the country code (for example, 1 for the US or Canada), then the area code and number. If calling European countries whose phone numbers begin with 0, you'll usually have to omit that 0 when you dial.

Tips: If you bring your own mobile phone, consider getting an international plan; most providers offer a global calling plan that cuts the per-minute cost of phone calls and texts, and a flat-fee data plan.

Use Wi-Fi whenever possible. Most hotels and many cafés offer free Wi-Fi, and you'll likely also find it at tourist information offices, major museums, and public-transit hubs. With Wi-Fi you can use your phone or tablet to make free or inexpensive domestic and international calls via a calling app such as Skype, FaceTime, or Google+ Hangouts. When you can't find Wi-Fi, you can use your cellular network to connect to the Internet, send texts, or make voice calls. When you're done, avoid further charges by manually switching off "data roaming" or "cellular data."

It's possible to stay connected without a mobile phone. To make cheap international calls from any phone (even your hotel-room phone), you can buy a prepaid international phone card in Spain (called a *tarjeta telefónica con código).* Dial the toll-free access number, enter the card's PIN code, then dial the number. Calling from your hotel-room phone without using an international phone card is usually expensive. Though they are disappearing in Spain, you may still find public pay phones in post offices and train sta-

Sleep Code

Hotels are classified based on the average price of a standard double room without breakfast in high season.

$$$$	**Splurge:** Most rooms over €170
$$$	**Pricier:** €130-170
$$	**Moderate:** €90-130
$	**Budget:** €50-90
¢	**Backpacker:** Under €50
RS%	**Rick Steves discount**

Unless otherwise noted, credit cards are accepted, hotel staff speak basic English, and free Wi-Fi is available. Comparison-shop by checking prices at several hotels (on each hotel's own website, on a booking site, or by email). For the best deal, *book directly with the hotel.* Ask for a discount if paying in cash; if the listing includes RS%, request a Rick Steves discount.

tions. For more on phoning, see www.ricksteves.com/phoning. For a one-hour talk on "Traveling with a Mobile Device," see www.ricksteves.com/travel-talks.

Sleeping

I've categorized my recommended accommodations based on price, indicated with a dollar-sign rating (see sidebar). I recommend reserving rooms in advance, particularly during peak season. Once your dates are set, check the specific price for your preferred stay at several hotels. You can do this either by comparing prices on Hotels.com or Booking.com, or by checking the hotels' own websites. To get the best deal, contact my family-run hotels directly by phone or email. When you go direct, the owner avoids the 20 percent commission, giving them wiggle room to offer you a discount, a nicer room, or free breakfast. If you prefer to book online or are considering a hotel chain, it's in your advantage to use the hotel's website.

For complicated requests, send an email with the following information: number and type of rooms; number of nights; arrival date; departure date; and any special needs. Use the European style for writing dates: day/month/year. Hoteliers typically ask for your credit-card number as a deposit.

Some hotels are willing to make a deal to attract guests: Try emailing several to ask their best price. In general, hotel prices can soften if you do any of the following: offer to pay cash, stay at least three nights, or travel off-season.

Some hotels include Spain's 10 percent IVA tax in the room price; others tack it onto your bill. When asking about prices, it's smart to check about the room tax.

PRACTICALITIES

> # Restaurant Price Code
>
> I've assigned each eatery a price category, based on the average cost of a typical main course (or 2-3 tapas). Drinks, desserts, and splurge items (steak and seafood) can raise the price considerably.
>
> **$$$$**   **Splurge:** Most main courses over €20
> **$$$**   **Pricier:** €15-20
> **$$**   **Moderate:** €10-15
> **$**   **Budget:** Under €10
>
> In Spain, takeout food is **$**; a basic tapas bar or no-frills sit-down eatery is **$$**; a casual but more upscale tapas bar or restaurant is **$$$**; and a swanky splurge is **$$$$**.

Eating

I've categorized my recommended eateries based on price, indicated with a dollar-sign rating (see sidebar). By our standards, Spaniards eat late, having lunch—their biggest meal of the day—around 13:00-16:00, and dinner starting about 21:00. At restaurants, you can dine with tourists at 20:00, or with Spaniards if you wait until later.

For a fun early dinner at a bar, build a light meal out of tapas—small appetizer-sized portions of seafood, salads, meat-filled pastries, deep-fried tasties, and so on. Many of these are displayed behind glass, and you can point to what you want. Tapas typically cost about €5-10 a plate. While the smaller "tapa" size (which comes on a saucer-size plate) is handiest for maximum tasting opportunities, many bars sell only larger sizes: the *ración* (full portion, on a dinner plate) and *media-ración* (half-size portion). *Jamón* (hah-MOHN), an air-dried ham similar to prosciutto, is a Spanish staple. Other key terms include *bocadillo* (baguette sandwich), *frito* (fried), *a la plancha* (grilled), *queso* (cheese), *tortilla* (omelet), and *surtido* (assortment).

Many bars have three price tiers, which should be clearly posted: It's cheapest to eat or drink while standing at the bar *(barra)*, slightly more to sit at a table inside *(mesa or salón)*, and most expensive to sit outside *(terraza)*. Wherever you are, be assertive or you'll never be served. *Por favor* (please) grabs the attention of the server or bartender. If you're having tapas, don't worry about paying as you go (the bartender keeps track). When you're ready to leave, ask for the bill: *"¿La cuenta?"*

Tipping: To tip for a few tapas, round up to the nearest euro. At restaurants with table service, if a service charge is included in the bill, add about 5 percent; if it's not, leave 10 percent.

Transportation

By Train and Bus: For train schedules, visit Germany's excellent all-Europe website (www.bahn.com) or Spain's RENFE (www.

renfe.com). Since trains can sell out, it's smart to buy your tickets in advance at a travel agency (easiest), at the train station (can be crowded, be sure you're in the right line; you'll pay a five percent service fee at the ticket window), or online (at www.renfe.com). Be aware that the website rejects nearly every attempt to use a US credit card—use PayPal; or from the US try www.ricksteves.com/rail. Futuristic, high-speed trains (such as AVE) can be priced differently according to their time of departure. To see if a rail pass could save you money, check www.ricksteves.com/rail.

Buses pick up where the trains don't go, reaching even small villages. But because routes are operated by various competing companies, it can be tricky to pin down schedules (check with local bus stations, tourist info offices, or www.movelia.es). For dirt-cheap long-distance bus fares, check out www.flixbus.co.uk.

By Plane: Consider covering long distances on a budget flight, which can be cheaper than a train or bus ride. For flights within Spain, check out www.vueling.com, www.iberia.com, or www.aireuropa.com; to other European cites, try www.easyjet.com and www.ryanair.com. To compare several budget airlines, see www.skyscanner.com.

By Car: It's cheaper to arrange most car rentals from the US. If you're planning a multicountry itinerary by car, be aware of often-astronomical international drop-off fees. For tips on your insurance options, see www.ricksteves.com/cdw, and for route planning, consult www.viamichelin.com. It's also required that you carry an International Driving Permit (IDP), available at your local AAA office ($20 plus two passport-type photos, www.aaa.com).

Superhighways come with tolls, but save lots of time. Each toll road *(autopista de peaje)* has its own pricing structure, so tolls vary. Payment can be made in cash or by credit or debit card (credit-card-only lanes are labeled *"vias automáticas"*; cash lanes are *"vias manuales")*. Spaniards love to tailgate; otherwise, local road etiquette is similar to that in the US. Ask your car-rental company for details, or check the US State Department website (www.travel.state.gov, search for Spain in the "Learn about your destination" box, then click on "Travel and Transportation").

A car is a worthless headache in cities—park it safely (get tips from your hotelier). As break-ins are common, be sure all of your valuables are out of sight and locked in the trunk, or even better, with you or in your hotel room.

Helpful Hints

Emergency Help: For **police** help, dial 091. To summon an **ambulance**, call 112. For passport problems, call the **US Embassy** (in Madrid, tel. 915-872-200) or the **Canadian Embassy** (in Madrid, tel. 913-828-400). If you have a minor illness, do as the locals do and go to a pharmacist for advice. Or ask at your hotel for help—they'll know of the nearest medical and emergency services. For other concerns, get advice from your hotelier.

Theft or Loss: Spain has particularly hardworking pickpockets—wear a money belt. Assume beggars are pickpockets and any scuffle is simply a distraction by a team of thieves. If you stop for any commotion or show, put your hands in your pockets before someone else does.

To replace a passport, you'll need to go in person to an embassy (listed earlier). Cancel and replace your credit and debit cards by calling these 24-hour US numbers collect: Visa—tel. 303/967-1096, MasterCard—tel. 636/722-7111, American Express—tel. 336/393-1111. In Spain, to make a collect call to the US, dial 900-99-0011; press zero or stay on the line for an operator. File a police report either on the spot or within a day or two; you'll need it to submit an insurance claim for lost or stolen rail passes or travel gear, and it can help with replacing your passport or credit and debit cards. For more information, see www.ricksteves.com/help.

Time: Spain uses the 24-hour clock. It's the same through 12:00 noon, then keep going: 13:00, 14:00, and so on. Spain, like most of continental Europe, is six/nine hours ahead of the East/West Coasts of the US.

Siesta and Paseo: Many Spaniards (especially in rural areas) still follow the traditional siesta schedule: From around 14:00 to 17:00, many businesses close as people go home for a big lunch with their family. Then they head back to work (and shops reopen) from about 17:00 to 21:00. (Many bigger stores stay open all day long, especially in cities.) Then, after a late dinner, whole families pour out of their apartments to enjoy the cool of the evening, stroll through the streets, and greet their neighbors—a custom called the paseo.

Sights: Major attractions can be swamped with visitors; carefully read and follow this book's crowd-beating tips (visit at quieter times of day, or—where possible—reserve ahead). Opening and closing hours of sights can change unexpectedly; confirm the latest times on their websites or at the local tourist information office. At many churches, a modest dress code is encouraged and sometimes required (no bare shoulders or shorts).

Holidays and Festivals: Spain celebrates many holidays, which can close sights and attract crowds (book hotel rooms ahead). For more on holidays and festivals, check Spain's website: www.spain.info. For a simple list showing major—though not all—events, see www.ricksteves.com/festivals.

Numbers and Stumblers: What Americans call the second floor of a building is the first floor in Europe. Europeans write dates as day/month/year, so Christmas 2019 is 25/12/19. Commas are decimal points and vice versa—a dollar and a half is 1,50, and there are 5.280 feet in a mile. Spain uses the metric system: A kilogram is 2.2 pounds; a liter is about a quart; and a kilometer is six-tenths of a mile.

Resources from Rick Steves

This Snapshot guide is excerpted from my latest edition of *Rick Steves Spain,* is one of many titles in my ever-expanding series of guidebooks on European travel. I also produce a public television series, *Rick Steves' Europe,* and a public radio show, *Travel with Rick Steves.* My website, www.ricksteves.com, offers free travel information, a forum for travelers' comments, guidebook updates, my travel blog, an online travel store, and information on European rail passes and our tours of Europe. If you're bringing a mobile device, my free Rick Steves Audio Europe app features dozens of free, self-guided audio tours of the top sights in Europe, plus radio shows and travel interviews about Spain. You can get Rick Steves Audio Europe via Apple's App Store, Google Play, or the Amazon Appstore. For more information, see www.ricksteves.com/audioeurope.

Additional Resources
Tourist Information: www.spain.info
Passports and Red Tape: www.travel.state.gov
Packing List: www.ricksteves.com/packing
Travel Insurance: www.ricksteves.com/insurance
Cheap Flights: www.kayak.com or www.google.com/flights
Airplane Carry-on Restrictions: www.tsa.gov/travelers
Updates for This Book: www.ricksteves.com/update

How Was Your Trip?

To share your tips, concerns, and discoveries after using this book, please fill out the survey at www.ricksteves.com/feedback. Thanks in advance.

Spanish Survival Phrases

Spanish has a guttural sound similar to the J in Baja California. In the phonetics, the symbol for this clearing-your-throat sound is the italicized *h*.

English	Spanish	Pronunciation
Good day.	Buenos días.	**bway**-nohs **dee**-ahs
Do you speak English?	¿Habla Usted inglés?	**ah**-blah oo-**stehd** een-**glays**
Yes. / No.	Sí. / No.	see / noh
I (don't) understand.	(No) comprendo.	(noh) kohm-**prehn**-doh
Please.	Por favor.	por fah-**bor**
Thank you.	Gracias.	**grah**-thee-ahs
I'm sorry.	Lo siento.	loh see-**ehn**-toh
Excuse me.	Perdóneme.	pehr-**doh**-nay-may
(No) problem.	(No) problema.	(noh) proh-**blay**-mah
Good.	Bueno.	**bway**-noh
Goodbye.	Adiós.	ah-dee-**ohs**
one / two	uno / dos	**oo**-noh / dohs
three / four	tres / cuatro	trays / **kwah**-troh
five / six	cinco / seis	**theen**-koh / says
seven / eight	siete / ocho	see-**eh**-tay / **oh**-choh
nine / ten	nueve / diez	**nway**-bay / dee-**ayth**
How much is it?	¿Cuánto cuesta?	**kwahn**-toh **kway**-stah
Write it?	¿Me lo escribe?	may loh ay-**skree**-bay
Is it free?	¿Es gratis?	ays **grah**-tees
Is it included?	¿Está incluido?	ay-**stah** een-kloo-**ee**-doh
Where can I buy / find...?	¿Dónde puedo comprar / encontrar...?	**dohn**-day **pway**-doh kohm-**prar** / ayn-kohn-**trar**
I'd like / We'd like...	Quiero / Queremos...	kee-**ehr**-oh / kehr-**ay**-mohs
...a room.	...una habitación.	**oo**-nah ah-bee-tah-thee-**ohn**
...a ticket to ___.	...un billete para ___.	oon bee-**yeh**-tay **pah**-rah ___
Is it possible?	¿Es posible?	ays poh-**see**-blay
Where is...?	¿Dónde está...?	**dohn**-day ay-**stah**
...the train station	...la estación de trenes	lah ay-stah-thee-**ohn** day **tray**-nays
...the bus station	...la estación de autobuses	lah ay-stah-thee-**ohn** day ow-toh-**boo**-says
...the tourist information office	...la oficina de turismo	lah oh-fee-**thee**-nah day too-**rees**-moh
Where are the toilets?	¿Dónde están los servicios?	**dohn**-day ay-**stahn** lohs sehr-**bee**-thee-ohs
men	hombres, caballeros	**ohm**-brays, kah-bah-**yay**-rohs
women	mujeres, damas	moo-**heh**-rays, **dah**-mahs
left / right	izquierda / derecha	eeth-kee-**ehr**-dah / day-**ray**-chah
straight	derecho	day-**ray**-choh
When do you open / close?	¿A qué hora abren / cierran?	ah kay **oh**-rah **ah**-brehn / thee-**ay**-rahn
At what time?	¿A qué hora?	ah kay **oh**-rah
Just a moment.	Un momento.	oon moh-**mehn**-toh
now / soon / later	ahora / pronto / más tarde	ah-**oh**-rah / **prohn**-toh / mahs **tar**-day
today / tomorrow	hoy / mañana	oy / mahn-**yah**-nah

In a Spanish Restaurant

English	Spanish	Pronunciation
I'd like / We'd like...	Quiero / Queremos...	kee-**ehr**-oh / kehr-**ay**-mohs
...to reserve...	...reservar...	ray-sehr-**bar**
...a table for one / two.	...una mesa para uno / dos.	**oo**-nah **may**-sah **pah**-rah **oo**-noh / dohs
Non-smoking.	No fumador.	noh foo-mah-**dohr**
Is this table free?	¿Está esta mesa libre?	ay-**stah** ay-stah **may**-sah **lee**-bray
The menu (in English), please.	La carta (en inglés), por favor.	lah **kar**-tah (ayn een-**glays**) por fah-**bor**
service (not) included	servicio (no) incluido	sehr-**bee**-thee-oh (noh) een-kloo-**ee**-doh
cover charge	precio de entrada	**pray**-thee-oh day ayn-**trah**-dah
to go	para llevar	**pah**-rah yay-**bar**
with / without	con / sin	kohn / seen
and / or	y / o	ee / oh
menu (of the day)	menú (del día)	may-**noo** (dayl **dee**-ah)
specialty of the house	especialidad de la casa	ay-spay-thee-ah-lee-**dahd** day lah **kah**-sah
tourist menu	menú turístico	meh-**noo** too-**ree**-stee-koh
combination plate	plato combinado	**plah**-toh kohm-bee-**nah**-doh
appetizers	tapas	**tah**-pahs
bread	pan	pahn
cheese	queso	**kay**-soh
sandwich	bocadillo	boh-kah-**dee**-yoh
soup	sopa	**soh**-pah
salad	ensalada	ayn-sah-**lah**-dah
meat	carne	**kar**-nay
poultry	aves	**ah**-bays
fish	pescado	pay-**skah**-doh
seafood	marisco	mah-**ree**-skoh
fruit	fruta	**froo**-tah
vegetables	verduras	behr-**doo**-rahs
dessert	postres	**poh**-strays
tap water	agua del grifo	**ah**-gwah dayl **gree**-foh
mineral water	agua mineral	**ah**-gwah mee-nay-**rahl**
milk	leche	**lay**-chay
(orange) juice	zumo (de naranja)	**thoo**-moh (day nah-**rahn**-hah)
coffee	café	kah-**feh**
tea	té	tay
wine	vino	**bee**-noh
red / white	tinto / blanco	**teen**-toh / **blahn**-koh
glass / bottle	vaso / botella	**bah**-soh / boh-**tay**-yah
beer	cerveza	thehr-**bay**-thah
Cheers!	¡Salud!	sah-**lood**
More. / Another.	Más. / Otro.	mahs / **oh**-troh
The same.	El mismo.	ehl **mees**-moh
The bill, please.	La cuenta, por favor.	lah **kwayn**-tah por fah-**bor**
tip	propina	proh-**pee**-nah
Delicious!	¡Delicioso!	day-lee-thee-**oh**-soh

For hundreds more pages of survival phrases for your trip to Spain, check out *Rick Steves' Spanish Phrase Book.*

INDEX

INDEX

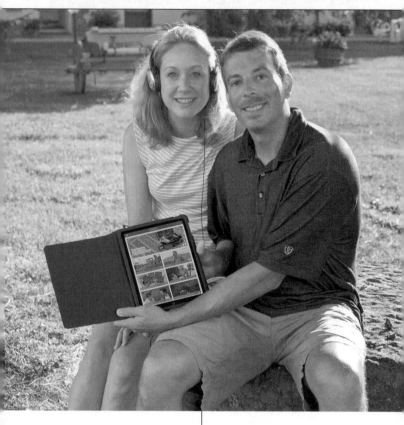

Explore Europe

At ricksteves.com you can browse through thousands of articles, videos, photos and radio interviews, plus find a wealth of money-saving travel tips for planning your dream trip. And with our mobile-friendly website, you can easily access all this great travel information anywhere you go.

TV Shows

Preview the places you'll visit by watching entire half-hour episodes of Rick Steves' Europe (choose from all 100 shows) on-demand, for free.

Radio Interviews

Enjoy ready access to Rick's vast library of radio interviews covering travel

tips and cultural insights that relate specifically to your Europe travel plans.

Travel Forums

Learn, ask, share! Our online community of savvy travelers is a great resource

for first-time travelers to Europe, as well as seasoned pros. You'll find forums on each country, plus travel tips and restaurant/hotel reviews. You can even ask one of our well-traveled staff to chime in with an opinion.

Travel News

Subscribe to our free Travel News e-newsletter, and get monthly updates from Rick on what's happening in Europe.

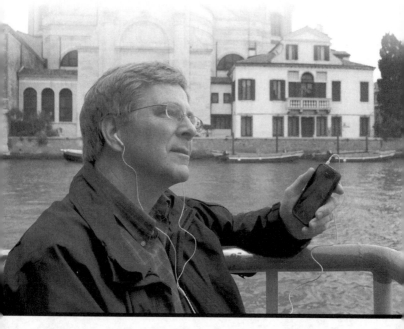

Gear up for your next adventure at ricksteves.com

Light Luggage

Pack light and right with Rick Steves' affordable, custom-designed rolling carry-on bags, backpacks, day packs and shoulder bags.

Accessories

From packing cubes to moneybelts and beyond, Rick has personally selected the travel goodies that will help your trip go smoother.

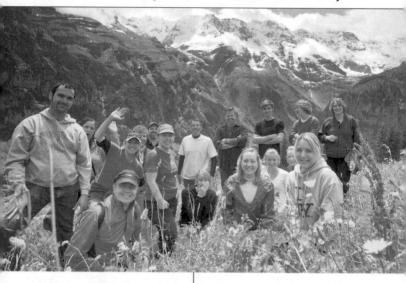

Save time and energy

This guidebook is your independent-travel toolkit. But for all it delivers, it's still up to you to devote the time and energy it takes to manage the preparation and logistics that are essential for a happy trip. If that's a hassle, there's a solution.

Rick Steves Tours

A Rick Steves tour takes you to Europe's most interesting places with great

with minimum stress

guides and small groups of 28 or less. We follow Rick's favorite itineraries, ride in comfy buses, stay in family-run hotels, and bring you intimately

close to the Europe you've traveled so far to see. Most importantly, we take away the logistical headaches so you can focus on the fun.

travelers—nearly half of them repeat customers— along with us on four dozen different itineraries, from Ireland to Italy to Athens. Is a Rick Steves tour the right fit for your travel dreams? Find out at ricksteves.com, where you can also request Rick's latest tour catalog. Europe is best

Join the fun

This year we'll take thousands of free-spirited

experienced with happy travel partners. We hope you can join us.

See our itineraries at ricksteves.com

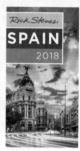

BEST OF GUIDES

Full color easy-to-scan format, focusing on Europe's most popular destinations and sights.

Best of France
Best of Germany
Best of England
Best of Europe
Best of Ireland
Best of Italy
Best of Spain

COMPREHENSIVE GUIDES

City, country, and regional guides with detailed coverage for a multi-week trip exploring the most iconic sights and venturing off the beaten track.

Amsterdam & the Netherlands
Barcelona
Belgium: Bruges, Brussels, Antwerp & Ghent
Berlin
Budapest
Croatia & Slovenia
Eastern Europe
England
Florence & Tuscany
France
Germany
Great Britain
Greece: Athens & the Peloponnese
Iceland
Ireland
Istanbul
Italy
London
Paris
Portugal
Prague & the Czech Republic
Provence & the French Riviera
Rome
Scandinavia
Scotland
Spain
Switzerland
Venice
Vienna, Salzburg & Tirol

HE BEST OF ROME

me, Italy's capital, is studded with
man remnants and floodlit-fountain
ares. From the Vatican to the Colos-
n, with crazy traffic in between, Rome
onderful, huge, and exhausting. The
ds, the heat, and the weighty history

of the Eternal City where Caesars walked
can make tourists wilt. Recharge by taking siestas, gelato breaks, and after-dark
walks, strolling from one atmospheric
square to another in the refreshing evening air.

ed *Pantheon*—which
est dome until the
ly 2,000 years old
y over 1,500).

of Athens in the Vat-
dies the humanistic
ce.

gladiators fought
rucher, entertaining.

 Rome *ristorante*,
ds at St. Peter's
 seriously.

, toss in a coin

Rick Steves guidebooks are published by Avalon Travel, an imprint of Perseus Books, a Hachette Book Group company.

POCKET GUIDES

Compact, full color city guides with the essentials for shorter trips.

Amsterdam	Paris
Athens	Prague
Barcelona	Rome
Florence	Venice
Italy's Cinque Terre	Vienna
London	
Munich & Salzburg	

SNAPSHOT GUIDES

Focused single-destination coverage.

Basque Country: Spain & France
Copenhagen & the Best of Denmark
Dublin
Dubrovnik
Edinburgh
Hill Towns of Central Italy
Krakow, Warsaw & Gdansk
Lisbon
Loire Valley
Madrid & Toledo
Milan & the Italian Lakes District
Naples & the Amalfi Coast
Northern Ireland
Normandy
Norway
Reykjavik
Sevilla, Granada & Southern Spain
St. Petersburg, Helsinki & Tallinn
Stockholm

CRUISE PORTS GUIDES

Reference for cruise ports of call.

Mediterranean Cruise Ports
Northern European Cruise Ports

Complete your library with...

TRAVEL SKILLS & CULTURE

Study up on travel skills and gain insight on history and culture.

Europe 101
European Christmas
European Easter
European Festivals
Europe Through the Back Door
Postcards from Europe
Travel as a Political Act

PHRASE BOOKS & DICTIONARIES

French
French, Italian & German
German
Italian
Portuguese
Spanish

PLANNING MAPS

Britain, Ireland & London
Europe
France & Paris
Germany, Austria & Switzerland
Ireland
Italy
Spain & Portugal

Avalon Travel
Hachette Book Group
1700 Fourth Street
Berkeley, CA 94710

Printed in Canada by Friesens
Fifth Edition
First printing November 2017
ISBN 978-1-63121-682-4

For the latest on Rick's lectures, guidebooks, tours, public radio show, and public television series, contact Rick Steves' Europe, 130 Fourth Avenue North, Edmonds, WA 98020, tel. 425/771-8303, www.ricksteves.com, rick@ricksteves.com.

The publisher is not responsible for websites (or their content) that are not owned by the publisher.

Rick Steves' Europe

Managing Editor: Jennifer Madison Davis
Special Publications Manager: Risa Laib
Assistant Managing Editor: Cathy Lu
Editors: Glenn Eriksen, Tom Griffin, Katherine Gustafson, Mary Keils, Suzanne Kotz, John Pierce, Carrie Shepherd
Editorial & Production Assistant: Jessica Shaw
Editorial Intern: Alexandra Ivy
Researchers: Amanda Buttinger, Robert Wright
Contributor: Gene Openshaw
Graphic Content Director: Sandra Hundacker
Maps & Graphics: David C. Hoerlein, Lauren Mills, Mary Rostad

Avalon Travel

Senior Editor and Series Manager: Madhu Prasher
Editor: Jamie Andrade
Associate Editor: Sierra Machado
Editorial Intern: Rachael Sablik
Copy Editor: Maggie Ryan
Proofreader: Suzie Nasol
Indexer: Stephen Callahan
Production & Typesetting: Christine DeLorenzo, Rue Flaherty, Sarah Wildfang
Cover Design: Kimberly Glyder Design
Maps & Graphics: Kat Bennett, Mike Morgenfeld

Photo Credits

Front Cover: Gran Via street in Madrid © Nacroba | Dreamstime
Title Page: Architecture at Plaza Mayor in Madrid © adamgolabek/123rf.com
Additional Photography: Dominic Arizona Bonuccelli, Rich Earl, Cameron Hewitt, David C. Hoerlein, Suzanne Kotz, Pat O'Connor, Gene Openshaw, Jessica Shaw, Robyn Stencil, Rick Steves, Robert Wright, Wikimedia Commons—PD-Art/PD-US. Photos are used by permission and are the property of the original copyright owners.